Character
&Destiny

Books By This Author

Evangelism Explosion
The God of Great Surprises
Truths That Transform
Turn It to Gold
Why I Believe
The Real Meaning of the Zodiac
Spiritual Renewal
Your Prodigal Child
Truth and Education
Delighting God
What If Jesus Had Never Been Born?
Learning to Live with the People You Love
Knowing the Whole Truth

Character & Destiny

A Nation In Search of Its SOUL

D. James Kennedy
with Jim Nelson Black

ZondervanPublishingHouse
Grand Rapids, Michigan

A Division of HarperCollins*Publishers*

Requests for information should be addressed to:
Zondervan Publishing House
Grand Rapids, Michigan 49530

Library of Congress Cataloging-in-Publication Data

 Kennedy, D. James
 Character & Destiny : a nation in search of its soul / D. James Kennedy, with James Nelson Black.
  p. cm.
 Includes bibliographical references and index.
 ISBN 0-310-44380-6
 1. Apologetics. 2. Secularism—United States. 3. United States—Moral conditions. 4. United States—
History—Religious aspects—Christianity. 5. Religion and science. 6. Evolution—Religious aspects—
Controversial literature. 7. United States—Religion—1960. I. Black, Jim Nelson. II. Title. III. Title:
 BR526.K46 1994
 239'.00973—dc20

94-13032
CIP

Edited by Mary McCormick
Cover design by John M. Lucas

94 95 96 97 99 00 01 02 03/❖DC/10 9 8 7 6 5 4 3 2 1

This edition is printed on acid-free paper and meets the American National Standards Institute
Z39.48 standard.

I dedicate this book
to the millions of godly Christian men and women
who are working and praying to restore the character of America
and thus ensure its destiny

Sow a thought and you reap an act;
Sow an act and you reap a habit;
Sow a habit and you reap a character;
Sow a character and you reap a destiny.

—Anonymous

The one who sows to please his sinful nature,
from that nature will reap destruction;
the one who sows to please the Spirit,
from the Spirt will reap eternal life.

Let us not become weary in doing good,
for at the proper time we will reap a harvest
if we do not give up.

—Galatians. 6:8–9

Contents

Introduction

A Crisis of Character

Today we are facing a "crisis of character" that is undermining every aspect of American life. This crisis is so severe that it amounts to a "new cold war." And the ethical and moral fallout threatens not only our political, economic, and intellectual well-being but our very "destiny" as a nation. It has been said that "God is in the business of building character," and that is true. But when any society chucks God out of its public life and slaps up a patchwork structure of humanism and idealism in the place of God, the soul of its people can only grow weaker and its character atrophy and die. The message of this book is that unless we wake up now and respond with moral conviction to these signs of the times, we face imminent and irreversible catastrophe.

For more than three centuries, moral values have been the life-support system of this country. The men and women who planted their standard on these shores in the year 1607 vowed to build here a nation founded on virtue and moral integrity. And during all those years their promises and plans held true. The American people brought forth on this continent a nation dedicated to liberty and justice, and they transformed a barren wilderness into a colossus among modern empires. Underlying all their hopes and ambitions was a consensus of values and a unity of vision. The founders were

11

committed to strong moral principles based on individual liberty and personal responsibility. They believed in honesty, integrity, and fair dealing, and the history of this nation for most of its first two hundred years demonstrates the vitality and indomitability of the American character.

But somewhere along the way, something changed. Today there are people in this nation who want to rewrite that history and revise the facts of our cultural and moral heritage according to a more modern politically correct view. They want to shake off the restraints and the responsibilities of Christian virtues and to guide the nation toward a new era and a new destiny—toward a new world order of cultural and moral diversity. Will the American people submit to these new ideas? Will we allow our history to be rewritten? Will we accept the view that this nation was founded by people who were imperialistic and corrupt? And will we allow all our traditional religious and spiritual values to be overthrown? And, most troubling of all, can this or any nation survive such a radical transformation?

REDEFINING AMERICA

The Greek philosopher Heraclitus said, "There is nothing permanent except change." It often seems that change is about the only thing we can be sure of anymore. Bill Clinton and the Democratic Party gained control of the White House and the Congress in 1992 by a mere forty-three percent plurality. They have never had the full support of the people of this country, and there are many dissident voices resisting their policies. Nevertheless, the democrats have promised to "reinvent" the American form of government and to "redefine" what it means to be Americans in this century. We have already been through so many shocking changes during just the past three decades. Can we tolerate more of the same? How much *change* can "one nation under God" endure before the framework of order and republican self-sufficiency collapses?

The writer Ellen Glasgow reminds us that "All change is not growth; all movement is not forward." Sometimes we are forced to move in a direction we did not intend to go; we have already allowed the government and the judiciary to overturn laws and historic moral principles and thereby place the American Constitution and all the people who subscribe to it in jeopardy. We are a nation as risk as never before in our history. Human life has lost its sanctity, and neither infancy nor old age is sacred any longer to the social reformers of our day.

Laws that once provided order and restraint are being tossed out by the high courts and by local magistrates, often by fiat. As a consequence, crime and immorality are rampant throughout the nation. Pornography has been legitimized; bizarre sexual practices are now protected as "rights." And the family is being torn asunder and redefined by the liberal policies of government. We are in the ironic position of being the richest nation on earth, with the highest crime rate, the highest incidence of murder and robbery, and the greatest percentage of its citizens behind bars of any nation. From coast to coast we are threatened by the greatest siege of barbarism since the fall of Rome.

Reform is not necessarily bad, and not all changes are dangerous. If responsible changes are made by men and women of strong character and moral vision, then things should improve; but if we turn over the reins of government to men and women of weak and questionable character, and if we empower people to rule this nation whose views are absolutely contrary to the beliefs of the founders and deliberately opposed to the principles that made this nation great, then the changes they bring about will not—indeed cannot—be for the better.

A great orator of the last century, Senator Henry Clay, said that, "Of all the properties which belong to honorable men, not one is so highly prized as that of character." Good character, like a good name, is a very valuable thing. Americans have always understood this truth. But today many people have apparently decided that character is a "personal matter." Highly visible and outspoken people in government and the media are trying to convince the American people that evidence of immorality and bad behavior among politicians and public figures should not influence our judgment of them, or our votes. But can this be true?

Heraclitus also said, "A man's character is his fate." And the Bible says we can judge a man by his character, "For as he thinks in his heart, so is he" (Prov. 23:7 NKJV). In Proverbs we read that "The character of even a child can be known by the way he acts—whether what he does is pure and right" (Prov. 20:11 TLB). If we believe that character has consequences, and if people who are indiscreet and immoral are allowed to rule the nation and make its laws, then what hope can we hold for the future? In a nation in which men and women of poor moral character make the laws, the law will necessarily become corrupt, lawlessness will increase, and the nation itself will fall. Those are the risks we face today.

A CRISIS OF MORAL AUTHORITY

In an influential column written in 1941, several months before America entered World War II, Henry Luce, the founder and chairman of *Life* magazine, said that "character is destiny." By that he meant that the boldness and vitality of the American character were this nation's best security for a bright future. On the continent of Europe, the world was being forced to deal with the dangerous ambitions and brutal tactics of dictators such as Hitler, Mussolini, and Stalin. Threatening the entire continent of Europe, the Axis powers unleashed an unimaginable holocaust of violent change upon the world. Some of our senior statesmen tried to keep America out of the war, but when the Japanese attacked Pearl Harbor on December 7, 1941, America was drawn in, and it was soon clear that we could not remain neutral in this great hour of crisis.

Under the leadership of General Dwight Eisenhower and the Allied commanders, the armed forces acted decisively and entered the war on two fronts, in Europe and the Pacific. By defying the voices of tyranny—very much as we had done during our own revolutionary war—the American military contributed a new level of strength, resourcefulness, and resolve to the beleaguered British and French forces. This was what helped turn the tide of battle. Eventually, America's youthful vitality won the day, and when the final treaty was signed in Tokyo Bay, on September 2, 1945, evil had been defeated and the United States of America was recognized as the most powerful social and military force in the world. In an address to Parliament, Winston Churchill said, "America stands at this moment at the summit of the world." And, at that moment, we did.

Half a century later, we know precisely how the great drama of the Second World War played itself out. We witnessed the fall of Germany, Italy, and Japan, and the triumph of democracy and freedom. But the world of the 1990s hardly resembles the world of the 1940s anymore. Who could have predicted the changes of just the past decade? While Europe and Asia are still searching for economic and social renewal, the United States matured in some ways but struggled in many others.

We have paid the price for our military unpreparedness and vacillation in places like Korea and Vietnam, while we have been reassured in some measure by the collapse of the Soviet Union, the destruction of the Berlin Wall, and our victory in the Persian Gulf War. The American character has been tested repeatedly, and our military power has proved superior time and time again.

But not all of America's wars have been fought with bullets, and not all are being fought on foreign soil. Our most difficult battles are the ones being fought right here in our own neighborhoods.

WARFARE IN THE SOUL

In addition to the many wars and police actions of this "American century," we have witnessed the development of countless new technologies and ideologies. Many of these innovations have been life-changing, though not many have been successfully assimilated within the culture. Television, cinema, the mass media are profoundly troubling. And even now, as we debate the various proposals for "change" being threatened by government, we are facing a host of new problems and reacting to a barrage of emotional challenges for which we often seem surprisingly ill-prepared.

The American character is being tested at the core of its very being. Beyond the merely physical challenges, we find ourselves confronted by weapons that are emotional, ideological, and spiritual in nature. In some ways, this nation has grown older and wiser, but we are still surprisingly immature, without much experience in soul-searching. Consequently, Americans of every age and every walk of life are facing an unprecedented assault on their consciences and character. This is what I would call a crisis of moral authority, which must also be seen as a crisis of faith waged on the battleground of the soul.

There is no doubt that America's physical resources and our current level of wealth are unprecedented in history. But the soul of the nation is being challenged today as never before. Are we able to cope with these dangerous pressures? Will we have the moral fiber to respond in time? All too often we are overwhelmed by emotional and moral questions, and all too often it is clear we are making all the wrong choices. Just consider the shocking decisions being handed out by judges and juries from coast to coast. Police officers are convicted of abuse of authority, while thugs and murderers are routinely let loose on the streets. In some cases, criminals are rewarded with large damage settlements and they become heroes to the underclass that preys on social disorder.

We are faced constantly by confusing and intimidating dilemmas. How are we to deal with the shocking rise of crime, violence, and abuse? Women and children are no longer safe in our cities and towns, or even in their own homes and churches. Children can be snatched from their bedrooms, and there is seemingly no way to maintain safety in public places. At the same time, our schools and workplaces are under increasing political assault, and the symptoms of radical change are everywhere. How can the men and women of this country make sense of their world when the values being thrust at them are so contrary to tradition and often so extreme? Are there any answers for our problems? Is there any hope?

The kind of muscular Americanism that saved us in time of war is no longer enough, it seems. What worked in war has no place in peacetime. We are beginning to seem like the ancient Trojans who were valiant warriors but who could not survive the peace. Are we only able to pull together in emergencies? The 1992 Los Angeles riots showed the whole world what insidious passions are lying just under the surface of the American character; but only a year later the Los Angeles earthquake demonstrated the exact opposite qualities, as people of every race and creed and class pitched in to help each other through the disaster. Which ones are we? Are we barbarians or humanitarians? Are we survivors or destroyers? And what triggers these contrary and unpredictable kinds of response?

We are facing many serious problems today—a gut check for the American character. The moral debate that confronts this nation will certainly affect, and perhaps even determine, the future well-being of this nation. But which will it be—chaos or compassion? Generosity or devastation? What will we become as a nation? How will the American people respond to the political challenges from the Right and the Left? Who are we really? And how should men and women of religious convictions respond to the evidence of spiritual crisis? And finally, where can we look for solutions to the emotional problems we face now on every hand and at every level of society?

A NEW ORDER OF THE AGES

In this book I want to take a hard and unflinching look at many of these questions. The work will explore the relationship between America's Christian heritage and our future hopes. If the warnings of George Washington and the great leaders of American history are valid, we already have many reasons to be worried about the prospects for this nation. The failure of American character and resolve is already a matter for serious concern, but when combined with a rise of lawlessness, growing immorality, corruption, and abuse in every area of society—and when compounded by the willful destruction of moral standards and ethical values—we have to recognize that we are in a state of national emergency. We cannot afford to look the other way any longer. There is too much at risk. We have to stare into the face of reality, and we have to recognize that the face in the mirror is our own. The future of this nation depends on what you and I decide today.

Do we understand what disasters inevitably befall nations that have lost their souls? Do we really perceive the risks ahead of us? Secular sociologists are trying to reinterpret the moral and social codes of this country without any reference to the Word of God or God's principles of righteousness. But history shows that such actions always lead to dishonor and destruction. Through His infinite grace, God has given us His Word as divine revelation. The Bible is an owner's manual for life on this planet, and to ignore God's Word is not only counterproductive but absurd. The deterioration of personal responsibility, the loss of moral perspective, and the weakening of our sense of purpose in life are problems no nation can survive. And the willful destruction of our religious heritage is a threat we cannot afford to ignore. How can we simply overlook the vandalism and crime in our cities? How can we avoid the plague of immorality that confronts us (and our children) so blatantly in films, periodicals, and television? These signs of disorder, if nothing else, should tell us that we are at risk and in an advanced state of moral decay. Will God turn His back upon us? Will He simply look the other way? Can He withhold judgment forever?

No one living in America today can deny the fact that we are standing on the sheer precipice of some sort of national disaster. We have been pounded by every calamity known to man. Just think of the storms that have struck the nation in the past twelve months. These are warnings, foretold by the Bible, that God is reaching the end of His patience with us. How long will we resist Him? How long will this nation continue in its sin? Unless we can restore some sense of moral vision and personal integrity and unless the people of this nation can come back to God's standards of righteousness, I believe I can say without stretching the truth at all, that within a very short time we will witness the end of life as we know it. What other conclusion can we draw from the facts at hand?

We are already a long way down the road to national disaster. Who could have predicted the changes of just the past ten years? Political, economic, cultural, social, and moral changes have reshaped the dimensions of our lives. For the time being, we still possess the greatest wealth and power of any nation on earth, yet we have lost control of our streets. We have the greatest military power of any nation in history, yet we are powerless to control the teen gangs or the plague of drugs, prostitution, and violence in the inner city. For the first time in history we cannot protect ourselves or our foreign visitors. Travelers from Third World nations are at greater risk in the streets of America than in their own underdeveloped homelands. Schools, workplaces, and homes are no longer safe, and the signs of deterioration are increasing daily.

People in all walks of life feel overwhelmed by the physical and emotional problems of our day. They are faced with unprecedented problems. How are they to respond? What is happening to American culture? In the pages to come I will take a hard look at each of these critical questions. I will examine the relationship between our heritage of freedom and our future hopes, discuss what I perceive to be America's *cultural mandate* to restore order and decency, and offer a plan designed to help the nation regain its strength of purpose, its moral convictions, and its security in the world.

If "a man's character is his fate," as the philosophers have suggested, then we must understand that what we believe and how we behave will determine what we can become. How we respond to all the challenges before us today will determine whether or not we can survive. Our destiny, both as individuals and as a nation, hinges on the decisions we make today. It is my hope that this book will challenge many people to reconsider their priorities and to return to the bedrock of faith in Jesus Christ. For the One who holds tomorrow will decide the destiny of the world. In due time, Christ will judge the nations, and we will be blessed or cursed based on the decisions we make today. The Lord of heaven has taught us the values upon which our destiny depends. He has given us every opportunity to repent.

GOD'S LOVE FOR AMERICA

Before turning to the first chapter, please let me offer one more word of hope and a challenge. God loves America. When you consider what He went through to bring our forebears to this magnificent land, and when you realize what He accomplished in bringing forth a new nation on this continent—a government founded on Christian principles and dedicated to life, liberty, and the pursuit of happiness—you have to realize that He had a dramatic vision and purpose for this nation. But God is also our loving parent, and His heart is broken by the way we have neglected Him, the way we have turned to our own selfishness, and our wicked and self-indulgent ways. He will not allow us to continue in rebellion forever.

Already we are witnessing God's judgment on the nation. Nature, which is His to control, seems to be turning against us. How much more obvious can it be? As Billy Graham has suggested in his newest book, *Storm Warning*, the storms of recent years—that even the insurance companies refer to as "acts of God"—must be seen as a warning from heaven. No, they are not the evidence of God's hatred for mankind but of His profound love. They are the reprimand of a loving parent. We are faced with the responsibility of either choosing God or denying Him. But God wants America to repent and return to Him, to love Him with all our hearts, and to love one another. Near the end of his long and fruitful life, Dr. J. B. Phillips wrote that after years of study and discipline he had finally discovered the meaning of life, and it could be summarized in these two points: "to love the Lord your God with all your heart, soul, and mind, and to love your neighbor as yourself."

These are the fundamental principles of the Christian faith as they were taught by Jesus Christ. And they are also the principles upon which this nation was founded. The tragedy of life in America today is not that we are in political and economic turmoil. This world has always been in turmoil. It is not that government or education or health care or the economy is in crisis, but that we have turned away from these two simple principles that can bring everything else back into balance.

We have turned away from the God who made us to a cold, materialistic view of His world. We have allowed a vain and rationalistic view of man to infiltrate our homes and schools and to rob us of faith in the great Creator who is the source of Truth. We have denied the reality of the soul, and ours spirits are dying; we have turned to gratification of the senses, and our bodies are dying. How long can this nation turn its back on God? And how much longer will God restrain His wrath? I can offer no more important message than this: America, the God who loves you wants you to come home. Please, come home to His love. Your rich inheritance is waiting.✶

Part I

The Cultural Mandate

1

A Nation at Risk

W hat happens when a nation has too much wealth, too much freedom, and too much time? Anyone looking at the changes that have taken place in this nation over the past twenty-five years would have to see that some sort of radical values shift has taken place. A quarter century ago, every school child understood the premise of Western culture. Our way of life was built on a tradition of great adventurers, great thinkers, great explorers, and great ideas. School children, indeed all Americans, were well-versed in the heritage of the United States, and they understood the backgrounds to this nation's hopes and dreams.

We have always been a culture that dares, that takes risks, that seeks bolder and brighter horizons. The idea that hard work and individual initiative would pay off and that personal sacrifice would lead to happiness and prosperity was born here—we called it the "American Dream." And while we were always searching for new challenges, we never lost sight of the achievements and the moral values of our founding fathers. Hard work and honesty were essential, along with faith in God and a commitment to our fellowman. We believed in the proud heritage of our American way of life, and our anticipation for tomorrow only increased our sense of reverence for the past.

Today, however, we can no longer take such attitudes for granted. Modern educators tell us they have examined the past and discovered evidence of malice aforethought. The founders, the great thinkers, the very culture and mind-set of all those "dead white European males" were perverse and imperialistic from the start. So teachers in our public schools and great universities have set out to "redefine" the world for our children and set the record straight. As Professor Allan Bloom has said, "openness" and "relativism" are the great insights of modern education. Students have been taught to believe that the most dangerous person in America is the "true believer"—the man or woman who actually believes in some standard of truth.

Bloom tells us that, according to the new "liberated" view, "The study of history and of culture teaches that all the world was mad in the past; men always thought they were right, and that led to wars, persecutions, slavery, xenophobia, racism, and chauvinism. The point is not to correct the mistakes and really be right; rather, it is not to think you are right at all."[1] In other words, everything is relative; there are no absolutes. These are the truths of the modern age. Consequently, millions of American students have no views or values they wish to defend, no firm belief in cultural or religious values, and no respect for traditions.

But what does all this revisionist history really mean? Has society simply run out of novelties and amusements? Are America's problems merely the result of too much luxury and too little sacrifice? Or are we actually witnessing the long-overdue debunking of the myths and illusions that kept us in darkness for all those years? Maybe the sociologists and liberals are right, after all. Maybe we just didn't know how unhappy we were! Or maybe this nation is simply out of time, and our experiment in democracy has failed.

Whatever it is, we can be certain that the changes taking place in the culture today are having a tremendous impact on the future hopes of American society. And if we can believe the bureaucrats in Washington, there is reason to believe that even greater changes are yet to come. Whether the nation's fixation on "change for the sake of change" will lead to some sort of "new world order" or, instead, to anarchy and outright collapse, remains to be seen. But there is no doubt that the long-range prospects for modern civilization will be affected profoundly by the events taking place around us.

THE VALUES SHIFT

In political events alone we see such an incredible contrast of opposites. Values we once took for granted no longer seem to apply. Black is white, left is right, and everything looks incredibly topsy-turvy. Three days after his inauguration in January 1993, the president of the United States signed executive orders expressing his desire to lift the ban on homosexuals in the military, to allow the bodies of aborted infants to be used in experiments called "fetal tissue research," to approve the use of the French abortion drug RU–486 in this country, to authorize abortions in U.S. military hospitals around the world, and to lift the restrictions imposed by the Bush Administration on "abortion counseling" at federally funded health clinics. In addition, during his first year in office the president appointed more than two dozen homosexuals and lesbians to high public office.

Throughout the history of civilization, and in every great society, a high code of ethics and morality has been a requirement for public office. A high priority has been given to the interests of traditional families founded on the vital bond of mother, father, and children. The family is the essential basic unit of civilization, while promiscuity and aberrant sexual behavior destroy lives, families, and nations. But the new president and his young, liberal, activist staff have gone out of their way to defy moral conventions and to break with every tradition of Judeo-Christian culture. When we see such radical changes taking place in the basic structures of society, we have to wonder what is going on in this country. What kind of nation are we, after all? Is this still "one nation under God" as we used to believe? Is it a noble experiment in democracy? Or is America, as the historical revisionists now claim, the ultimate expression of greed and repression?

Consider how language is being redefined in America's classrooms today. Advocates of "politically correct" speech have begun to rewrite the entire lexicon of Western thought and to invent a new vocabulary of "victimization," more suited to a cultural tradition of bigotry and exploitation. In his important book on the politicization of the university, *Illiberal Education*, Dinesh D'Sousa has said that, "Instead of cultivating in young people those qualities of critical thought and civil argument that are the essence of a liberal education, university leaders have created sham communities where serious and honest discussion is frequently drowned out by a combination of sloganeering, accusation, and intimidation."[2] A "liberal education" used to be based on the idea of *liberalis*, or freedom of thought and expression. But no more.

The game plan of the liberals in the universities has been to eradicate the past and indoctrinate the young men and women of this nation with a new view of society and a radical political ideology. According to these theories, there are no absolutes, no sources of ultimate truth and meaning, and all "values" are of equal importance. So, by this view, the principles of Mao Zedong are just as meaningful and reasonable as those of George Washington; and the tribal laws of the bushmen of the Kalahari are just as significant as the Mayflower Compact, signed by the pilgrims who settled America.

Thanks to the shoddy education they have received, most students have no means and no desire to challenge such fraudulent ideas. They have no grasp of history or ideas. They have been taught to respect "diversity" and "multiculturalism," and they have been taught that their heritage of freedom gives them plenty of "rights" but few responsibilities. There are no causes they are willing to fight for, no great and noble truths they would die for. Millions of young American have been stripped of their past and, very possibly, their future as well.

As students are infused with these revolutionary ideas, they lose any sense of esteem for American heritage, for the values of Western civilization, and for the virtues and the beliefs that made this nation unique. And because they have no sense of history, they are easy prey for radical beliefs and practically any political theory being palmed off by their liberal teachers and professors. The prevailing orthodoxies of the "cultural elite" have become the models for behavior and belief, and the emptiness in the souls of young people today is just one indication of the damage that has already been done.

THE INTELLECTUAL GULAG

The collapse of educational standards is just one more expression of a society turned in upon itself—a nation at risk. Clearly, this situation is not new, and it is not over, but it *is* a visceral warning that the American culture is undergoing a major change. Professor Charles Sykes, in his book *A Nation of Victims*, suggests that the meaning of "right and wrong" is being redefined by the secular society. To remove the restraints of the Christian religion and traditional moral values, educators have instilled the ideas of "behaviorism" and "modern psychology," which hold that behavior is simply the result of conditioning. Bad behavior is not sin but merely nonproductive action. Crime is the result of poor socialization. And to overcome such problems, we don't need churches but more "therapy." The psychologist, not the pastor or the priest, is the healer of our souls.

The rise of the "therapeutic culture" in America, says Professor Sykes, amounts to the ascendancy of a substitute faith—its roots are certainly in the false theology of humanism. "Filling the vacuum created by the decline of institutional faith and the collapse of the moral order it has provoked," Sykes observes, "psychoanalysis has assumed many of the functions traditionally performed by religion, and has done so by translating many of the theological and existential issues of human life into therapeutic terms." According to the intellectuals, the care of the soul is the task of science. And the principal institution of this new "therapeutic culture" is the pseudoscience of psychology—that is, the no-man's land of moral equivocation conceived by Sigmund Freud, Alfred Adler, and Carl Jung, all of whom were hostile to the Christian religion.[3]

But the most visible effect of this "psychologizing of culture" has been to create a "society of victims." Suddenly, our universities are overrun by new "sensitivities" for the plight of the downtrodden and the "underprivileged"—for what the liberals define as the casualties of the insensitive white-male-dominated American culture. But, suddenly the system has begun to feed on itself. Once the people could see that society's "victims" were receiving their "rights" and "entitlements" in terms of dollars and cents, promotions, scholarships, awards, and other privileges not available to ordinary hard-working Americans, the "in" thing to be was not an industrious, honest, reliable, middle-class citizen but a "victim."

"In the society of victims," says Charles Sykes, "individuals compete not only for rights or economic advantage but also for points on the 'sensitivity' index, where 'feelings' rather than reason are what count." And he adds that the new attitude of sensitivity is so finely tuned that "it can detect racism in the inflection of a voice, discover sexism in a classroom's seating pattern, and uncover patriarchal oppression in a mascara stick or a Shakespeare sonnet."[4]

In many of America's great universities, our brightest young men and women are no longer educated in the great traditions of Western civilization. Instead, the campuses have become virtual concentration camps, intellectual gulags, for indoctrinating destructive ideas of political correctness and historical revisionism. Socialism, which destroyed Eastern Europe and the Soviet Union, has now become the fundamental truth on the American university campus, the public school classroom, the national welfare system, and every other agency touched by the federal bureaucracy. And now that we are facing the highest level of social change in history, the people of this country are under assault by an administration that is determined to "reinvent" our democratic values and to create a dangerous new "politics of meaning" that threatens to "redefine" all the sacred institutions and beliefs of this nation.

THE DECLINE OF PUBLIC EDUCATION

The public schools in this country are in even greater danger than the universities, since the dangerous theories of educators are being used to corrupt the minds and morals of our children while they are still so young and impressionable. Held in a virtual stranglehold by the liberal, highly activist teachers unions—including especially the National Education Association (NEA)—American elementary and secondary schools have become dangerous ghettos of violence, apathy, and ignorance. The dismal state of public education today is directly responsible for the growing illiteracy of the nation, while educators concentrate on programming young children as pawns of some radical new idea of life in the "new world order."

Today, we have more than twenty-five million illiterates in this nation. Each year, more than 2.5 million young people who graduate from the public schools are functionally illiterate. They cannot read above a third-grade level; they cannot do simple mathematics; they cannot keep a checkbook; and in some cases they cannot even use a public telephone without assistance. More than twenty-five million adults read so poorly they cannot understand the warning label on a bottle of poison or follow the directions on a bottle of aspirin.

A 1989 study by Chester E. Finn, the former Assistant Secretary of Education, found that only five percent of seventeen-year-olds could read well enough to understand technical documents, literary essays, or works of history. Only six percent could solve math problems with more than one step, and only seven percent could draw a logical conclusion from a list of science facts. In a comparison of the educational attainments of students from the United States and nineteen other industrialized nations, American high school students scored dead-last or next to last in every single category. Sadly, American students had the highest level of self-esteem and the lowest intellectual attainments of all students tested. They did not know how ignorant they really were, and perhaps they didn't even care.

The National Commission on Excellence in Education, a group of scholars and researchers concerned with the dismal failures of public education in this country, produced an "Open Letter to the American People" in 1983 that warned of the dangers ahead if these educational trends are not somehow reversed. This report, subtitled "A Nation at Risk: The Imperative for Educational Reform," concluded that "the educational foundations of our society are presently being eroded by a *rising tide of mediocrity* that threatens our very future as a nation and a people." They blamed the erosion of standards on the failed ideas of public-school educators, shoddy educational methods, and a loss of focus on the critical skills and educational attainments that had always been considered essential in this country. The Three R's have been replaced by the three *S*'s—*sensitivity*, *self-esteem*, and *sexuality*.

And what is the fallout of all this negative programming? In his book, *Why Johnny Can't Tell Right from Wrong*, William Kirk Kilpatrick reports that as many as 525,000 attacks, shakedowns, and robberies occur in our public high schools each month. Every day, more than sixteen thousand crimes are committed in or near our schools. And despite the increase in metal detectors, spot-checks, and "pat-downs" by principals in the schools, still as many as one hundred-thirty-five thousand students carry guns to schools each day, and twenty percent of students (one out of every five) carry some type of weapon for protection.

But the problem doesn't end at the school door. We learn that the suicide rate among young people has gone up three hundred percent since the 1960s; drugs, alcohol, and promiscuous sexuality have become commonplace. While students and even teachers are routinely beaten, raped, and robbed in the schools, the biggest concern of many administrators is a program called "values clarification," which promotes "value neutral thinking." And the principal values they wish to clarify are "cultural sensitivity" and "safe sex."

But even here the system has failed. In 1991, more than 1.1 million teenagers became pregnant. And a growing number of teens today say they are experimenting with bisexuality because "It's cool!" One trend analyst for a major advertising company recently suggested that bisexuality will be the newest fad of the nineties among young people. But rather than a negative, many advertisers see this as a positive sign that will be good for business, opening up all new areas for marketing new fashions and other promotional ideas. So much for "values clarification."

William Kilpatrick makes a very good point. He says that none of us would allow ourselves to be treated by an untrained doctor, no one would fly with an untrained pilot, and we do not want untrained soldiers guarding our country. Yet we have accepted the notion that men and women, boys and girls, can be good without any training in good behavior and responsible citizenship. "We have succumbed to a myth," he says, "that morality comes naturally, or at most, with the help of a little reasoning." But it is unmistakably clear today that the educational and moral experiments of the past three decades have failed miserably. The authority of a "greater good" and a "higher power" is no longer invoked. But when God is banned from the schoolrooms of America, the souls of our young people are bound to become impoverished. The shocking level of violence and destructive behavior on the campus is only an indication of the degree to which the souls of the young have been mauled and abused by the system.

The author adds that many Americans seem to believe their children will be able to deal with moral issues with the flimsy materials given them by today's secular education, but *that* simply is *not true*. Yes, students are much more aware of political and social issues today. They know all about the environment, the arms race, the dangers of nuclear weapons, sexism, racism, and politically correct concerns. But they do not know right from wrong. The crime, violence, promiscuity, and destructive behaviors killing young people today in record numbers are all the proof we need. But this is not the only area where change is needed.

ARE WE LOSING THE DREAM?

In a speech to economists in Washington, D.C., in June 1992, James Schreyer remarked that America is the first country ever founded on a dream. The hopes of the men and women who came to the New World energized this nation and created something far greater than any other nation or empire had ever achieved. The dream is this, he said: "Give people personal and economic freedom and they will create the opportunities—and make the effort and the sacrifices to pursue them." Freedom and opportunity, effort and investment, risk and reward, plus the infinite potential of the individual human mind and spirit—these are the elements of what we have always known as the "American Dream." But underlying this magnificent idea is the requirement that we must also have *faith*. The economist says that "People have to feel secure in their freedoms if they are to use them. It isn't enough to be a prosperous country—which we are. We must also recognize how we became prosperous, and then continue stoking the spirit that got us here."[5] If we lose our history, we will lose our connection to the future. We must rediscover our heritage and recommit ourselves to our common goals.

But how do we do that? The speaker suggests that we abandon the "politics of envy" created by the liberal policies of government and the universities and return to the tried-and-proven "politics of growth" upon which the nation was built. Second, he says, we must restore open and free competition. This has always been the essence of American-style capitalism. Not "managed competition" but open competition shaped by the dynamics of the free market system. That is not what the current administration wants. Of course, they want "price controls," and they want many levels of government intervention—with policies that are more suited to a socialist economy. Economists and business people recognize the obvious threats represented by such bureaucratic restraints, and they are nervous about them. That is one of the major reasons for today's shaky stock market.

Despite all the pessimism that surrounds us, we still have the most dynamic economic system in the world. "It's fashionable to disparage the 1980s," says Mr. Schreyer, "to portray them as a decade of greed that sent us tumbling down the road to ruin." But what the 1980s actually gave us was the longest sustained period of economic growth in modern history and a level of performance "so formidable that the Soviets threw in the towel. In the face of our strength and determination, they concluded the costs of empire had become too great." The American Dream is so powerful that, even during the current weakness, it is able to vanquish all competitors. But think what could happen if government would simply get out of the way and let this marvelous system work as it was designed.

In less than one decade, from 1982 to 1990, the gross domestic product of this nation grew by nearly a third. American manufacturing increased by fifty percent; exports nearly doubled; and eighteen million new jobs were created, not by government but by industry. Schreyer told his audience that, "We have the world's highest standard of living, the world's best universities, the world's best medical care. Wherever you go in the world, the currency most in demand is the U.S. dollar. We are the world's number-one exporter . . . and we are still the number-one destination of choice for aspiring emigrants from every corner of the globe." The proofs of the success of "Reaganomics" and the stimulus to business engendered by twelve years of Republican leadership are easy to find. The evidence is everywhere. But the Keynsians, socialists, university intellectuals, government bureaucrats, and others who harbor anti-American sentiments deny that fact. They want to hide it. For them, success on the free market is economic oppression, and individual achievement is exploitation.

Despite the success of the American economy in those years, many people have fallen for the idea that only the rich made money in the eighties and that the middle and lower classes suffered. But this is not true. A study conducted by *Money* magazine showed that the main reason the number of middle-income Americans decreased during the eighties was that the number of upper-income Americans increased dramatically. In other words, the American Dream paid off in a big way, and the bureaucrats who trade on misery, suffering, and increased dependency on big government hated it.

RESTRAINING THE MONSTER

What the "doom and gloom" prophecies of political pundits really demonstrate, the economists tell us, is not the death of the American Dream but the political ambitions of elected officials who want desperately to convince the people of America that we are no longer capable of self-government—that we need professional bureaucrats and "experts" and government officials to tell us what to think and how to live. The growth of centralized government is a direct result of the deliberate drift toward totalitarianism in this nation. Truly, we are "a nation at risk" for many, many reasons. And one of the greatest threats to America's future is the unchecked growth of government.

A report in the *New York Times* in 1992 suggested that the nation and the economy suffer in proportion to the meddling of government in our private lives. Their study compared the performance of the Dow-Jones stock averages when Congress was in session and when it was in recess. The statistics showed that in the forty-five years from the end of World War II to 1991, the level of the Dow was 17 times higher when both houses of Congress were out of town. In 1990, Roger Kimball wrote the book *Tenured Radicals: How Politics Has Corrupted Our Higher Education*, showing how education is being threatened by government interference. But the politics of the United States Congress is every bit as harmful to business as it has been to the schools and universities. Yet, the members of Congress continually legislate bizarre policies contrary to the interests of business and contrary to the prospects of the people whose livelihoods depend upon economic stability. Ultimately, that includes all of us.

By manipulation of economic policy, by tinkering with the law, by questionable diplomacy, and by reducing the rights and responsibilities of the individual states—rights established by the Constitution—the federal government has taken unto itself unprecedented and virtually unlimited powers. And since the principal interest of the legislators is our pocketbooks, taxation and increased public welfare are the areas on which they concentrate their attentions. We must stop to ask ourselves, What right does government have to consume more than forty percent of the entire wealth of this nation? What right do Congressmen and lawmakers have to siphon off $1.5 trillion of America's wealth every year for government spending while at the same time running up a $4.4 trillion national debt? This is a shocking situation, yet, in the thrall of the liberal media and the facile smiles of political candidates, no one rebels! Why? Are we witnessing the end of Western civilization? Has the consumer society gone mad? What's happening to America? Where is our willpower? Where is our sense of indignation and outrage?

For one thing, the sources of personal convictions have been weakened to the point that moral judgment is often of no value. Every nation that has ever existed has been built upon some sort of religious foundation. Whether it is the Hinduism of India, the Islam of Saudi Arabia, the Confucianism of China, the Shintoism of Japan, the Judaism of Israel, or even the religion of atheism in the Soviet Union (which was based on the spiritual veneration of Marx and Lenin), every nation has had some form of religious commitment that contributed to its greatness. But while the government, the courts, the ACLU, the liberal American Bar Association, and the Trial Lawyers of America are doing everything in their power to strip away our moral values and religious rights, the government is stripping Americans of their property, their incomes, their rights of self-determination, and ultimately their hopes for the future.

RELIGIOUS LIBERTIES

On the Merv Griffin program some years ago, I had the unfortunate experience of following ABC newsman, Sam Donaldson, and I had to sit next to him on the couch. The whole time that Merv was talking to me and asking me questions, Donaldson would not stop talking. He kept interrupting our conversation and at one point put his hand on my shoulder to get my attention. I wanted to turn around and say to him, "Sam, you had your chance, now just shut up." Of course, I couldn't do that, so he finally cut in on our discussion of America's religious heritage. Basically, he said he didn't accept my view of history. There may have been "some few Christians" around when this country was founded, he quipped, but of course they gave us "a secular government."

"Some few Christians!" Well, the numbers were all on my side this time. As late as 1776 fully ninety-eight percent of the people in this country professed to be Protestant Christians; 1.8 percent said they were Roman Catholics; and .2 percent said they were Jewish. Now, if you add those numbers up you will find that 99.8 percent of the people in this nation declared themselves to be Christians.

As an indication of the beliefs of all thirteen colonies at that time, the Constitution of the State of Delaware required that all office holders swear in public, "I do profess faith in God the Father, and in the Lord Jesus Christ His only Son, and in the Holy Ghost . . . and I do acknowledge the Holy Scriptures of the Old and New Testaments to be given by divine inspiration." In 1931, the United States Supreme Court declared, in the case of *United States v. Macintosh*, that "We are a Christian people." And in 1952, even the liberal justice, William O. Douglas, declared from the bench that "we are a religious people and our institutions presuppose a Supreme Being." Until the 1960s, nobody in America ever doubted the truth of such statements.

Gallup surveys over the past two decades reveal that a consistent eighty-five percent of the people in this country still claim to be Christians. While that may be down from the 99.8 percent total of the eighteenth century, there is little doubt that more people in this country have a Christian heritage and support Christian beliefs than any other religious or moral doctrine. In the nation of Israel, which is widely recognized to be a religious nation, less than twenty percent of the people claim to be Jewish. As many as seventy percent have no religious beliefs, and as few as ten percent can realistically be called "observant Jews" who actually attend synagogue. But can anyone deny that Israel is a Jewish state? Does anyone resist the right of Israelis to follow the Jewish religion or for the Knesset to enact laws and policies that uphold the principles and beliefs of the Jewish faith?

In India just over eighty percent of the people claim to be Hindus, twelve percent are Muslims, about three percent are Christians, and the remaining five percent are Sikhs, Buddhists, Jains, and other minorities. No one doubts that India is a Hindu nation. No one resists the right of India's parliament to pass laws and public policies that encourage, support, and draw upon the religious beliefs of their people. Yet, in the United States, where eighty-five percent of the people are at least nominally Christians, and where the founding principles of the nation were established by a 99.8 percent Christian majority, and where those same principles gave rise to the most prosperous, most tolerant, and most virtuous nation in all of history, we are told, "You have no right to legislate your morality."

Still, isn't it interesting that a country with a 99.8 percent Christian majority actually gave the people more religious liberty and more "freedom of expression" than any other country in history? So, instead of being narrow-minded and repressive, as modern secularists claim, the application of Judeo-Christian principles in the laws and policies of this nation actually provided great freedom for people of all persuasions. It allowed other religions to worship and proclaim their faith without fear of intolerance. No other nation can make such a claim. The First Amendment to the Constitution requires that government stay out of religious matters and that government should not be allowed to set up a "state religion." But atheists and civil libertarians have used this amendment to strip society of its religious heritage and moral convictions. And all the anti-religious groups who rise up and scream about the dangers of our claiming to be a Christian nation are trading on fears and threats and charges that are patently ludicrous and untrue.

In no other country—and certainly not in the Soviet Union in their heyday—*has there ever been greater freedom of thought and expression*. In no other nation has there been greater freedom to worship as we please. In fact, it is in secular America today that our First-Amendment freedoms are most endangered. Free speech is being destroyed by the doctrines of "political correctness." Freedom of thought is endangered by socialist programming in the schools and the government. Free trade is in danger, and freedom from government interference in our private lives is in even greater danger of disappearing.

THE ROLE OF RELIGION

In a fascinating book written after his visit to America in 1820, the French statesman Alexis de Tocqueville was, frankly, amazed at what he found here. Having come through a bloody revolution of its own, France had overthrown the monarchy and the church and established a new atheistic form of government. The result of the French Revolution was very different from that of the American Revolution, but as Tocqueville traveled in the United States, he was stunned by the openness, the honesty, and the general sense of happiness and prosperity among the American people.

In his important book, *Democracy in America*, Tocqueville described America as the world's greatest political experiment. Moral values, which he calls "habits of the heart," were the backbone of civilized society. These values, or *mores*, were based on Christian principles. "In the United States," he said, "republicans value mores, respect beliefs, and recognize rights. They hold the view that a nation must be moral, religious, and moderate all the more because it is free."[6]

The Frenchman went on to say, "I do not know whether all Americans have a sincere faith in their religion, for who can know the human heart?—but I am certain that they hold it to be indispensable for the maintenance of republican institutions. This opinion is not peculiar to a class of citizens or to a party, but it belongs to the whole rank of society."[7]

What most astonished him was that, unlike France, where religion was a source of conflict, religion in America was the glue that held the nation together. The Enlightenment in France had taught the people to distrust the church, but in America religion was the key to good citizenship and agreement on all important issues. De Tocqueville said that America is "the place where the Christian religion has kept the greatest power over men's souls; and nothing better demonstrates how useful and natural it is to man, since the country where it now has the widest sway is both the most enlightened and the freest."[8] In France, religion had been considered the enemy of liberty, but in America, as George Washington expressed it, religion and morality were the "twin pillars of freedom."

In light of all the assaults on the traditional values and beliefs of this nation, some people believe that sometime before the end of this decade the United States is going to crash and burn. Mounting debt, both public and private, along with rising crime and immorality, are just too enormous, and many believe we cannot recover in time to stop the coming crash. Very soon the nation's debt load and the escalating interest on the federal deficit are going to consume the entire federal budget, which means that we will see a cut-off of Social Security, Medicare, Medicaid, and all the other welfare programs. Will the people be prepared for that situation when it comes? Can we go cold turkey when all these so-called "safeguards" of the welfare state are finally removed?

In 1929, people were jumping out of tall buildings, but that is not going to happen in 1999. Instead of jumping, you'll be thrown out of the window after you've been robbed. Morals have changed so much, and conditions are so different from what they were seventy years ago, that I would not be at all surprised to see the same kinds of riots that destroyed whole neighborhoods in Los Angeles in 1992 break out in every city in this nation at that time. Even now, we are not that far away from such a prospect.

If we do not see a restitution of values, morals, and the religious foundations of society in the next few years—along with a renewed commitment to "justice" and realistic punishment for convicted offenders—then there is absolutely nothing to save us from such a catastrophe. The welfare state will not save us. Science cannot save us. More police, more prisons, more threats will not save us. *Only a return to Christian virtues can save us now*. And so long as Christianity and the moral foundations of this nation are banned from the public square, the option of God's grace is simply not available to us. Without God we all fail, and surely ruin will come upon us.

THE LOSS OF WILL

America's problems in the late twentieth century have all come about because we have abandoned the Word of God and turned our backs on His law. Debt is one of the most obvious indicators of our moral and political insolvency. Today we are borrowing money from our children and grandchildren to maintain our own standard of living; whereas, the Bible says that inheritances must go from the fathers to the children. We are to give greater hope to those who follow us, not less. But we are not giving inheritances to our children. There isn't going to be anything to give them. Instead, we are leaving them our debts and an outrageous level of interest that the next generation will simply never be able to pay.

In his book, *The Coming Economic Earthquake*, Larry Burkett says that the United States government has three options. The first is to renege on our debt and let the nation go bankrupt. Literally, the government goes bankrupt, and when it does, it becomes persona non grata to the entire international community. Nobody will lend such a government any more money, so we would become a pariah nation to the rest of the world. The second possibility, Burkett says, is that Washington will just turn up the printing presses and inflate the economy with "funny money." This is what has happened in many Third World nations, such as Argentina and Zaire, and it inevitably leads to chaos and some kind of calamitous crash. It was also what happened in Germany in 1923 with disastrous effect.

The third possibility suggested by Burkett is that the politicians in Washington will become responsible statesmen, cut their spending back to reasonable levels, and pay off the national debt. That is obviously the only logical choice, but does anyone really believe that will ever happen? I certainly do not. The public has the power to demand that government take this third course. We can demand, by our votes and our powers of persuasion, that legislators heed the warnings while there is still time. We can pass a balanced-budget amendment. We can also use "term limits" as a weapon, if you will, to force Congress to get with the program. But, alas, the people have shown no better resolve on these issues than the bureaucrats and legislators. In the final analysis, we are *all* to blame.

As Senator Warren Rudman said when he left office in 1992, the American people are not really committed to the idea of deficit reduction. They talk about it, and they say they want it, but in reality they have become complacent, self-indulgent, and too interested in getting something for nothing from government. In 1993, more than fifty percent of all Americans were receiving some sort of financial assistance from government. Rudman said that he and four other senators had agreed that it was absolutely essential to cut government spending and get a grip on the deficit. They understood that it would be fatal to the nation if they did not do that. So they went home, told the people they wanted to cut spending and take positive steps to restore the economy, and all five of those senators were voted out of office by their constituents.

Clearly, we cannot continue to put all the blame on the politicians. If the American people actually were to say that they want to get a grip on government, and really mean it, then something would happen. If they were to tell their congressmen that they will no longer put up with any further deficit spending, and say, in so many words, "If you vote for anything that will add to the deficit, you're going to be voted out of office," then Congress would get rid of the deficit tomorrow. But, the fact is, the American people are saying, "No, don't cut mine, Congressman. I've got my snout in the public trough, and it's going to stay there!" What most Americans seem to be saying is, "If you turn off the tap on my benefits, your political career is finished!"

So this is a major part of the problem. Are the American people really serious about change? Are we so committed to our own greed that we can't stop our feeding frenzy even to save the nation from destruction? This nation has been on a spending binge for too many decades, and if we still can't see the truth, then, without a doubt, we will lose everything. And, along with Larry Burkett, I fear that the day of reckoning is not very far away.

After the Great Depression, people used to sing a silly tune that said, "Oh, the world owes me a living." The song was actually saying that government handouts are dangerous and unrealistic. Even in the depths of the Depression, the hard-working people of America didn't want welfare, they wanted jobs. Later, when I was a young man, we used to hear the expression, "There's no such thing as a free lunch." We understood that good things come from hard work, not government giveaways. But today, too many people have apparently come to believe there is not just a free lunch but free breakfast, dinner, and a midnight snack.

If we had gone to the Soviets ten years ago and told them that communism wouldn't work and that they needed to abandon that failed ideology before it destroyed their country, they would have laughed in our faces and probably thrown us into prison. It took an absolute financial disaster to make them see the truth. I fear that may be where this nation stands today. People with clear vision and a knowledge of history are screaming, "Watch out! The path we are on leads to self-destruction." But it seems that no one is willing to do what it takes to correct our course and restore the sanity, self-reliance, and moral restraint needed to stop this impending collapse.

These are the same symptoms you might observe in an alcoholic. It's not until he hits bottom that he's ready to give up his self-destructive habit and turn his life around. At this moment I have to wonder if the American people, or the American Congress, are willing to look in the mirror and take the hard steps that are needed to save the United States from collapse. Do we have to wait until our economy crashes completely, as it did in the Soviet Union? If so, is there any guarantee we can recover the next time? There are many nations that would love to see us utterly destroyed. There are outlaws and gangs within this nation, and militant Third World powers without, who would love nothing better than to prey on this country once we become weak and defenseless. Is that what we are waiting for? Is that what we have to look forward to? Will that be America's destiny?

CHALLENGING OUR ASSUMPTIONS

Our nation is at risk as never before, but the remarkable fact is that most of us can agree on the problems. We know that crime is out of control. We know that moral and religious values are in jeopardy. We know that bureaucracy is mushrooming and that government is already trying to confiscate the wealth of the nation. We also know that the government's social

39

programs have failed miserably and that every public institution is a threat to individual freedom and the right of self-determination. What we are fighting about is not the issues but the solutions to these problems. We cannot agree on the steps to be taken to bring this nation back into balance.

The simple fact is that everything that government subsidizes gets worse. *The way to restore the freedom of the individual is to get government out of our private lives.* If we want to reduce the effectiveness of the system, get government involved; but if we want to come back to the peace and prosperity of the American heritage—the kind of openness, honesty, happiness, and tranquillity that Alexis de Tocqueville observed in the nineteenth century—then we must empower those institutions that made America the great nation it once was.

As Charles Sykes observes in his important work, the fundamental concern in all of these issues is the matter of *character*. It is not a question of freedom or rights or restraint of white male domination but of character. Character is the cultivation of habits that are sound, supportive, and sensible. Character cares about the success of others, and the general well-being of the nation. Character is critical of dishonesty, shoddy attitudes, and immoral behavior. It stands up to tyranny and flees from compromise. Truly, a strong moral character is essential to the health and happiness of our nation and to each individual in it, but do we have the resolve to make character once more a priority in our lives?

The apostle Paul said, "we also rejoice in our sufferings, because we know that suffering produces perseverance; perseverance, character; and character, hope. And hope does not disappoint us, because God has poured out his love into our hearts by the Holy Spirit, whom he has given us" (Rom. 5:4–5). What he is saying is that through endurance and strong character, we can have hope for the future, regardless of how perilous the situation may seem. And we must also see that the way to possessing all these remarkable qualities is through strong faith and strong moral convictions. Jesus Christ said, "I am the way, the truth, and the life," and He declared that the Word of God shows us the way to victory and renewed hope. Do we still believe these words?

Clearly, we are living in troubled times. The earth is being ravaged by fires, floods, earthquakes, and other natural disasters; our cities are overrun by violence and racial strife; incurable diseases are raging out of control; the economy is in shambles, and government is invading our homes and private lives as never before. Public education has failed our children, and it has stripped them of the basic intellectual tools required for survival in modern society. Their classrooms have become institutions for propagandizing and demoralizing the young against the wishes of their elders. And on top of everything else, we are in a nationwide crisis of character. So what is our hope for the future? When we talk about "character and destiny," can we really expect to maintain any degree of faith in the future? In light of all the dangers around us, can we honestly expect some sort of moral and intellectual renewal?

My immediate and unequivocal answer is Yes. There is hope. Looming ahead of us, like a brick wall, are a new century and a new millennium that suddenly seem more ominous than we could ever have imagined a decade ago. There is no justice in the land. There is little faith and less peace, but there *is* hope, because our hope is in Jesus Christ, the Prince of Peace, who holds tomorrow in the palm of His hand.

I want to stress that beyond all the distress and anxiety we feel, the source of our strength has never changed, and it has never been closer than now. Our salvation can be found today, at this very moment, and with no further debate. It is right where it has always been: in a renewed commitment to the Savior of the world, and to the Lord who is the author of our hope and the finisher of our faith. The sooner the people of the world return to this fundamental truth, the brighter our future and our destiny will be.✺

NOTES

[1]Allan Bloom. *The Closing of the American Mind: How Higher Education Has Failed Democracy and Impoverished the Souls of Today's Students* (New York: Simon & Schuster, 1988), 26.

[2]Dinesh D'Dousa, *Illiberal Education: The Politics of Sex and Race on Campus* (New York: Vintage, 1992), xiii.

[3]Charles J. Sykes, *A Nation of Victims: The Decay of the American Character* (New York: St. Martin's, 1991), 49.

[4]*Ibid*, 11f.

[5]William A. Schreyer, "The Century of the American Dream," (address to the Economic Club of Washington, Washington, D.C., June 4, 1992). Reprinted in *Vital Speeches of the Day*, vol. 59, no. 6 (Nov. 1, 1992).

[6]Alexis de Tocqueville, *Democracy in America*, trans. George Lawrence (New York: Harper & Row, 1969), 395.

[7]*Ibid*, 293.

[8]*Ibid*, 291.

2

The Cultural Mandate

Fall is a busy time for most of us. At the end of the summer, when people are back from their vacations, they start getting into their usual routine of work and school and all the familiar patterns of life. If you have children, then you know how busy it can be, shopping, planning, getting each member of the family back on schedule, and also trying to keep everything in balance. The last thing you need is a major shock.

It was just such a time when a young family in our area sent their five-year-old son off for his first day at kindergarten. Of course, they were hopeful and excited, seeing their son take this first important step into the world of education. So, when Johnny got home from school that first day, his mother asked eagerly, "Johnny, what did you learn in kindergarten today?" Well, how much can a youngster learn on his first day of kindergarten? His mother expected that he might have learned his teacher's name, where he would sit in the class, and things like that. He would probably know some of the rules: not to hit the other children, to listen attentively when others are speaking, and to share toys and crayons. He would learn where the restroom is. But, what did Johnny learn on his first day of school?

"Well," the little boy hesitated slightly then said to his mother, "we learned you can't even prove that Jesus ever lived."

Imagine the shock on his mother's face. "What?" she said. "You mean your teacher told you that Jesus Christ is not real? She said that He is just a made-up story?"

"Well," the child answered, "she said nobody knows if Jesus was a real person or not, and she said you and Daddy can't prove it, either."

Does that story shock you as it did me? Does it strike you as outrageous that of all the things Johnny could have learned on his very first day in kindergarten he was taught that Jesus Christ is a myth?

Well, I was angry when I heard about that, and so were Johnny's parents. I said that it was not only shocking and outrageous, but it was illegal. No teacher has the right to assault a child's faith or his religious values. I suggested that the parents should get an attorney, go to the school board, and if some sort of satisfactory answer were not forthcoming immediately, they should sue the school. The law is on their side in this matter, and they would win.

The idea of separation of church and state has been abused by judges and juries for the past fifty years, but one thing is undeniably clear: If teachers in public schools can't teach Johnny about Christianity and if they can't say that Jesus Christ is alive today or that faith in God is a good idea, then they certainly cannot teach their students the exact opposite, either.

CHURCH AND STATE

The First Amendment to the Constitution says, "Congress shall make no law respecting the establishment of religion or forbidding the free exercise thereof." The specific and obvious meaning of that statement is that government has no control over the church and no authority in religious matters. In many countries there are official state religions. Almost all Muslim countries have declared Islam as the state religion. In a few countries, the Roman Catholic tradition has been declared a state religion. In colonial times, the official religion of the state of Massachusetts was the Anglican or Episcopalian form of Christianity. The English Civil War in the seventeenth century was a bloody struggle to determine, among other things, what the official religion of Great Britain should be.

The first Americans wanted to prevent that kind of clash, so the Constitution of the United States clearly teaches that the government may not set up a "state church" and legislators may not interfere in the affairs of the various churches in any way. There was to be religious liberty and tolerance of all faiths. Today the courts have pushed this policy to a ridiculous extreme by suggesting that even state-supported schools are somehow an arm of government. I do not totally agree with that policy; but even so, by their own standard the statements of that kindergarten teacher are a breach of the constitutional principle and a violation of law.

But what is most disturbing to me about a story like this is that only one child in thirty went home and told his mommy what happened. His mother and father were upset, and they immediately sat down with Johnny and told him the truth and explained to him what the Bible says and why the teacher was wrong in her opinion. But, in all likelihood, there were twenty-nine other children who did not get to hear the truth. The rest of those children all went home and, in many cases, I'm sure, their mothers didn't ask them the same question; or perhaps the parents weren't sure themselves what the Bible says, and they said, "Well, I guess that's true." So here are twenty-nine innocent children whose view of God will be damaged for the rest of their lives, perhaps forever.

But there are other consequences of this situation that are not immediately visible. For example, what happens the next time Mommy says, "Okay, it's time to get ready for Sunday school, Son"? What happens when the child says, "No, I don't want to go to Sunday school"? Why should he want to go to church? After all, he thinks, all they do there is talk about a religion that is nothing but made-up stories, and probably none of them are true! If nobody can prove that Jesus Christ ever lived, then what is the point of Christianity?

Maybe he won't rebel against his family or the church while he's still a small child, but what happens when he turns thirteen or so, and natural adolescent rebellion begins? He has been taught that Jesus Christ is a fable—that God is not real, that there is no eternal truth, and there is nothing beyond this moment he can believe in. So what else should he do? If we subscribe to the secular humanist view of life, then we need to understand that rebellion against both God and man is natural. It is inevitable. And I suspect this is a large part of the problem with the destructive behaviors and the low self-esteem of many young people today. If we teach children that they are nothing but animals and that they have evolved from the lowest forms of life, how then can we blame them when they behave like animals? Public education teaches children that their ancestors swung from trees, and then teachers and administrators are surprised when the children behave like apes.

THEFT OF THE SOUL

I also insist that a child who has been lied to in this way has been violated and abused by his public school teachers. He has been morally abused in a way that many in our society would not even recognize today. And perhaps that is really the saddest part of all, and it is more tragic than we will ever know. American society has been abused for the last fifty years. We have been told that God is dead and that religion has no place in our lives. We live in a cold, mechanistic world. Time and chance control everything, and God is dead. How can anyone possibly be surprised when millions of men, women, and children, whose souls have been stolen from them in this fashion, live and die in the most dismal and hopeless manner?

The truth is that the historical evidence that Jesus Christ lived and conducted his ministry just as it is described in the Gospels, is one of the most incontestable facts of history. I assure you, no historian in the Western world would put his reputation on the line by making the claim that Jesus Christ did not exist or that there is no proof He ever lived. The life and death of Jesus of Nazareth is one of the most well-documented and provable facts in history.

The first-century historian, Josephus, described Jesus as "a doer of wonderful works," and he affirmed that Jesus was crucified by order of the Roman governor, Pontius Pilate, and that Christ appeared to His followers "alive again the third day, as the divine prophets had foretold."[1] Josephus was a wealthy man who held a high position among the scholars of his day, and he was allowed to accompany the Roman legions throughout North Africa, Palestine, and Europe. His object was not to invent fables but to relate the true history of the events during those momentous years. His unambiguously clear and objective report on the reality of Jesus Christ is just one of many authentic proofs of Christ's life and times. Biblical scholars have studied the Gospels, the book of Acts, and the letters of Paul for centuries, and they have attested to the reliability of the accounts in the Scriptures. Jesus was a real person, and His claims have changed the world.

Skeptical intellectuals want to deny these facts, however, because they are inconvenient. If laws prevent thieves from stealing, then thieves will want to get rid of the laws or to ignore them. And if the Bible declares that "the wages of sin is death," then the sinner wants to declare the Bible false, or at least make himself believe that it does not apply to himself. But wishing does not make it so. There is a dreadful reality to sin that no amount of bitterness or theorizing or self-delusion can deny. There is an eternal reality, and there is an immediate reality. The eternal reality of sin is a life apart from God in eternal punishment. At least a part of the immediate reality is the destruction of lives we can see all around us, through violence, disease, civil unrest, and all the other symptoms of chaos in society.

THE REALITY OF SIN

The biologist, Sir Julian Huxley, was once asked on a British television show why the theory of evolution was so readily accepted by the scientific community. "I suppose the reason we leaped at *The Origin of the Species*," the scholar replied, "was because the idea of God interfered with our sexual mores." Many scientists were shocked and angered by Huxley's off-the-cuff remark. They didn't deny that his statement was true. After all, there is no scientific proof of evolution. But they didn't want to tell the whole world that their acceptance of the absurd notions was actually motivated by their lust and their rejection of God. Modern secularists and agnostics do not want to admit that the Christian religion is true, because that would mean that they are sinners; and they have no intention of giving up their right to sin.

But this is an old, old story that has repeated itself throughout the history of civilization. You might think of it as a sort of neoclassical sandwich that keeps reappearing in new disguises every now and then. The ancient world was very religious. People understood the reality of heaven and hell, acknowledged the reality of God, and knew that life has an eternal dimension that extends beyond the present. There was great debate over the proper form of religions and strife between the various cults and religions of the day, but it was not until the Gnostic heresy arose in the mid-first century A.D., at about the time that the apostle Paul was on his missionary journeys in Asia Minor, that people began to see man as the source of his own salvation.

The Gnostics claimed that there is a duality in the universe, a warfare of good and evil, and that through intense spiritual discipline and intellectual attainments, humankind could attain a perfect knowledge of the divine. During the second and third centuries, Gnosticism became a major heresy. The church fathers roundly condemned its teachings, but it did not die out. The same idea of the perfectibility of man comes back to haunt society time and time again. It appeared in the Renaissance as the idea of "humanism," then it lost credibility during the Reformation. It returned during the Enlightenment in England and France but lost support once again during the nineteenth century. Today the neoclassical idea is very much alive and even dominant in our culture in the ideas of "secular humanism." The warfare today between church and state is just one more expression of this ancient debate. Basically, it is an age-old warfare between the Bible and the classical ideal of the perfectibility of man—an optimistic and wishful idea that has no basis in fact.

The White House has made no secret of the fact that they intend to get control of our children as early as possible to get them programmed for their new vision of society. Adolf Hitler had the same goal. Whenever people believe that the state holds the answer to all our needs, they think nothing of changing traditions or of breaking down the unity of the family by turning parents and children against each other. If they can get control of children in their most impressionable years, teach them their radical theories and program their minds, then one day they can gain control over the whole of society once and for all. When you see secular programming in the schools through textbooks, reading material, assignments that make a virtual religion out of environmental studies as well as of video and computer materials that have a scientific New Age point of view, you can be certain that this is a deliberate and highly sophisticated attempt to take control of the nation by controlling the minds of the next generation of young people.

History teaches that great nations are seldom if ever destroyed by invaders or other outside forces. Wars and invasions may be involved in their final collapse, but nations fall because of compromise of their own foundational beliefs, loss of faith in the values that made them great, and the lawlessness and disorder that arise as a result. Make no mistake: *Unless people rise up and demand a return to moral standards, this nation will be destroyed from within.* Secular humanists have already taken over the public-school system. They are teaching an insidious and dangerous doctrine, and the young people who are constantly exposed to the destructive teachings of those amoral and anti-Christian educators have been exposed, as it were, to a deadly virus that will eat away at their souls. Unless the antidote of faith and a return to our historical views and values is applied, this nation will surely die of the infection.

One very obvious biblical principle that was incorporated in the founding of this country, which sets it apart from other revolutions, is a theological view of man. The French Revolution saw man as basically good. In the Russian Revolution, Marx saw man as basically good. The humanists also view man as perfectible. The American Revolution, on the other hand, took the Christian view that man is basically sinful and corrupt. The common belief expressed by Lord Acton that "power corrupts, and absolute power corrupts absolutely," would not even exist if man were capable of perfection. If man's nature were naturally noble, then the more power he attained the greater his nobility would be. But, in fact, power does allow man to attain his true nature, but his nature is corrupt. Charles C. Colton put it even more graphically when he said, "Power will intoxicate the best hearts, as wine the strongest heads. No man is wise enough, nor good enough to be trusted with unlimited power." We should add that only the transforming power of faith and Christian virtue can restore balance to the equation.

CHECKS AND BALANCES

When I took civics in junior high school, none of the theological principles behind the topic were ever taught. I now believe that lack of insight deprived the study of history of its deeper significance and its moral consequence. They did tell us that power is divided between three branches of government—the executive, legislative, and judicial—and these are further moderated by a complex system of checks and balances. There were, by design, limitations on the power of each branch, and the powers designated to the branches were specifically enumerated by the Constitution so that no branch of government could take unto itself rights and privileges it should not possess. And all powers not specifically granted to the government were to reside either with the individual states or with the people.

Why did the founders go to such pains to create these restraints and limitations on the government? Because they knew that one day there would be people who would try to monopolize the system and wield greater authority than they should. Some feared that the executive branch, which is the office of the president, might try to take control of everything. A president with too much power could make himself dictator and try to take control of the entire nation. Some people feel we came very close to that under Franklin Roosevelt. Others feared that the Congress might try to rule the nation and take unfair advantage of their law-making authority. I believe we are seeing expressions of that danger today. And others, like Jefferson, feared that the judiciary would try to legislate from the bench and change the laws of the land to suit their personal preferences, thus taking away the essential rights and responsibilities of the people. We have been living under that dark mantle for the past forty years.

As children we were also taught that these checks and balances were designed to make sure that each branch of government had just enough power to do its job but not enough to wreak havoc on the nation. Unfortunately, the laws have been modified to such a great extent over the past three decades that we are no longer as secure from the federal bureaucracy as we once were. The principle of checks and balances is routinely abused, and government has ignored those founding principles. They have expanded their own authority more and more, without the limitations specifically ordained by the founding documents of the nation.

At one time, as you may remember from your study of history, there was an intense battle in the Congress over the issue of states' rights. Thomas Jefferson argued that all powers and rights not specifically granted to the federal government should reside with the states. That is constitutional. Why did he push so hard for this principle? Because he knew that "power corrupts and absolute power corrupts absolutely."

And of course, the first ten amendments are an expression of the same desire to restrain the lust for power. Why were the first ten amendments created? Again, it goes back to the biblical view of man, to the corruption of human nature, and to the problem of sin. Both George Washington and Patrick Henry absolutely insisted upon a Bill of Rights, and the ten amendments that make up the Bill of Rights were designed to protect the people from government, not the other way around.

In his letter to the Baptist congregation in Connecticut, in which he first used the term "a wall of separation between church and state," Thomas Jefferson was not implying that the church should be restrained but that government could have no religious function. This is, of course, where we get the concept that has been extended beyond all reason by civil libertarians and atheists in our time. The wall, as Jefferson perceived it, was there to restrain the government, not to penalize the church.

Maybe you can think of it as like King Kong, in the movie, when the giant gorilla is brought to this country and put on display. He is there on stage, bound with steel manacles, and under all kinds of restraints. The chains are there to protect the people from the monster. Well, like King Kong, the government is constantly tugging at its chains trying to see how much it can get away with, and before one knows it, the monster has broken his manacles and is reaching right into the hotel and taking people out of their rooms. The next thing, he has come up through the elevated train tracks and has the people trapped inside the cars, and he's shaking them up and down and killing them by the dozens. Suddenly the people are no longer protected from the monster.

The First Amendment was to protect the people from the government, but the "wall of separation" affects people on both sides of the wall. Anytime you hear the concept of the separation of church and state being talked about these days, it is never in regard to maintaining the restraints on government; instead, it is always talking about what Christians and churches cannot do. The government and the bureaucrats who hang around government want to limit what ministers and religious people can do, so they have reversed the meaning of the term. They started by making it a two-way street, where both church and state were protected from each other. But now they have turned it completely around so that the purpose of the First Amendment is perceived as protecting the government from religious people. And that is the opposite of what it was *intended* to be.

THE RESTRAINT OF TYRANNY

A reporter called me one day to get some information on one of our programs, and during the conversation he brought up the subject of the separation of church and state, speaking as if the phrase were a constitutional term. So I told him, "You know, that's not really in our constitution." He seemed a little surprised, and he said, "Well, that's what my Constitution teaches."

I said, "No, it isn't. It's very different." I told him, just as I have described it, that the first ten amendments are one-way streets to protect the people from the government, and that the wall of separation impedes people on both sides of the wall.

He paused a moment, then he said, "That's ridiculous! That's not the case at all."

So I said, "Have you ever stopped to think what comes in the very next section? After the first two clauses concerning freedom of religion, the First Amendment goes on to say that Congress shall make no law abridging freedom of speech or press or the right to assemble and petition for redress of grievances. So, in that section, comes the constitutional guarantee of *freedom of the press*." He didn't say anything, so I said, "You see, that provision of the amendment was meant to protect the press from hindrance or from any intrusions by the government."

The reporter still wasn't saying much, so I continued. "Suppose we change that wording just a little and say that what the framers of the Constitution really meant was that there should be a 'wall of separation' between press and state. Now that means that the government can do nothing against you, but you can do nothing against the government. In other words, as a reporter, you can't say anything or write anything against the government because that would be a violation of the 'wall of separation between press and state.' And if that were the case, my friend, you and many of your fellow reporters would all be in jail right now."

He said, "You know, I never thought of that before."

But that is the true sense in which these amendments were passed. When James Madison introduced the amendments of the Bill of Rights to the House of Representatives on June 8, 1789, he called them "securities for liberty" and said they were designed to "declare the great rights of mankind." Nothing in them was meant to suggest that they were meant to safeguard the state from the church or to protect the government from the press. They were to protect the people against the abuse of power by the branches of government.

The idea of a "separation of church and state" as it now exists was never a part of American jurisprudence until the ACLU lawyer, Leo Pfeffer, wrote and presented the ACLU's brief on the question of law in *Everson v. Board of Education* in 1947. Pfeffer's statement was given to Chief Justice Hugo Black, who submitted it as his decision in the Everson case. That was the first time in the history of the United States that such a thing had ever been done, and on that day two new concepts entered into American jurisprudence: the separation of church and state, and the notion that this is a secular nation. Having thus imported those alien concepts into American law, the ACLU then proceeded to take out its judicial hammer and bash Christianity for the next forty-five years. Justice Black not only presented the opinion but cast the final and deciding vote in a 5–4 decision. So, by the vote of one man, this country was dislodged from its Christian foundations and made into a secular nation.

It really is tragic what that one case has done to this country. After we had just been through the Second World War, after God had blessed the nation so bountifully, and after He had preserved us in so many ways, then all of a sudden we turned our backs on God. And the tragedy is that the United States has grown further and further from God ever since, and today many people in this country are desperately searching for something to believe in. It is as if we were stripped of our heritage of faith and belief, leaving America's souls empty. Today we are a nation in search of our soul and, short of a miracle, or some sort of spiritual awakening, our hopes for the future seem poor indeed.

A CALL FOR RENEWAL

As important as it is to reflect upon the various disturbances and difficulties that plague this nation today, and as much as we need to examine the undeniable crises that confront modern culture, ultimately the restoration of America is secondary to the call for *repentance* and *renewal*. The urgent need of the church today is to fulfill the Great Commission worldwide and continue the building of the kingdom of God. Our duty, whatever else may happen in this nation or around the globe, is to tell men, women, and children that Jesus Christ is the living truth and our only hope of salvation. Jesus said, "I am the way, the truth, and the life. No one comes to the Father but by me" (John 14:6). The only way we can ever have peace with God is to acknowledge that truth and receive Christ as Lord of our lives.

I believe, however, as our founding fathers said, that God in His infinite wisdom and providence reserved this nation, separated by two oceans from the civilized world of that day, until such a time as this. I believe He set this land and these people apart as the last best hope of people on earth. His purpose was to establish here a godly nation built upon Christian principles, a nation capable of maintaining religious and political freedom and serving as a model of faith and fruitfulness to the rest of the world. It was His plan that a great nation might flourish here as no other nation had ever done, so that it might provide a beacon of hope to people everywhere.

For many years this country was an example to the whole world, just as Alexis de Tocqueville described it. Tragically, we have turned our back upon our patrimony in large measure—at least in the upper echelons that control the essential institutions of the country. We have abandoned the godly principles set forth by our founding fathers, and now we are suffering the consequences of apostasy and doubt, which are already grievous and which portend even more ghastly suffering and loss. In the next decade we may see disasters and destruction upon this nation beyond anything we could every have imagined. Unless we come back to God, we may well witness the loss of everything we cherish.

There is such a desperate need for this country to repent of its ungodliness and return to its religious foundations. I believe there is still hope that we might prosper once again and grow, and that we may not have to endure the wrath of God. But remember that the Bible says, "Blessed is the nation whose God is the Lord" (Ps. 33:12). That is a great promise of hope. But it also says, "The wicked shall be turned into hell, and all the nations that forget God" (Ps. 9:17 KJV). Those are the two options we face today. We can choose God and reap a harvest of renewed blessings, or we can choose the vanity of man and the secular life promised by the state—and reap a harvest of doom. *We must get right with God.*

THE DIVIDED CULTURE

There are some people in our society, however, who do not see the renewal of faith and our historic republican values as reclaiming a nation but almost as an alien effort to take over a nation to which we have no prior claim. When we conducted our three-day conference entitled "Reclaiming America" at Coral Ridge Presbyterian Church in January 1994, the church was surrounded by demonstrators, gay-rights activists, and other radical pressure groups, who said we were trying to deny their freedom. The press acted as if we were aliens trying to invade the nation with beliefs and views that are foreign to the American culture.

The problem is education. At least since the mid-sixties, we have been robbed of our history, and as a consequence, anyone under the age of forty who has simply accepted without questioning the liberal public-school curriculum, or anyone who allows the media to determine his or her beliefs, has no idea what the legitimate roots of this nation are. If we are going to reclaim America's birthright of freedom, we must also reclaim our heritage. That means getting rid of the "politically correct" doctrines of the humanists and returning to the great traditions of history, literature, and language that have stood the test of time.

The only way to do that, many people believe, is to get our children into Christian schools that are not infected with the humanist and New Age disciplines. Today there are already more than three million students in Christian schools around this country. Ironically, if you went back just one hundred years you would find that all students in American schools were in Christian schools. They were not called Christian schools in those day—they were called public schools. All school children, for more than two hundred years, were taught principles of faith as a central part of their education, and they were the best-educated and best-behaved young people in history.

To remember how Christian the schools in this country truly were, one has but to recall that in 1890 the Roman Catholic Church started its own school system. Why? Was it because of the secular element in the schools? No. It was because the public schools were so overwhelmingly Protestant that the Catholic families and their priests felt they needed to start their own school system in order to make sure their own point of view was expressed. So we have, indeed, come a long way from the beginning of this nation.

It is, of course, the contention of probably most people that this nation began basically as a Christian nation. The Mayflower Compact was the first draft of a United States Constitution. At least, it was the first attempt at a general covenant among the settlers, and it was written in the captain's quarters on board the Mayflower just a few days before landing at Plymouth, Massachusetts. That famous document, sometimes referred to as the "birth certificate of America," stated that they set out in this great undertaking to establish the first colony on the northern parts of Virginia "for the gloire of God, and the advancements of the Christian faith." Even though they did not quite get to the northern parts of Virginia, it is why the first settlers came.

That was in 1620, and there are documents from succeeding decades that make the same sorts of statements. The same statements were made in 1643, when delegates from the colonies joined together to sign the New England Confederation. Today we are told that this was not intended to be a Christian nation, but read what the colonists said: The New England Confederation says, "we all came into these parts of America with one and the same end and aim, namely, to advance the Kingdom of our Lord Jesus Christ and to enjoy the liberties of the Gospel in purity with peace." Yes, we have come a long way since those times; unfortunately, much of it has been downhill. And the battle rages on.

A CIVIL WAR OF VALUES

I saw a graph recently that absolutely astounded me. It showed two lines, one representing the rise of illiteracy in America, the other showing the rise in what was pejoratively called "fundamentalism." The latter terms was, of course, meant to suggest all forms of evangelical Christianity. The implication was that the rise of Christianity had brought about a rise in illiteracy. It makes me wonder if those who prepare such graphs are totally ignorant of all the tests that have been conducted across the country, comparing the scores of students in Christian schools with those of students in the public schools? Generally, students in Christian schools average almost two grades higher than those in the public school system. In addition, they score from fifteen to twenty-five points higher on all standardized exams. That is not a boast. It is not wishful thinking. It is the simple truth, and test after test confirms that fact. But why is it true? Is it because Christians are smarter? Is it because Christian-school teachers are so much better? No. It is because the loss of Christian morality, the loss of a Christian worldview, and the loss of a moral purpose in life has resulted in a tragic loss of perspective, which leads to a decline in educational standards.

An objective of this book is to examine the dilemma of "a nation in search of its soul." Why is it that the most radical ideas appeal to the intellectuals? Those who supposedly should be the clearest thinking, most well-read, and most experienced people in our society, want to "change" society in keeping with some utopian model. In his book *Populism and Elitism,* Jeffrey Bell says that the reason for the current culture war that is raging in American society is not the conflict between church and state or between religious and secular society but the struggle between the common people and the intellectuals. The average American simply wants to live a good life in a comfortable sort of way. But the elitists, bureaucrats, and intellectuals want something radically different. They want a man-made paradise.

Why do these so-called elites want to destroy the traditional culture of America? Well, I think that there are two major streams at work here, and they go back to the time of Christ, and before. In the third and fourth centuries B.C., the Greeks attained the Golden Age of ancient culture. In Plato's *Republic*, it is very clear that the philosopher was proposing a communal, socialistic type of government. He talks about getting the children out of the homes to be taught by the state. So the intellectual ideal of Greek philosophy was Communist, or at least socialistic. But later we see the emergence of Christianity, which stressed the "priesthood of the individual believer." The apostle Paul said, "It is for freedom that Christ has set us free." And he told the believers in Asia Minor, "Stand firm, then, and do not let yourselves be burdened again by a yoke of slavery" (Gal. 5:1). Earlier, in his second letter to the church at Corinth, the apostle had said, "where the Spirit of the Lord is, there is freedom" (2 Cor. 3:17). So at the foundation of the Christian faith is the idea of freedom.

In the first century, Christians shared their goods and they did some things communally as a result of their incredible excitement over the Gospel and their love for one another, but it was clear from the start that faith is an intensely personal matter between us and God. Society has no voice in our salvation. The church cannot save us. Baptism or communion or good works cannot save us. Each person must come to his own hour of decision and confess belief and faith in Jesus Christ. Short of that there is no hope and no salvation. So this view, which Martin Luther made even more vocal during the Protestant Reformation, was clearly an enormous contrast to the socialist view of the Greeks and the Gnostics. But these two streams of belief have been in conflict ever since.

After the Emperor Constantine made Christianity the official religion of the Roman Empire in the fourth century, the teachings of the Christian church were spread throughout the known world. The Holy Roman Empire in Europe, which continued in one form or another for a thousand years, was founded on Christian teachings, but in the thirteenth and fourteenth centuries there was a revival of classical learning. During the Renaissance, the writings of Aristotle were rediscovered, along with the teachings of Plato and Socrates. Then the Reformation came along and called everyone back out of the Dark Ages to the Gospel. As I said early in this chapter, all of modern history, at least for the last five hundred years, has been the record of conflict between the worldviews put forth by the Renaissance and the Reformation.

Wherever classical teaching is in vogue, you will find socialism, which calls for communal thinking. But wherever Christianity is taught, freedom and individualism prevail. I have no doubt that without the Christian beliefs and values of our founding fathers—rooted in their strong belief in freedom and individualism—this great nation, as it has been over the past two hundred years, would never have come into existence. The pilgrims took an unbelievable risk in coming to a New World in search of freedom, and their quest was motivated first and foremost by their faith in God.

THE POST-CHRISTIAN AGE

Yet, today we are still enduring this age-old conflict in Western society between Reformation and Renaissance beliefs. Clearly, the Enlightenment in France was another expression of the Renaissance's bearing bitter fruit. Had they known their historical models, the men and women of the Enlightenment could have had a preview of coming attractions by simply looking back at the fruits of secular ideology in ancient times. In Greece and Rome, as well as in the succession of wars and disasters ever after, they could have had a portrait of the ghastly results their vision has produced. But they were not looking. They were misled.

Today, these same views are being spread throughout America's schools and universities. As we have seen, it is even coming down to the kindergartens. Consequently, we now live in what liberals love to call the "post-Christian era." As I mentioned in the first chapter, fully eighty-five percent of the people in this country still profess the Christian faith. More than 106 million people attend church on an average Sunday in America. We have moved far from the traditions of Christian faith and morality of a century ago, but this is certainly not yet a post-Christian era like that of Germany or France or England today. *But it is coming.* In the major institutions of education, government, science, and the arts, we are witnessing the imposition of a post-Christian view of life. It now dominates in motion pictures, television, and every other form of entertainment. Most people would agree that, in comparison with the America of the 1950s, we are in a post-Christian age. But the war is not over.

It's amazing how unbelievers have taken over all of the significant areas of influence, even the libraries. Horace Mann, who was one of the first to try to eliminate religious and moral instruction in the schools, said that his purpose was to get education out of the hands of the clergy, where it had always been since the founding of this country. And it is very informative, in reading the writings of the various leaders of the public school movement, how they occasionally leave the window open, as it were, and let people know what is really going on inside their minds. I think of Dr. Paul Blanshard, a humanist educator who wrote a book on the separation of church and state, saying that "Our schools may not teach Johnny to read properly, but the fact that Johnny is in school until he is sixteen tends to lead toward the elimination of religious superstition. The average American child now acquires a high-school education, and this militates against Adam and Eve and all other myths of alleged history."

So, here and in many other similar statements, we see the view of the humanist tradition. Here is the neoclassical ideal of the perfectibility of man without the intervention of God. It may sound noble and scientific. It may even sound feasible. But it is contrary to the truth of human experience and, without a doubt, it is contrary to the great Christian tradition that brought forth this great nation. *To lose that source of authority now is truly tragic.*

Think of all the lost centers of influence that we simply did not understand or appreciate. Think of all the lost opportunities for giving people a moral foundation for life and for enriching their hopes for the future. When the motion picture was first invented in the 1890s, one of the early pioneers of the new process suggested that it would be a wonderful instrument that could be used and developed by the Christian leaders of America. Unfortunately, the churches didn't understand it and didn't see the potential. They refused the offer. Just think about losing the opportunity for motion picture films. I also think of the times, just after World War II, when General Douglas MacArthur wired the churches of America to bring ten thousand Christian missionaries to Japan because the people of Asia were ready for the Word of God. But few came. They didn't have the vision. Either they couldn't come up with the resources, or they didn't see what might happen if they missed this opportunity. So they didn't go.

The inventor of the motion picture offered his invention to the church, but no one knew what to make of it. They let it go to the entertainment industry and to Hollywood instead. The churches and missionaries did not go to Japan because they did not know what to make of it. Today Japan is one of the least Christian nations on earth. In both cases, we lost tremendous opportunities. For whatever reasons, the Christian church abandoned its cultural mandate and lost the chance to change history. Are we ignoring other opportunities just as remarkable today? Are we overlooking something of equal importance?

THE CULTURAL MANDATE

Whenever a president or an elected official wins public office by a landslide, it is said that they have a "mandate from the people" to carry out their campaign objectives. The cultural mandate, as I see it, is a challenge to all Christians from God Himself to carry out the Great Commission and to fulfill their commitments to "redeem the time." The first commandment that God ever gave to mankind, as recorded in Genesis 1:28, was the command to be fruitful and multiply and replenish the earth. Humans were to subdue the earth and have dominion over the fish of the sea and the fowl of the air. They were to exercise authority over every living thing. Today there are people that criticize Christians who hold such a view. They say it is just an excuse to exploit the earth and to indulge in greed and imperialism. But the doctrine of stewardship was a mandate from God that has never been revoked or countermanded.

You may wonder how this teaching applies to us, in the last decade of the twentieth century, when practically every inch of the earth's surface is under someone's dominion. First of all, we are still to be fruitful and multiply and replenish the earth. The passage does not say we are to have dominion over other men but over the earth and all the things in it that are created by God. Would God be saying to unregenerate people today that they are to rule the earth? I don't think so. He is speaking to those of us who have been recreated into the image of God and who are being refashioned by Him.

As the Christian hymn says, "This is my Father's world," and we should endeavor to give glory to God in His own world. What has happened so often in the cultural institutions of our society is that they have been taken over by unbelievers who have produced monstrosities that give glory not to God but to Satan. Consequently, God is robbed of His rightful glory in His own world. How much glory does God get out of Hollywood? Out of television? Out of the National Endowment for the Arts? How is God treated in our museums, libraries, and public-school systems? How is He treated by political and government leaders? The very thought is frightening.

If God has been expelled from the schools, that is certainly bad news. But unbelievers have attempted to expel God from His own world, and Christians have stood by silently while all this has happened. As long as Christians continue hiding out in their churches and homes with the doors locked, the secular world is going to continue trying to expel God from every place they possibly can. God is sovereign, and He will decide how far they will be allowed to go, but perhaps He has allowed them to go so far so He can find out just how committed to Him His people truly are. Yes, God will win in the end—there is absolutely no doubt of that. But has He given us this moment of tribulation to try our spirits and allow us to share in His ultimate victory? Christians of an earlier era allowed so many great marvels and so many lost opportunities to pass them by. Are we in danger of losing this opportunity as well?

I encounter far too many people who have a split personality about the authority of God. On one hand, they believe the Great Commission and agree that they should support the work of evangelizing the lost. But when it comes to influencing the culture with Christian values—and when it comes to speaking out from a framework of Christian values in cultural, social, and political situations—they run for cover. If God is God, then He is Lord of all. He is not just the Source of salvation but the very Wellspring of life. If God rules in our hearts, then He must also rule in our heads—every day and in every way. If you believe that God can save a lost soul, then you must believe He can save our lost world. If Jesus Christ is the Lord of the Great Commission, then He is absolutely and without question the Lord of the *cultural mandate*.

Believe me, if we concede the field of battle to the atheists, secularists, and humanists of our day, they will take everything we will give them. Throughout the history of this nation, liberty has been maintained by Christian men and women who have taken a stand and said, "You may go this far and no farther." Unless Christians today stand firm in their faith and preserve this nation with the same sort of resolve, we may indeed lose everything.

As I say this, allow me to clarify my perspective and my use of the term "cultural mandate." There are some people who subscribe to some of these same principles of Scripture as a "dominion covenant." That is the view that Christians were given the authority to take control of all aspects of public and private life and to occupy the kingdom until Christ returns. That is a more militant idea than I have in mind, and it is not my belief or my intent. I think that teaching gives the impression that Christians believe they are to lord it over unbelievers, and I believe that only isolates us even further. In reality, that is certainly not what Christ was saying in the Great Commission, which was His last statement on earth. He said, "Go and make disciples of all nations, baptizing them in the name of the Father and of the Son and of the Holy Spirit, and teaching them to obey everything I have commanded you. And surely I am with you always, to the very end of the age" (Matt. 28:19–20). We are not to simply hold on to our faith and rule the world, but we are to share our faith and love with all mankind and, together, we are to live in peace until Christ returns.

The first statement of God to Adam and Eve, and the last statement of Christ to His disciples, was to go into all the earth and take the "good news" of God's love to all people. We are to evangelize the people of all nations. But we must also disciple the nations—that is, to teach them to observe all things that Christ has taught us. And since God speaks and has spoken on almost every conceivable issue of human life, we need to bring that word to bear. That's what I mean by the cultural mandate. We are to influence the world for Christ.

THE CHANGING SCENE

Bertrand Russell once said, when God and His purpose for the universe have been gotten rid of, it "frees me up to pursue my erotic desires." That is the principal motivation of those who deny God's reality—their own selfish desires. But observe how things have changed in just a few years. If you go back to 1950, the biggest problem between the church and the rest of the world was not abortion. Abortion was no problem at that time. It was frowned on by everyone, and it was against the law. The biggest problem wasn't the godlessness of public school textbooks. That wasn't a problem at that time, and no one was pushing New Age ideas or any of the generally accepted views of sexuality and immorality we see in the schools today.

Sex education in kindergarten and the idea that Jesus Christ may have been a mythical figure were simply not an issue. We had prayer and Bible reading in schools, so there was no conflict over those issues. They certainly weren't giving out condoms in schools, and sexual permissiveness was minimal compared to what it is today. Teenage pregnancy was a rarity and a disgrace. Homosexuality was invisible and did not exist to any significant degree at that time.

So what has changed? Is it the church that has changed? No, it is the world. And it is the enormous change in the views and values of secular Americans that represents such a great danger to our future as a nation. For one thing, the morality of the common man has slipped so far that the things people accept today as "normal" would have been considered an abomination to church members a half century ago.

Little by little, the world has changed, and its values have infiltrated the church. Sin has become common, and compromise is too easily accepted. The church simply closed its eyes and never saw the danger that was looming just ahead. Christians felt safe in their holy huddles, and they withdrew into the cloisters, saying, "Well, we'll just take care of our own and give up everything outside these doors. We'll maintain the sanctity of our own home and churches." But what happened as a result of that kind of thinking? Marauders came and took everything that wasn't nailed down. Now, neither the home, the church, the neighborhood, nor the world is safe, and Christians bear much of the blame for this situation.

The enemy is outside today, banging on the door, trying to get in and enter your bedroom and despoil the privacy of your home. Not only that—they're trying to take control of your children. I recently saw an article that proclaimed that the secular educators are going to start taking children out of the home from the first minute they begin to toddle, so that they can begin training them up for life in a new secular world order.

In 1850, virtually every newspaper in this country was run by Christians. All the schools, academies, and great universities were run by Christians. The law and the federal and local judiciaries were all either Christian or Jewish, and all these institutions attested to the great liberty and justice in this country at that time. But 1848 was a momentous year for the world. In that year, the *Communist Manifesto* was first published by Karl Marx, and the French philosopher, Auguste Comte, published his work on "logical positivism," which was another secular answer to the meaning of life. In the United States, the women's movement began with a "Declaration of Sentiments" at a conference in Seneca Falls, New York.

That was also the year the California Gold Rush began, and many other changes were taking place in the world at that time. Eleven years later, in 1859, Darwin published *The Origin of the Species*. And even though it wasn't until the turn of the century that all these things suddenly had enough momentum to challenge the historic values and foundations of society, their impact continues to this day, and they are evidence of the turmoil in America's soul.

THE MONSTER YET LIVES

In our day, it looks as if communism may be dead as a major political system. We don't know for certain that it is dead forever, but we assume that it is. Liberals are saying in print that communism is dead. It has been declared dead in Russia, and in Europe. But, ironically, communism and socialism live on in the American government today. Communism is alive in American jurisprudence, in the law schools and universities, and it lives in many other covert places all over this nation. We must even say that it is alive in many of our churches, and in American homes, and it is alive in what your children are learning in the classroom. The essential danger of communism is not its economic theories or its ideals of communal property but its denial of the reality and transcendence of God. The worker's paradise was a man-made vision of peace on earth. Today we know that the Communist vision of paradise was really hell on earth; but the ideology has not disappeared.

While the whole world has been rejoicing over the demise of communism and the dismantling of the Berlin Wall, a small group of people has been working day and night to make sure the flame of communism does not expire. They are putting out papers that say communism is alive and well and that true believers must not give up hope. They are like the Grinch that stole Christmas. Everybody is rejoicing, but these people are saying, "No, stop rejoicing! Communism is not dead, it's alive!"

Just a few years ago there were as many as ten thousand Communist professors in American universities. The average person never saw any of them, and many would doubt the truth of that statistic. But I can assure you it is true. When I was a doctoral candidate at New York University, my sociology professor's first comment on the first day of class was, "I want you to understand that I am a Communist, and I will be presenting all this material from a Communist perspective." I couldn't believe my ears. I was shocked to hear such an open admission from a man who obviously wanted to see the destruction of this nation. But nobody in that class even blinked an eye.

Later, when I was concluding my dissertation, I went back to meet with my doctoral committee, and I found that there was some kind of fair going on in and around the campus, which is right at Washington Square, at the southern end of Manhattan. All the streets around the university were blocked off. The traffic was blocked, and there were tables that went down the middle of the streets for at least a mile through Greenwich Village. There were thousands of people on the sidewalks, in the streets, all of them standing around looking at the stuff on the tables. Bands were playing on every corner. It looked like a big county fair or a major festival of some kind.

I thought, *Well, this is interesting. I wonder what's going on here.* So I worked my way through the crowd to get to one of the tables, and there were all the books they were selling: *Das Kapital* by Karl Marx, Chairman Mao's *Little Red Book*, as well as many other books, pictures, and pamphlets honoring Communist heroes such as Ché Guevara, Fidel Castro, and others. One after the other, every table on that enormous mall was set up as a tribute to the most despicable tyrants and villains of our age. For the New York intellectuals, that was clearly a commonplace idea. For me, it was a symbol of the danger that is always there. And I see America in a similar situation today. Communism is dead, right? Gorbachev and the arms race are all gone, right? Maybe, maybe not. The real danger we face may very well be that we are being lulled to sleep by those who are telling us that the Soviet Union has collapsed, while, in fact, the monster yet lives.

I will be one of the first to say that we ought to rejoice in the victories won over the past five years, but we must not forget that the ideologies of our enemies have not all died out. They may be found today on the great university campuses and in the halls of government. Remember that after the Allied victory in World War II, after peace was declared and all the treaties had been signed, we found that there were still pockets of resistance in some of the islands in the Pacific. In one case, one lone Japanese soldier continued his vigil for twenty or twenty-five years without knowing that the war was over.

Well, there are still pockets of resistance throughout this nation. In some cases they are preaching outright communism; in others they are preaching "deconstructionism" and "post-structuralism," and other modern ideologies that hold that traditional Western values—and certainly anything to do with Christianity—are dangerous to their humanist ideals. There are still some very adamant Marxists out there working for the overthrow of this nation. But all the ideas coming from the secular establishment are dangerous to faith, and we ignore these threats at the greatest possible risk to our future security. *Our cultural mandate is to stand by our convictions against all odds, and to know that, in Christ, we shall overcome the world.*

NOTES

[1]Josephus, *The Antiquities of the Jews*, XVIII, iii, 3.

3

Speaking Out for Freedom

When Dan Quayle spoke at our conference on faith and democracy in January 1994, an event called "Reclaiming America," he spoke of
the great tradition of freedom in this nation. The former vice president
reminded those present—along with the millions who saw his address on
nationwide television—that the patriots who founded this country were people of strong character and moral vision. He said, "Great Americans throughout our history have been those who strove to make this a more moral country. Trying to solve human problems with a more human blueprint."

But today, Quayle noted, there are many who say that Christians
are the problem. They say Christians have no right to express their views in
public, or to "force their values on others." But the history of this nation is
the story of Americans who have banded together to overcome adversity. In
tough times, it has always been the churches and the individual believers
who have fought to stop prejudice, to end slavery, to uphold civic virtues, to
feed the hungry, and to support those in need. "That isn't a conspiracy," said
Mr. Quayle, "I call it good citizenship." Christians believe that to do any less
would be inexcusable.

The vice president went on to say that "The day we quit trying to make America better is the day we stop being Americans." And he added, "The founders of this country would have agreed with that. They, like us, were a diverse group, with various and at times bitterly opposing theological views. But they had a common unifying principle. They all assumed that the nation's freedom depended upon its character. In short, they believed that to live free, the people had to live morally."

Economists today tell us that the United States still has the highest gross national product in the industrialized world. We have more automobiles, more VCRs, more fine homes, and more luxuries than any other nation. Unfortunately, those statistics don't reveal the tragic conditions in the soul of this nation. Beyond all the numbers, there is a terrible loss of moral values in this land that is ripping the nation apart, a fact that every citizen knows only too well. Mr. Quayle said, "Over the last thirty years or so, our culture has changed dramatically. The divorce rate has quadrupled. Teen suicides have doubled. Drug abuse moved from the fringes of society into every neighborhood. Violent crime jumped more than five hundred percent. Every one of these social problems, and many more, can be traced back to the same underlying malady: an abrupt decline in family life and a terrible weakening of the family structures." We all know these facts. We read about them in the headlines, but for some reason the problems are only getting worse, not better.

Given all these intractable problems, Christians have no other option. They have to speak up, and they have to be involved in offering solutions. Throwing more money at problems such as these will not solve them. Government will never be able to solve any of these problems, because they are moral problems that affect the depths of the human soul. And that is an area that can only be touched by faith.

Dan Quayle said, "We have to speak up and speak out for those family values that sustain the American character—responsibility, integrity, hard work, fidelity, and compassion. Most of all, we have to live those values in our own lives." Christians do have the answer, because we know the One who heals and restores lives. Not to speak, and not to hold up a new standard in such a time, would be unthinkable. And despite the harangues of the media and the secularists, people of faith must demand their rights to be heard. That is what the principle of religious liberty is all about. That is what it means to speak out for freedom.

A HIGH VIEW OF FAITH

One Sunday night a few years ago, a missionary came to our church in Fort Lauderdale just prior to the breakup of the Soviet Union and told a fascinating story about the reactions of the Russian people to Christianity. After living and working in Russia for a long time, the missionary had gone through a long and complicated process of getting permission from the Department of Education to distribute Bibles to one of the large high schools in the capital. This was an unusual opportunity, and he didn't want to make any mistakes, so he was careful to follow all the rules and to be very precise.

When the appointed day came around, he gathered up all his boxes of Bibles and transported them to the large old building in the center of the city and, with the help of a small group of Russian and American Christians, he carried them up the long steps into the school. As he entered the building, the principal came out to see what was going on and stood watching as the missionary stacked the bulky cardboard boxes on the cold stone floor.

The principal was a man of medium height, stocky shoulders, square jaw, short-cropped hair, steely gray eyes, and the look of a KGB Colonel. It was clear that no one dared cross this man. But the missionary reached over and handed him a copy of the Bible, with the name printed very simply on the cover, *The Book of Life*. The school official accepted the book but said nothing. Then, after looking briefly at the volume in his hand, he said, "Thank you for this book on religion. I have been thinking about teaching a course on religion next year, and I'm sure it will be helpful."

That was a very gracious reply under the circumstances, but the missionary said, "Excuse me, sir. But there seems to be some misunderstanding." The stocky man looked at him intently. "This is not a book on religion," the missionary told him, "it is a Bible."

Suddenly the principal's eyes opened wide in amazement. "What?" he said. "A Bible? This is a Bible?" The missionary stepped back, his heart starting to beat faster. He was afraid he might be in trouble now. No one had ever been allowed to pass out Bibles in a Russian high school before. Had he made some kind of mistake? But he looked back at the principal and nodded. "Yes, sir, it is a Bible."

All of a sudden the principal clasped the book to his chest and said, "A Bible! I don't believe it. Thank you, thank you! We were once a great Christian nation here in Russia. But we turned our backs upon God, and we have destroyed ourselves. Now, you have given me this book, this Bible. Thank you very much!"

When I first heard this story, I was filled with emotion. What a difference from the reactions of so many Americans today, who live in the "land of the free." We have liberty, we have Bibles, we have the Word of God, and it means so little to so many people. What a terrible shame. The conversation between the missionary and the school principal took place in Moscow, in the heart of Communist Russia, more than a year before the fall of the Iron Curtain. Those people, starved for the truth, understood instinctively that only the grace of God could save them. They knew that when they had the truth of the Christian faith, they were free. But when the Word of God was taken away from them, they became slaves of the socialist state. Is there any doubt that the Russian principal had a better understanding of the great value of Christianity than many people in this country today? Is there any doubt that God will surely bless any man and any nation who cherish Him in that way?

Those words should ring in our ears. *We were once a great Christian nation, here in Russia. But we turned our backs upon God and we have destroyed ourselves.* We can say much the same words: We were once a great Christian nation here in America, but we have turned our backs upon God and are well on the way to destroying ourselves, our nation, and our rich heritage of freedom. Is there any doubt that God will bring judgment upon the nation that turns its back upon Him?

The evidence of our self-destruction is all around us today. In Los Angeles, thousands of angry men, women, and teens took to the streets in the fall of 1992. Angry because a jury's verdict was unsatisfactory, they burned their own neighborhoods, beat and killed at least forty-four people, and unleashed a holocaust of violence and rage upon this nation. Later, we saw the reports of the gunman who killed six people and wounded twenty-three on a subway train in New York City, and the shocking story of a madman in Petaluma, California, who kidnapped a twelve-year-old girl from her bedroom, then raped and killed her.

The nation followed the news of Lyle and Eric Menendez, two brothers from a wealthy Los Angeles family, who confessed to brutally murdering their parents because they had withheld money and privileges from them. On two separate occasions, sympathetic juries could not agree that the young men were even guilty of any crime. And we have seen an endless string of mass murders and serial killings in every corner of this nation for nearly thirty years. Men crazed by pornography, or by addictions of various kinds, have taken the lives of dozens, even hundreds, of innocent men, women, and children. That is what life has become in the richest nation on earth.

During one ten-year span, more than 7,600 people were murdered on the job in this country. And while the senseless killing of tourists in Florida was making all the headlines, many others were being victimized in less-visible and less-publicized crimes. A Dade County Commissioner, along with his wife who was a Florida state representative, was robbed at gunpoint in 1993. The thief took five hundred dollars in cash and drove away in the commissioner's car. In 1992, the Manager of Dade County was robbed by a gun-wielding hoodlum. And a former Miami Chief of Police fired at burglars who broke into his home. In 1990, the mayor of Miami had to use his own gun to chase burglars from his home.

THE LOSS OF STANDARDS

What is happening to America? What is going on? Can't something be done to stop the madness? While all this is happening, we have seen an incredible rise in the rate of births to unwed mothers. Today, more than one-third of all births in this nation are to women without husbands, including twenty-two percent of all births to white women and sixty-six percent of births to black women. In the inner city, the rate of illegitimacy is as high as eighty percent.

America, the land of the free. "The home of the brave," we once called it. The richest, proudest, most dynamic nation on earth is producing a whole generation of people who have never known a father. In Los Angeles there are more than 7,800 police officers patrolling the streets, but the violence, rape, murder, and devastation continue. They cannot stop it. No amount of surveillance can stop it. Someone asked an LA police officer how many gang members there are in Los Angeles today. "We have a hundred thousand names in our records," the officer replied. "But how many of those people are currently active in gang activities?" he was asked. The officer said, "A hundred thousand, and almost every one of them is armed and dangerous."

The tragedy of illegitimacy, the rise of crime, the growing illiteracy, and all the other problems that cause us so much concern are but warning signs that we have turned our backs on God and are destroying ourselves. The secular society should be crying out to the church, begging Christians to step in and offer solutions. The president of the United States should be appointing a task force of Christian ministers and parachurch organizations to come up with a blueprint for solving America's moral problems. All over America, armies of concerned Christians should be mobilizing to attack the evil and the godlessness that are rampaging through the streets of this nation. Evangelists should be bringing the love of God and the truth of the redeeming power of Jesus Christ to every city and town—to the inner cities and the suburbs. But the nation does not want to hear from Christians. It has turned its back on God. It doesn't want to hear what God can do for America. And what the media demands from Christians, as I have said before, is our silence.

It was very interesting to see all the articles that appeared in the media prior to and during our "Reclaiming America" conference. The reporters told their subscribers and their broadcast audiences that the Christian community is trying to cram their idea of "family values" down America's throat. If we were Communists or socialists trying to infiltrate the government and destroy the economic capacity of the country, chances are they would have ignored us, or simply smiled. The secularists and the atheists in the media have enormous "tolerance for diversity" so long as your form of diversity does not include faith in God. They have little patience with Christian ideas about God, or anything else.

But the reporters all accuse us of waging a "culture war" upon America. I admit that there is a culture war going on and getting hotter all the time. Indeed, I am also glad to say that I often find myself in the thick of it. But the media are not being entirely honest, for they never mention who actually started the war.

On the last night of our 1993 conference, I was with Vice President Quayle, standing before a whole battery of television cameras and reporters, trying to respond to their questions about our agenda and our views on the state of American culture. As we offered our comments and listened to the way the reporters phrased their questions, one thing was very obvious: The idea that America was founded as a Christian nation was alien to most of them. In fact, it was something that was threatening to even mention.

I realized that if we had been sitting there spouting dirty words, or talking about any of the vile things that can be seen on television these days, they would have been totally unaffected. But to suggest that Christians had founded this nation and that the Declaration of Independence, the Constitution, the Bill of Rights, and all the other founding documents were specifically Christian in their design and purpose, was perceived as an obvious threat.

But the fact is, the United States of America *was* conceived and brought forth by Christians, and history tells that story in no uncertain terms. At least, the authentic history of America, the history that I learned as a child and the history that has been taught to young men and women for more than two hundred years tells that story. Anyone who reads about the values upon which this nation was founded understands perfectly well that this was, from the start, a Christian nation.

The culture war that is raging in America was started by those who have a different ideal and a different agenda for this country. Christians and other conservatives are simply trying to protect and preserve what is our own: a nation discovered, tamed, founded, defended, and nurtured from infancy to greatness by men and women of faith. No, we will not give up without a fight, and for that reason we are accused of waging a culture war upon America. We did not start the culture war, but we have a profound commitment to this nation and its values, and we *will* stand up for them. And, little by little, the truth is getting out.

ANTI-CHRISTIAN BIAS

Paul Vitz, the renowned professor of psychology at New York University, headed a blue-ribbon panel appointed by President Reagan in the mid-eighties to examine the history and social studies textbooks used in our public schools. After their in-depth study, the group concluded that there is a sense of paranoia on the part of textbook authors and publishers concerning the religious foundations of this country. Almost all references to the Christian heritage of this nation have been expurgated from textbooks, and all other teaching materials in our public school classrooms. History has been rewritten to exclude that vital perspective.

Since there is no mention of the Christian involvement in the founding of America, we have tens of millions of people in this country who do not have the foggiest idea where this country came from or who started it. And because of that liberal censorship, it is almost impossible to talk to anyone who grew up with that distorted view. The students of the "liberated" generations are so illiterate and so chronically biased in their understanding of their own history that nothing you say can penetrate their built-in censorship grid. Since I am frequently quoted by the press and interviewed by television reporters on these issues, I long ago learned that the truth will always fall on the censors' cutting-room floor, and the "objective" reporters will use only those sound bites they feel they can twist to present their own point of view and to discredit yours.

When Dan Quayle and I were being grilled by the media, we both knew there would be no effort to be objective or fair on the part of the reporters. If our words made it onto the news, they would be scrambled, taken out of context, and skewed to present our views as being absurd and out-of-touch. Nevertheless, since we had a whole roomful of news people, I thought it might be a good idea to turn that press conference into a classroom. So, I told those young people—some for the first time in their lives—that "all of the Pilgrims were Christians." That's why they came to America in the first place—for religious liberty.

I know of no other nation in the world that was founded by a group of people who so uniformly professed a common belief, but not everyone can grasp that fact. Recently, while speaking to a young woman, I casually mentioned the name of Patrick Henry. She looked at me with a blank expression and asked, "Who is he?" I said, "You mean you've never heard of Patrick Henry?" I couldn't believe my ears, but then I remembered that the history of this nation has been hidden and rewritten by liberal educators. And what a great loss!

Patrick Henry, the golden-tongued orator of the American Revolution, was the man whose impassioned speech at the Virginia Assembly on March 23, 1775, was the spark that ignited the American Revolution. In the peroration to that dramatic speech, he said, "Is life so dear or peace so sweet as to be purchased at the price of chains and slavery? Forbid it, Almighty God." Then he added, "I know not what course other men may take, but as for me, give me liberty or give me death!" Those are words that should ring in the pages of history. They are the words that struck the first chord of the Revolution.

There was absolute silence in the room when Henry concluded his remarks. The distinguished patriots and founders were stunned. For almost a full minute, silence filled the hall, and then one voice and then another was heard, and another saying, "Yes, he is right. We must be willing to risk our own security for the welfare of the nation. Without freedom, life is not worth living." And suddenly the cry rang out, "To arms! To arms!" Thus, in that hour, the heritage of American freedom was born. The triumphs of George Washington at Valley Forge and the final defeat of the British at Yorktown in 1781 were only the physical expressions of the liberty that had been awakened by Patrick Henry's impassioned words.

But how many people today know what else that great founder had to say? On another occasion, he proclaimed, "It cannot be emphasized too much or repeated too strongly that America was not founded by religionists, but by Christians; not upon religions, but upon the gospel of Jesus Christ." It was not founded by religionists, he said—it was founded by Christians. Those are Patrick Henry's words, but many Americans have never heard them. Their heritage of faith and freedom has been stolen.

AMERICA REVISED

Today, anyone under the age of forty is likely to be completely oblivious to the truth that this was a nation conceived and brought forth by Christians. In the first important work on historical revisionism in this country—which is the practice of revising the history textbooks of our public schools to accommodate the new liberal interpretation of America's past—Frances FitzGerald said that once history was permanent, etched in stone, and a permanent expression of the American culture. If it seemed dull, that was because it was so widely accepted. It was simply history. But today, everything has changed. History has been revised by liberal educators, and the nation is much the worse for what is being done to its noble past.

FitzGerald writes, "The society that was once uniform is now a patchwork of rich and poor, old and young, men and women, blacks, white, Hispanics, and Indians. The system that ran so smoothly by means of the Constitution under the guidance of benevolent conductor Presidents is now a rattletrap affair. The past is no highway to the present; it is a collection of issues and events that do not fit together and that lead in no single direction. The word 'progress' has been replaced by the word 'change'; children, the modern texts insist, should learn history so that they can adapt to the rapid changes taking place around them. History is proceeding in spite of us."[1]

Despite the eloquent description of the dismal condition of the modern history texts, FitzGerald's book goes on to suggest that it is all right to use history as a tool, so long as the tool is socially and politically expedient. While she describes very well the way "progressive" educators have manipulated texts for their own biases—following the lead of John Dewey and the social activists of the last century—she argues that Christians are doing the same thing from their own conservative, biblical bias. Like so many others, she overlooks the fact that George Washington, Thomas Jefferson, Benjamin Franklin, Patrick Henry, James Madison, John Adams, and many of the most prominent names among the founding fathers had pre-cisely the same conservative, biblical bias.

The most perceptive assessment of the damage being done in our schools today was offered by author David Horowitz, in his address in Toronto to the very liberal, very politically correct Modern Language Asso-ciation, in December 1993. In his brilliant analysis of the crisis of values in the universities, Horowitz called a spade a spade and laid the guilt for the plague of historical revisionism and moral relativism squarely at the feet of the liberals and intellectuals of the West. "The intellectual level of the Amer-ican university," he said, "is at its lowest ebb in its three-hundred-year his-tory, less academically free than when colleges were run by religious puritans. Its mission was once the disinterested pursuit of knowledge and the education of moral character. Today it has been redefined by a generation of radicals so that its tasks have become political indoctrination and cultural deconstruction. The American university is now part of the problem rather than the solution."

But the failed ideologies of the elite in the schools and universities, Horowitz points out, are not simply a new way of thinking. Liberals love to make people think they are onto something new and different. But, in fact, the rhetoric coming out of these educators is just a new visitation of the dangerous ideas of Hitler and Stalin, brought back in modern dress.

Horowitz says, "The oppressive apparatus of the new campus thought control is justified by the prospect of 'eliminating racism, sexism and classism'—that is, by the same fantastic vision of a liberated future that inspired the Nazi and Communist disasters." But the roots of "deconstructionism," and the other destructive ideologies in the universities have even deeper and darker roots. "Marx himself identified the radical's affinity with the Great Destroyer, invoking Mephistopheles' dictum: 'All that exists deserves to perish.' What is the radical's imperative but the Devil's choice: To sever the past from the future, to annihilate what is for what will be."

In his brilliant assessment, Horowitz points out the true source of the liberals' attempts to redesign the American value system. That source is not merely sentimental thinking. It is not just the liberal desire to be generous to the weak and "disadvantaged." In fact, at the bottom of the "change" movement is a deep desire to dismantle this nation and to sever average Americans from their heritage of faith and freedom. The obvious implication is that at its foundation, this is the work of the Enemy himself. Horowitz quotes from the words of

Mephistopheles, the Devil in Goethe's drama, *Faust*, when he declares, "All that exists deserves to perish." That statement is the central belief of the philosophy of nihilism, the root of all the destructive political theories of this century—including socialism, communism, and deconstructionism. The desire to destroy everything that exists, and to "change" and "reinvent" the history of the nation, is first and last the work of the Destroyer who is the enemy of America's soul.

I cannot stress forcefully enough how vital it is for the honest, law-abiding, tax-paying, tradition-respecting people of this nation to heed what men like Horowitz and his colleague, Peter Collier, are saying. As ex-radicals themselves, having been the editors of the leftist magazine, *Ramparts*, during the sixties and seventies, and having been friends and supporters of the Black Panther movement and its key leaders, these men know what they're talking about. They have seen inside and outside the movement with incredibly clear vision, and they have come back to the other America to say, "Wake up, America! The enemy is at your door."[2]

Not all the educators in our public schools and universities are deliberately deceitful, not all of them want to destroy this nation, but many do. The major teachers' unions certainly do. The National Education Association has a very sophisticated training program and a great deal of literature informing its members how to defeat the "religious right" and to wage war on traditional "family values" in this nation. And the vast majority of the men and women in education today have bought into this leftist ideology and are repeating the lies that will, if left unchecked, destroy this nation. Please, make no mistake about that.

THIS CHRISTIAN NATION

After examining every document pertaining to the foundation of this country over several years, the Supreme Court drafted the Trinity Decision of 1892 and concluded that "this is a religious people." They said the bulk of the historical literature shows, beyond a doubt, that "this is a Christian nation." Theirs was one of the most exhaustive studies of the historical and philosophical foundations of American law ever made, and the Court's statement was the only logical conclusion that could be drawn from the records of this nation. They spent ten years on the study and reached a momentous decision.

But to make such a statement today causes reporters, newsmen, and many politicians to go ballistic. America, a Christian nation? They act as if Christians started the culture war and have done so in order to impose bigotry and censorship upon the world. They give the impression that we are beings from an alien culture, or perhaps even from some alien planet, who are attacking the secular status quo.

For three hundred years this has been a Christian nation. It is only in the last fifty years that the hostile barrage from atheists, agnostics, and other secular humanists has begun to take a serious toll on that heritage. In recent years, they have built up their forces and even increased their assault upon all our Christian institutions, and they have been enormously successful in taking over the "public square." Public education, the media, the government, the courts, and even the church in many places, now belong to them.

Christians did not start the culture war, but we are saying that it is high time for Christians to defend their spiritual liberties and to help restore the moral foundations of this nation. But while we didn't start the war, by the power of God's Holy Spirit, by the strength of the Gospel, and by the passionate commitment of Christians to share in the struggle, we are going to end it. That is a fact, and the Bible assures us of victory.

On the morning after Dan Quayle's address at the Reclaiming America conference, the newspaper said, "Vice President Quayle was inside speaking about family values and the protesters outside were preaching tolerance." I had to go back over the line twice to see if I had read it correctly. We are for "family values," teaching the importance of a stable home and solid community standards, and *we* are intolerant? But outside on the street were five hundred gays, mostly men, who have as many as three hundred different sexual partners in their brief lifespans. They have no serious family commitments and disavow all the traditional virtues and moral standards of this nation. They march in parades, screaming profanities, they thrust themselves before the television cameras in all sorts of vulgar and obscene poses, shouting four-letter words, but they are all for "tolerance." What am I missing?

Today, gays and their supporters have their own churches and clubs, and they preach their ungodly, immoral vices there. No one from our community goes around to their clubs, their churches, their bathhouses, or their homes and private establishments to scream at them and call them names. We don't follow them in the streets and tell them that they are intolerant. We don't scream profanities, throw condoms or bags of AIDS-infected blood and tell them they are corrupt and living in sin. But they do those things to us. So, who is being intolerant?

The Christian church is being forced to defend itself against the blatant, premeditated, willful, and malicious attack of those determined to overthrow the freedom and spiritual values of this nation. They want to overturn all the fundamental beliefs of the American way of life so that they can justify their own immoral lifestyles. To accomplish this goal, they have designed a radical and totalitarian agenda to seize control of the media, to hold government leaders and other opinion makers hostage to their point of view, and to vilify conservatives and Christians who disagree with them, and to brand us as evil and intolerant. This is the kind of distortion they are using, and in some quarters it is working just fine—just the way they designed it. They are methodical, relentless, and absolutely irreverent, and millions of Americans have bought into the lie.

THE DESTRUCTIVE AGENDA

Their destructive agenda is very straightforward. They are determined that we shall not encourage families to be monogamous. We must not expect husbands to be faithful to their wives or wives to be faithful to their husbands. In a country where half of our marriages are failing, they want to do everything in their power to destroy the other half as well. Throughout the entire history of mankind, the single most essential custom of society is that men and women should be united in marriage.

To bear a child out of wedlock has always been considered a very shameful thing and a cause for reproach. Illegitimate children may not inherit the property or the privileges of their fathers, and because often they will lack the social skills and moral conditioning so necessary to good citizenship, they have been relegated to second-class status in every society known to man.

Today, recent statistics prove that this kind of dysfunction has not changed, despite the burgeoning number of illegitimate births in this nation. Young people who do not have fathers of their own seek ersatz fathers in gangs. These are the people who rage across our cities wreaking chaos and mayhem. As discussed in earlier chapters, much of the crime in this nation is being committed by children without fathers. We say that the destructive capacity of immorality is wrong, and the reason for the ancient prejudice against children born out of wedlock was to ensure that each child will have an honorable place in society. It was designed to stigmatize promiscuous behavior and the practice of bearing children out of wedlock. And the numbers all show that the proponents of that view were correct. As Christians, we are not to forget the unfortunate children, or the mothers, who find themselves in this circumstance. Yes, we want to show love and compassion, and we want to give them God's own word of hope. But the *practices* must be stopped. Illegitimacy is *wrong*. It is a sin, and it destroys nations.

Christians believe in and practice tolerance, but you must remember this: Tolerance is the last and only virtue of the completely immoral society. The people who have violated every code of decency imaginable, who trample the law of God, who expose their wickedness before the entire world in their parades in our major cities, and even in the nation's capital, sodomizing each other in public for all the world to see—these people have no other virtue left except their absolute tolerance of wickedness.

Currently the only virtue in America is tolerance, and the only sin of a sin-soaked society is the failure to be tolerant, so the media declares. But do not forget that Almighty God is not tolerant of sin. God has said that He will turn the wicked into hell. We must either repent of sin or we must perish in flames. There is no gray area there.

The time has come for us to reclaim America. But the media are incensed at the mere suggestion that Christians founded this nation. How can they be incensed by the truth? History is very clear: *Christians built this nation*. And what's wrong with Christians' reclaiming the nation their ancestors founded? "Well," one reporter blasted, "because of all the censorship that (the homosexuals) have gone through!" Is anyone counting the number of times that the Christian message has been censored by the liberal media in the past thirty years? Is anyone counting the calumnies that have been heaped upon ministers, Christian teachers, evangelists, and other public figures who have spoken for moral behavior? Does anyone remember the blistering attacks on Dan Quayle when he had the audacity to suggest that children are better off in two-parent homes?

Today the time has come for Christians to get up off the ropes and take the initiative in the culture war. We have been bruised and battered long enough by our ruthless enemies. Unlike the principal in the Russian school, we cannot say that we have utterly destroyed ourselves. There are many people who are still enjoying many aspects of American life. I also remember the words of Dr. Francis Schaeffer, who preached one of his very last sermons shortly before his death, from my own pulpit in Fort Lauderdale. He said that the problem in America is that Christians are seeking peace and prosperity while watching their culture slide down the slippery slope into hell. The culture is self-destructing, and Christians are doing almost nothing about it. Former Secretary of Education William Bennett, in a speech at the Heritage Foundation in December 1993, said that the greatest problem in America is not economic or legal but spiritual apathy. We have not cared enough to get involved and try to pull the nation back from the edge of the abyss.

If we have any understanding about what's going on around us, then we must get involved. We must take up spiritual armaments and join the fray. If the Soviets could only have seen what was happening in their country ten years sooner, they would have said, "We are destroying ourselves," and they might have turned to democratic and spiritual solutions in an orderly fashion, and perhaps they could have saved their nation from utter chaos. But, as we look at what is going on in this nation, our first reaction is to look away. We don't want to face the fact that we are in chaos and the Enemy is pushing us to the edge of the chasm.

If Christians do not begin to do something to change the state of crisis in this nation, we are going to see both peace and prosperity utterly demolished before our eyes. We cannot continue to add a quarter-to-a-half-trillion dollars in new debt each year without paying the piper very soon. We cannot continue to pour endless sums down the ratholes of debt and welfare and government waste—and expect our economy to survive. And peace? What will happen when the welfare spigot is turned off? When the federal government is bankrupt—which many people believe will happen in this decade—scenes worse than anything we witnessed in the Los Angeles riots will be a common occurrence in every major city in America.

AND THEY FORGOT GOD

The sad part of this story is not that radicals and New Age idealists want to dismantle this nation, to rub out religion, to overturn all standards of morality and decency. There have been such people among us since the Garden of Eden. The tragedy is that while Francis Schaeffer was warning us about these things, and while others with the same hope and vision for our country were giving us wise counsel, we were sitting in the pews nodding our heads, and saying, "Oh, yes, it's bad. We believe you, Brother." But we forgot all about it and walked away unmoved. At the first sign of conflict, at the first accusation from the media, at the first instance of conflict, we felt embarrassed, and we simply walked away.

We who should care the most, we who should be crying out at the top of our lungs, and we who should be on our knees before God, imploring heaven for the strength and vision to turn back the onrushing tide of moral disintegration in every quarter, in every occupation, and in every city and town—we simply walked away from the fight. Instead of accepting the taunts and the wounds of the enemy, too many of us apparently decided that our own personal peace and prosperity should come first. We abdicated our Christian duty to "occupy" in the name of Christ.

Scripture tells us that if we allow these things to take place, then we are the ones who will be held accountable by God for the loss of this land of liberty. The Bible tells us in no uncertain terms that "The nation that forgets God will be turned into hell." That means, first of all, that the land will be turned into a literal hell, right here on earth; and then, when we can no longer endure the degradation and squalor that has come upon us, the nation will be turned into the next hell, which will be the final destruction.

How much more forcefully can I say it? The time has come, and it is long overdue, when Christians and conservatives and all men and women who believe in the birthright of freedom must rise up and reclaim America for Jesus Christ. I have said it many times and in many ways. I have said it on radio and television broadcasts from Coral Ridge Presbyterian Church, and I have said it in public before the media. No doubt I will continue saying it, without shame or apology, until we see the nation brought back to its senses.

In the end, Jesus Christ is the only person in this world who can bring America back to its place of moral and intellectual integrity. The character and destiny of this nation are His to command, but He will not do it unless we demonstrate our faith and conviction by physical and spiritual action. The song says, "We are His hands; we are His feet." Our Lord has the power to do whatever He wants, and He is never powerless. But He has given us the great honor and privilege of representing Him on this earth, and He has given us this hour to show what we are made of.

Consider this lesson: When the children of Israel were being held captive in Egypt under a religion and a way of life that was abhorrent to them, Moses and his followers became a thorn in the flesh to Pharaoh, beseeching God and bringing down terrible plagues upon the nation. But Pharaoh's heart was hardened, and he would not change his ways or allow the Israelites to leave. But as the Israelites continued to pray, to resist, and to cause untold miseries for their masters, the ministers of Pharaoh finally came running to him, pleading with him to give the Israelites their freedom. Pharaoh's officials said to him, "Let the people go, so that they may worship the LORD their God. Do you not yet realize that Egypt is destroyed?" (Ex. 10:7). I suggest that we must be just as persistent and as unbearable to our adversaries as the Israelites were to Pharaoh, and we must be relentless until the wicked officials of our own time relent and flee. The issue is freedom, the freedom of our faith and convictions, and the freedom of our American heritage. No amount of resistance or verbal abuse should stop us from speaking out for what is ours by right.

SPIRITUAL WARFARE

Perhaps another example from history will help to illustrate our situation. There was an especially dark hour during the Second World War when the Japanese forces had taken over most of the Pacific. It seemed there was no stopping them. Day after day they captured new territory, moving into Korea, China, and the Philippines. They were on their way to Australia, and it looked as if they would soon own the entire Pacific theater. In Europe, Hitler's Panzer Divisions had crushed Czechoslovakia and Poland. They had already moved through France, and there, too, it looked as if the enemy would take all of Europe and perhaps England, as well. I remember that time. It was a dark and frightening hour for the world.

But then, in the providence of God, the Allied forces challenged the Japanese at Midway Island, and after a prolonged and bloody battle, the backbone of the Japanese carrier fleet was destroyed, and we were able to muster our forces and carry on until we had won absolute and total victory. Yes, we suffered many casualties. Yes, there were tears and sorrow and great concerns at every stage, but the victory was *won*. In Europe, the Nazis and the Axis powers had covered the entire continent, and it would be only a matter of time until they crossed the North Sea into Britain.

But then the Allies launched what has become known as the great D-Day Invasion on the beaches of Normandy, and the largest armada in the history of the world landed on the shores of France. Then came the Battle of the Bulge and the crossing of the Rhine, and all of a sudden the tide was turned and the forces of liberty were triumphant. By prayer and persistence, by tenacity and incredible bravery, the American and British forces crossed into the heartland of Germany itself and soon rejoiced in victory.

The truth of our situation is not hard to see. We are beleaguered. The enemy is all around us and is winning most of the highly publicized skirmishes of the culture war. But the time has long passed to begin to do something about it. What can we do? What will you do? How will you and I and all the valiant Christians among us reclaim this nation and the world for Christ?

Here is the answer. First, we must carry out the Great Commission. We must proclaim the Gospel of Christ to every person. Now, that is not a passive task, as we know. But it is the essential first phase of the Christian's battle plan because the problem at the heart of all our struggles is the fact that men are wicked and do not know the truth. The Bible says, "The heart is deceitful above all things, and desperately wicked; who can know it?" (Jer. 17:9). People who hate Jesus Christ and who hate Christians will also hate His Word. They have never been converted—that is their problem and ours!

Unless we can reach out to the lost in such a way that they can see their own wickedness, as dark and ugly as it is, we have not truly entered the struggle. The Great Commission calls every believer to reach out to the lost, to proclaim the Gospel, and to make disciples. That means, allow the power of God to transform our enemies into our friends so that those who were once against us are now *for* us, fighting for moral values and righteous living throughout this land. The Bible also says, "Eye has not seen, nor ear heard, nor have entered into the heart of man the things which God has prepared for those who love him" (1 Cor. 2:9). Great and unfathomable blessings await those who come to the loving arms of Christ. But unless we give them that message of repentance and hope, they cannot hear. And unless they hear, they cannot be changed.

A VISION OF BATTLEMENTS

Do you recall the story of the little Presbyterian church in San Francisco that refused to compromise the truth of God's Word? Attacked by homosexual activists who not only surrounded the church but grabbed and pulled at members and their children, trying to drag them out into the streets, the people were terrified. They had to lock and bolt the doors of the church, but the gays outside were taking chairs and heavy lawn furniture and beating on the doors, screaming curses and blasphemous insults at the believers inside. They screamed, "We want your children. We want your children." And there is no telling what evil they would have done had they actually broken through into the sanctuary. The pastor used the podium microphone to record the sounds that poured through those doors into the church, and Dr. James Dobson broadcast that tape all across America and the world on more than a thousand stations so that Christians and others could hear what wickedness and what great evil is within the hearts of men.

This is a true story, my friends, and it happened in enlightened America in open-minded San Francisco, in modern 1993. But more than the pain and suffering of those local believers—those godly men and women with the courage to stand for the truth—it was also a dramatic symbol of what is really happening to this nation. Are we going to wait until that day comes to every town and every church in America? Will we wait until they come through the door and stand in all their wicked arrogance—like the abomination of desolation foretold by Christ in the book of Matthew—in the holy places of this world? I pray it will never happen. But, in such a time, we must hear these powerful words once again:

> For our struggle is not against flesh and blood, but against the rulers, against the authorities, against the powers of this dark world and against the spiritual forces of evil in the heavenly realms. Therefore put on the full armor of God, so that when the day of evil comes, you may be able to stand your ground, and after you have done everything, to stand. Stand firm then, with the belt of truth buckled around your waist, with the breastplate of righteousness in place, and with your feet fitted with the readiness that comes from the gospel of peace.
>
> — EPHESIANS 6:12–15

We need to share the Gospel, and we need to be prepared to stand against the forces of wickedness in this world. Have you been obedient to the commission given to you by Christ Himself? He says to every one of us, "Go and share the Gospel with every creature."

But secondly, we are to get involved in our culture in the various spheres of activity in our schools and PTAs, and in city and country government. We need to run for office. We need to be registered to vote. We need to write letters. We need to get active in every area of daily life. Someone asked me recently, "Do you really think that Christians should be involved in politics. Isn't that dirty business?" For some reason I felt inclined to say, "Yes, of course, you're absolutely right! Christians have no place in such a dirty business. We should leave it to the atheists and the secularists, so they can run the country their way. Otherwise you wouldn't have anything to complain about!" My friend got the point and recognized that we must be involved in the dirty business of making the policies and setting the rules, whether we like it or not. Otherwise, the wicked and godless will be more than happy to do it for us.

That is, in all truth, the problem today, and we have more than enough to complain about. At what point will you make the decision to become involved? Will you recognize Christ's call on your life? Will you reach out in love to those who are lost, and then, in the power of His might, get involved in the battle for America's freedom? Will this day and this hour be the turning point in your life?

A CHALLENGE TO THE FAITHFUL

I urge each man and woman reading this book to declare before God that you will do your part—to swear by the power of God's indwelling presence that, from this day forward, you will do more to get the Gospel to other people—that you will do more than you've ever done before to speak up for the values and beliefs upon which our nation was founded. I ask you to seek God's guidance and to ask Him to show you how you can do more to influence the society in which you live with the principles of Christ. What the unchristian world, and especially the media, demand of you is simply your silence. Are you willing to accept their dictates? Are you willing to turn over your nation, your neighborhood, your home, and your family to them? I assure you, if you abdicate your responsibility, that is precisely what they will take, and they have no intention of giving up without a fight.

I remember with a certain degree of sadness the decade of the seventies and early eighties in which Christians supposedly stood up for their rights. We were no threat to Satan. We were no threat to the liberals. We were no threat to the media. We were a joke. We were the "silent majority," and we became exactly what they wanted us to be—silent. But I will be silent no longer, and I will not be ashamed of Him upon whom my hopes of heaven depend. I declare before heaven that I will speak the name of Christ and not be ashamed. I will speak for the principles of Christ, and I will tell them I have had enough with of "the sliming of America." Will you join with me in that pledge?

Every single program the secular elites have laid their hands on has contributed to the degradation and perversion of this nation. Their ideas are utter failures. The statistics and the news reports say it loudly, and the world should hear: Secularism and liberal politics have destroyed this nation, and now it is time for Christians to reclaim the nation for Jesus Christ.

The men and women who established this land were not looking for a new world order, but a New World for religious freedoms. They discovered a new continent, and they brought forth a new nation where the Gospel of Jesus Christ could go forth and provide a workable, practical standard for daily life. That is our heritage, and as their spiritual and biological descendants, we have every right to speak out and to proclaim our birthright to the entire world. This is our land. This is our world. This is our heritage, and with God's help, we shall reclaim this nation for Jesus Christ. And no power on earth can stop us.

Benjamin Franklin, whom many wish to consider a secular man and a deist, believed in life, liberty, and the pursuit of happiness. He believed that the experience of freedom was ennobling and that the American experience of freedom could be instructive to all nations everywhere. It was with that hope that Franklin once wrote, "God grant, that not only the love of liberty, but a thorough knowledge of the rights of man, may pervade all the nations of the earth, so that a philosopher may set his foot anywhere on its surface, and say, 'This is my country.'"

Those words of the great patriot should be a strong challenge to believers in this land who have been silent too long. Today we stand on that conviction and, in the name of our Savior, we proclaim this nation, our birthright, to be our country. And we proclaim that one day that same vision of liberty and justice shall, indeed, cover the earth, and the love of God shall be spread abroad in every land and every heart.❦

NOTES

[1]Frances FitzGerald, *America Revised: History Schoolbooks in the Twentieth Century* (New York: Random House, 1979), 10f.

[2]Everyone who wants to know why and how the leftist movement infiltrated the halls of power and the institutions of higher learning should read Peter Collier and David Horowitz, *Destructive Generation: Second Thoughts about the Sixties* (New York: Summit Books, 1989). This is the most perceptive, honest, and hard-hitting book I have ever seen on this subject by men who have impeccable credentials both as scholars, authors, and as former participants in the dismantling of America.

4

Reclaiming Our Heritage

A woman I had never met before came up to me after the Sunday service and said that she was a missionary to Romania and needed to speak to me about an unusual situation involving an elderly pastor and his young son who were trying to spread the Gospel in Bucharest, the capital city, but who were under intense political pressure from the dictator, Nicolae Ceausescu. The Communists were threatening to kill these two men because they had spoken out against the government. The woman asked if I would write a letter to Ceausescu and urge him not to harm them.

To say I was surprised by her request would be an understatement. In the early 1980s, we knew very little about what was going on behind the Iron Curtain. The Communists had a lock on everything over there, and I wasn't even sure that a letter from an American minister would even get through. But the woman insisted. She said she had prayed about it, and since our television broadcast is seen around the world, and because even in Romania they are concerned about Western opinion, she believed that a letter from me would have a positive impact.

Well, I wasn't as confident as she was, but I wrote the letter anyway. I described the situation as I knew it, told the Romanian dictator of my interest in this matter and urged him to have compassion on those two men. I added that the eyes of the world would be on the situation, then I forgot all about it.

It was at least seven years later that I received a letter from that same woman. At first I did not recognize her name or remember anything about our brief encounter. She said, "Do you remember when we spoke after the Sunday service, and you agreed to write a letter to Romania?" As I searched my memory, I vaguely recalled that meeting. But then, as I continued reading her words, I was surprised by what else she had to say. She described the way all the various events unfolded over the turbulent months and years leading up to the winter of 1989. The picture she painted was graphic and compelling.

She said, "I want you to know that after you wrote your letter, the government backed off of their threats to kill those two men. And even though they continued to harass and persecute them, the younger man went on to become a pastor in his own church in the city of Timisoara, Romania." It seems the pastor was preaching the Gospel and telling the people that the government was corrupt, and he challenged the people to pray that God would intervene in the political situation and bring about a change. So he was declared a dissident, and the government ordered the local bishop to transfer him to a remote village where he would no longer pose a threat to them. But the members of his congregation were outraged, and they were joined by as many as twenty thousand local citizens who staged a massive protest in the streets around the church, blocking the entrance, and preventing the Securitate, the secret police, from taking the minister away.

But while all those people were gathered in the streets, police with high-powered rifles had been stationed on the tops of the adjacent buildings. When they opened fire on the crowds, they killed or wounded as many as two thousand people. It was a terrible massacre. But, as God would have it, that was the spark that set all the other events in motion that would eventually lead to the fall of Nicolae Ceausescu and bring about the end of the Communist regime in Romania.

Within just two weeks, I learned, the government of Romania had fallen, and on Christmas day, 1989, Ceausescu and his wife, Ilena, were dead, executed by a firing squad for crimes against the people. Many bloody stories began to come out about all the evil he had done, including the criminal exploitation of women and children. A committee of free democrats was then named to lead the country, and in less than a month democracy was chosen as the official political system of the nation. Little by little, the same process began to reproduce itself throughout Eastern Europe; and that momentum led ultimately to the fall of the Soviet Union.

In her letter, my one-time visitor of nearly a decade earlier said, "You would be interested to know that the young minister that I spoke to you about is the pastor of the church that was at the center of all the controversy. His name is Laszlo Tokes, and today he is a national hero and the most visible Christian leader in all of Eastern Europe."

I said to myself, Isn't it amazing how God works in the most mysterious ways, His wonders to perform? At the time, I doubted that any good would come of my letter or that the Communist dictator would ever read it. Of course, I will never know for sure what influence that simple request may have had. I do not know for certain that it was ever received. But the fact remains, Ceausescu and his henchmen backed off for some reason, surely inspired by the hand of God, and if the prompting of that caring woman, or of my letter, had any effect, then I am grateful to have had some small part in those events.

NEVER TOO LITTLE

That experience tells me something else, too, which I think is critical to recognize in times like these when our own nation is under assault from a dangerous liberal minority. It says that if we endeavor to serve the Lord, and if we try to be faithful even in the least of things, God can use our efforts, however small or great they may be. We have no way of knowing what consequences will come of our labors; but in God's providence, no work for the kingdom will be in vain, and no labor of love will go unrewarded.

This also brings to mind the story of another occasion when a group of elders got together for their last meeting of the year in the wee kirk of Blantyre, a small church in the south of Scotland. This was in the early part of the nineteenth century when many people were leaving that tiny country to emigrate to America. As the elders reviewed their various activities and accomplishments for the year, the elderly pastor said that he felt he should hand in his resignation and leave the ministry. The church didn't seem to be growing any more. Very little was happening, and nobody had been converted in more than a year.

But one of the men interrupted him and said, "Pastor, there was that one little boy, you know. There was at least one boy who came to the Lord under your teaching this year, and maybe others."

"Oh, yes," the minister said. "That is so. Little Davy did come, but that's just one wee lad. Is that enough for a year's work?" Little Davy, as it turns out, was David Livingstone, who went on to become a famous medical missionary to Africa. And by the mid-nineteenth century, David Livingstone had done more than any other person to bring Christianity to the people of Africa and to open up the Dark Continent to the light of the Gospel. The Scottish minister may have led only one small child to Christ, but just imagine how many lives he touched indirectly. *In the hands of God, even little can be more than enough.*

In Romania, a simple letter may have been just enough to preserve the life of the one man who could rally his nation to freedom and democracy. In a tiny church in Scotland, one solitary decision for Christ may have been just enough to bring the Gospel message to tens of thousands on the continent of Africa. Later in his life, David Livingstone said, "All that I am I owe to Jesus Christ, revealed to me in His divine book." The pastor at his home church in Scotland had introduced him to the Word, and from that Word he found the strength that helped him to change the world. So I ask, What is the little that you can do? What can you do today that may have an impact for the kingdom? What would you give for the future of faith and freedom in this nation?

During the Civil War, Abraham Lincoln said at Gettysburg that this is a nation "conceived in liberty and dedicated to the proposition that all men are created equal." He went on to say that they were engaged in a great Civil War testing whether this or any nation "so conceived and so dedicated can long endure." Today, we are engaged in another war—another struggle even more fundamental in character than that one. The question before us today is not whether men are created equal but whether they are created at all—whether they are creatures made by God with certain inalienable rights, or whether they are merely an accident of time and chance. Whether, indeed, this is a nation under God which can have a new birth of freedom, or a nation whose tradition of character and destiny has come to an abrupt end. Today this nation is facing some of the most fundamental challenges in the history of mankind.

THE CHALLENGE OF INVOLVEMENT

If you decide that the best solution to the challenges before us today is to cover your eyes and assume that someone else will take care of it, then be assured that everything you treasure will be lost. But if each one of us decides, by the grace of God, to stand on the principles of faith and do everything in our power to reclaim our homes, our communities, and our nation for Christ, then we will see the most thrilling reawakening imaginable.

Psalm 33:12 says, "Blessed is the nation whose God is the LORD." That is a marvelous statement that should give us hope—to secure God's blessing upon this land once again. But in Psalm 11:3 we read, "When the foundations are being destroyed, what can the righteous do?" There is no doubt that this is indeed a nation that was built upon a foundation of faith and the belief that the Lord is indeed the God of this nation. The great charters and founding documents proclaim that America was conceived upon the principles of God's Word, upon the teachings of Christianity, and for the advancement of the kingdom of Christ. But all of that is under attack today, as it has been for at least three decades.

The attack on our heritage has been so effective, as we saw in the previous chapters, that the historical revisionists of our day have all but removed every trace of our Christian heritage from the textbooks in our schools. Even the monuments of freedom in the nation's capital that bear the words of faith that inspired the patriots, and many of the inscriptions that point to the Christian origins of this country on our great public buildings, are being changed or removed. Will we stand by while the foundations of this nation are being destroyed? Will we allow the revisionists to dismantle our heritage?

When the foundations are destroyed, the righteous will have no place to stand. The only way to keep everything we believe in from being destroyed is to *get involved*. The first rule of warfare is to engage the enemy wherever you find him, and that is the challenge of every Christian today. Somehow, somewhere, we must all be involved.

Most of us can say that we were born in a Christian nation, but will our children and grandchildren be able to make the same statement? Francis Schaeffer used to say that unless we who have received this marvelous patrimony *do* something about it other than let it sift through our fingers like sand, then our Christian heritage will surely disappear before our eyes. At the moment, many people apparently feel they are protected. After all, we still have a fair measure of peace and prosperity. But there is no denying that our heritage of faith and freedom is under assault, and soon it may be lost forever unless we rise up in Jesus' name to reclaim the land.

There are those in this country today who are busily tearing down the foundations. Some of them can be found in the loftiest and most powerful places in the land, and they gnash their teeth at the mere suggestion that this is a Christian nation. Such people will not be satisfied until they have removed Christianity not only from our monuments but from our minds. Our task is to see that they fail in their mission to destroy the principles and foundations we cherish. Our job is to reclaim America for Christ, *whatever the cost.*

At a time when the nation was torn by bitter controversies and divisions, Abraham Lincoln said, "I know that the Lord is always on the side of the right. But it is my constant anxiety and prayer that I and this nation should be on the Lord's side." And that really is the proper balance. The challenge before us today is not just to recognize that we are in trouble. It is not just to smile and say, one way or the other, "the will of God will be done." There is no doubt that, in the end, God's will and purpose will be done; but our assignment is to be on the Lord's side and to be a part of His victory celebration.

God has ordained the outcome in our own struggles, but it is up to each man, woman, and child to lay out the strategies, to conduct the battle, and to claim the victory through faith and determination. God forbid that we who were born into the blessings of a Christian America should let our patrimony slip like sand through our fingers and leave to our children the bleached bones of a godless secular society. But whatever the outcome, one thing is certain: God has called us to engage the enemy in this culture war. That is our challenge today.

CONFRONTING DISBELIEF

While the Great Commission is God's plan for changing the human heart and bringing men, women, and children into the kingdom, the cultural mandate is the means by which we transform a godless society into a culture where the Spirit of Christ lives in every heart and where life can be lived to its fullest. God has given us the great privilege of being His junior partners in managing the affairs of this world, and our task is to bring out all the potentialities God has built into the world. When we live according to the patterns that God has ordained, we bring glory to the Creator, but we also attain our highest purpose and fulfill the potential that the Father has placed within us.

There are many forces in the world that dissipate our efforts, however. There are many enemies who do not want to see God's plans succeed; there are self-righteous people who have their own notions about how things should be done; and there are secular humanists who decided that mankind is all the god we need. All these forces operating in unison can be destructive to our hopes and dreams. Make no mistake, Satan does not want us to succeed. Our success is Satan's doom, so he takes advantage of our disunity and weakness. Therefore, we must resist, overcome, and break down the strongholds of evil.

Several years ago, a member of the Jehovah's Witness sect had visited one of our members and raised some difficult questions that caused some concern. Everytime our member would recite a verse of Scripture, the Witness would say, "Well, that's not what it says in the original Greek text," and she would retranslate the verse to mean what her leaders had said the verse should mean.

Well, the Witness lived right around the block from our member's house, so I decided to drop by to see her one day. Since she was in the habit of visiting people all the time, I thought it would be nice if I visited her for a change. Surely she would be happy to talk to a Christian minister. So I went over with my Greek New Testament, and I started talking, witnessing to her, and I mentioned Christ, the Son of God. I said, "In the Bible it does teach that Jesus is God, doesn't it?"

She said, "Oh, no, it doesn't."

So I said, "Oh, I thought that's what it said in John 1:1. Doesn't it say, 'In the beginning was the Word, and the Word was with God, and the Word was God'?"

She said, "Yes, but that's not what it says in the Greek."

"That's very interesting," I said. "I wasn't aware of that." So I handed her my Greek New Testament, and said, "Would you show me where it says Jesus is not God."

You could never imagine that anyone would do what she did with that book. She took my Greek New Testament, opened it up, and she started thumbing through the pages and looking at it. "What is this?" she said.

I said, "It's the Greek New Testament that you were just referring to."

She kept looking at it, and then she turned it upside down and she started thumbing through the pages again and she still couldn't make any sense of it, and she asked me again, "What is this?"

So, I said, "Well, as I said, that is the New Testament in Greek that you were referring to." She kept looking at it with her mouth open, staring at it, and then she turned it on its side and tried reading it upside down and backward, and I could see the tension rising.

She was really suffering with all this, so I said, "This is the New Testament in the original Greek language. As you said, this is the way it was originally written, and I'm simply asking that you show me where it says that Jesus Christ is not the Son of God, as you say." It was obvious to me—and now suddenly to her—that she didn't have a clue what the Greek New Testament said. But like a parrot, she had been going door-to-door and telling people, "The Greek New Testament says so-and-so." Programmed like a robot, she raised questions she could not answer, and she was sowing tares in the garden of Christ.

Finally, I said, "Ma'am, you have been going house-to-house in this neighborhood telling people the Greek New Testament says something that it does not say, and it is apparent that you don't even know what a Greek New Testament is when you're holding one in your hands. You can't read one single word in that book, and it is utterly hypocritical on your part to claim the Scriptures do not say what any student of Greek can assure you they do say." I wish I could say that the woman repented at that moment and came to Christ, but she did not. She had been programmed, and she wasn't about to question her instructions. I realized, of course, that she must have been mortified to be confronted by the truth of her ignorance, but I hoped that she would be conscence-stricken to the point that the next time she was tempted to tell somebody what the Greek New Testament says, she would at least think twice about it. And that someday, perhaps, she might have a change of heart.

CHALLENGING HYPOCRISY

Ironically, this was also the downfall of the founder of the Watch Tower Society, Charles Taze Russell, in the "miracle wheat" case in the early part of this century. Russell had been selling a grain called "miracle wheat" that, he said, would produce ten times as much as regular wheat. Farmers were sending in their money for this new grain, and it didn't work. It was just regular grain. But Russell made a serious mistake. He started selling it through interstate mail, with explicit claims about what it would do. As a result, he was hauled into court on charges of mail fraud.

During the trial, Russell kept saying that he had a divine revelation and the Bible says this or that, but he had no other proof. The only evidence was the clear fact that the grain did not produce a bumper crop, and many people felt they had been cheated. At last, after Russell had been claiming he had proof of his claims in the Bible, the prosecutor called his bluff.

"Oh, really?" he said. "Where is that passage in the Bible?" Russell told him the verse, so the prosecutor looked it up. He paused to read it aloud, and then said, "Mr. Russell, this verse doesn't say anything like that at all."

"Well, the English Bible is a bad translation. But that's what it says in the original Greek text," Russell declared.

Now, the prosecutor was a reasonably bright lawyer, so, he said, "Oh, I see. Are you an expert in the Greek text?"

Russell said, "Yes, I am. I'm an expert in the Greek text, and I'm telling you just what it says in the original Greek."

At that point, the prosecutor pointed out that Russell was still under oath. And he said, "Your Honor, the prosecution requests a recess until 10:00 A.M. tomorrow morning, at which time we will continue with this line of questioning." And the court granted the recess until the following morning.

By the next morning, the state had brought in a professor of Greek from the theological seminary, who could expound at length on the meaning of that or any other passage in question if he were needed. But, as it turns out, that wasn't necessary. The prosecutor took a copy of the Greek New Testament, opened it at random, handed it to the accused, and said, "Now, Mr. Russell, since you are an expert in the Greek New Testament, would you please read the first line on this page."

Russell said he couldn't do it.

"Mr. Russell, would you please read for us the first word in that line."

He couldn't do that, either.

"Mr. Russell," the prosecutor said once again, "would you please tell us what the first letter of the first word in the first sentence is."

And Russell still couldn't do it. So he was convicted of perjury and fraud and all the other charges against him, and the miracle-wheat case served to prove that his teachings were a fraud designed to victimize gullible people. As we have seen repeatedly over the past ten years, that sort of fraud is still with us, but we have the capacity and the responsibility to confront it. The English statesman, Edmund Burke, said, "All that is necessary for the triumph of evil is that good men do nothing." In spiritual and cultural matters alike, if deceit goes unchallenged, then evil will prevail.

My point is not the truth or falsehood of the Jehovah's Witnesses' teachings but to say that fraud must be challenged. We must be willing to wage warfare against sin and to call evil by its name. The Christian is called not only to do good in this world but to confront evil and fraud wherever they are found. Only those who are armed with the truth will be able to check the advance of lies and hypocrisy.

FIRST, THE BAD NEWS

When you stand up to falsehood, you have truth on your side, and fraud falls silent in the face of truth. The liberals and atheists in our society are in much the same situation. They have a pattern of rhetoric that they have memorized, but the minute you come against them with answers based on historical truth, they either fall silent or they revert to name-calling and childish rage. Look at the success of the conservative talk-show host Rush Limbaugh over the past few years. He is flamboyant, he is often abrasive, and his intimidation of liberals is calculated to drive them crazy; but he also has facts, figures, and practical answers based on meticulous research, and that frustrates the liberals no end. They are not angry because he argues with them but because he has done his homework and they can't argue back. He has answers, but he also has a massive radio and television audience, and the liberals simply do not know how to deal with him. We should all be just that well-prepared.

There are probably all sorts of people with a better, more in-depth understanding of the problems than Limbaugh, but their audiences are microscopic by comparison. I have heard Democrats and liberals crying because Limbaugh and the new conservative movement have generated such an avalanche of response. They are completely frustrated because people keep calling and faxing them at all hours of the day, demanding changes and demanding honesty. Whenever Rush Limbaugh describes what the liberals are up to and gives telephone numbers on the air, immediately the offices of Congress are deluged with calls and letters. The president's telephone lines are tied up for days.

I heard one liberal congressman complaining because, "None of these people ever bothers to see what *Time* or *Newsweek* or Dan Rather have to say about it. They just call or write because they heard it on Limbaugh!" But the poor man was missing the point. The public are saying that Dan Rather and the media, and all the other go-along liberals, no longer offer viable options. They are a big part of the problem. They are part of the liberal establishment that got us into this fix in the first place. They need to be swept out along with the Congress and the entire liberal bureaucratic network.

Limbaugh is not the only one with answers. There are many other people in this country who have answers. I would even say that many other people have better and more in-depth answers that Limbaugh, but he has helped restore balance to the national debate. A large part of his appeal is the winsomeness of the message. He's funny, he's irreverent, and people respond to him. But he has also helped show the nation that they can have a voice in government and will be heard if they have the courage to sound off. That is a message I passionately want Christians to understand as well. We not only have a voice, but we have moral values and a worldview prescribed by the Word of God. If we want to make changes in the world, then we have to get over our fear of embarrassment and reach out and change the culture. We have to speak up.

We don't always have to be on the attack, however. There are many things that can be accomplished through diplomacy and tact. There is an awful lot of doom and gloom out there, and we have a message of hope and optimism. In the long run, the Christian is the only person who can be optimistic. Liberals like to accuse us of being the doom-and-gloom people. But it is the White House that gives you doom and gloom. Just remember the hysteria they created—by convincing voters that everything was out of control and only a Democratic president and Congress could save them. What we can say is that, sure, we're going to give you some bad news. There is a lot of bad news around today. But the White House gives you bad news, Ross Perot gives you bad news, and everybody else is giving you bad news. Our bad news comes with a message of hope. We also have some wonderful good news, and that good news is the Gospel of Christ.

AMERICA IN THE BALANCE

It is obvious that we are dealing with a crisis of authority in this nation. What we are debating about is, "Whom do we want to be in charge?" What kind of authority will we recognize? Are we going to do it God's way, or will we settle for the secular humanist way? When Joshua was preparing the people of Israel to face the Amorites, he told them, "Choose for yourselves this day whom you will serve." The people could take the easy way out and accept the gods and moral standards of the aliens, or they could stand for the God of heaven, which meant they would have to go to war. But Joshua said, "As for me and my household, we will serve the LORD." The people joined with Joshua, and they went to war to defend their faith. And they won. Are we prepared to make that same choice?

We used to have laws against gambling in this country, but most of them have fallen by the wayside. Today, legal wagering, off-track betting, casinos, lotteries, and other kinds of wagering operations are robbing millions of people who can barely afford to pay their rent. We used to have laws against child pornography, but now the attorney general of the United States has supported changes to the criminal code so that many forms of child pornography can be published without fear of prosecution.

We used to have laws against divorce, but now a married couple with children can split up under the new "no-fault" laws, and millions of lives are being wrecked every year. We used to have laws against homosexuality, cohabitation, and other forms of perversion that are suddenly sweeping the nation and dragging people into the spiritual wasteland, and nobody is coming forward to stop America's headlong slide down a slippery slope into moral oblivion.

Today's trendy ethical agenda is based on a "new morality" designed by the secular humanists, which is simply the old morality of the Bible turned on its head. Ethics is fine, so long as they're not biblical ethics. Values are fine, so long as they are not Christian values. In his great book, *Crime and Punishment*, Fyodor Dostoevsky says, "If God is dead, then everything is permitted." That is the message of the new morality. God is dead and everything is permitted. And the degradation and emptiness of modern culture are the payoff of that degraded philosophy. We can't impose our morality on them. We can't hold up the Word of God as it has been taught for the past two thousand years, for that would violate the separation of church and state. Yet the humanists are imposing their view of morality upon the rest of us in the form of godless and destructive legislation, and the aftermath is all around us.

When people tell me, "You're trying to force your morality on other people," I often say, "I don't have a morality." There is no such thing as "D. James Kennedy's morality." The secular humanists have a morality. They have a "new morality" that they are very successfully imposing upon the nation by law, by practice, and by subtle insinuation upon the culture through the mass media and many other ways. But I have no morality of my own, and neither does any other Christian. We just accept the old morality of God as it was delivered in the Ten Commandments. So the debate being put forward by the humanists, that it is our morality against their morality (as if the two were even parallel), is clearly false. What we are talking about is not "their morality" and "our morality" but a humanly manufactured morality of liberal humanism versus the God-established morality given to mankind by the Creator of the universe. The God who made us and before whom we all must stand in judgment one of these days established the laws by which we should live. Who am I to argue with God?

Bertrand Russell rejected the Christian value system because, as he said, God's law treads upon his right of immorality. Am I right to pursue my own law? Russell did not say that God's law was unjust or invalid or untrue; rather, he just happened to like his own law better than God's. But isn't that the story of the human race? Creating a "new morality" in order to free mankind from the "old morality" ordained by God is simply a fraud, a charade. Man's new morality is nothing more or less than the old "immorality" that is designed, as Russell said, "to free me up to my own erotic choices." But just think of all the different descriptions and tricks people have come up with to justify what they are doing. "Values clarification" means establishing a new set of humanistic values based on secular morality. "New Age" means a "new theology" that disregards the old theology ordained by Jesus Christ. The "playboy philosophy," "liberation theology," and even Hillary Clinton's "politics of meaning" are all simply new terms for ancient heresies in modern dress—they are systems for denying God's perfect authority in order to invoke the fallible authority of man.

THE NEW LAW OF GRAVITY

Behind all of these pop movements is the ancient promise of Satan: "You shall not surely die, but you shall be as gods." And many people are deceived into believing that they can be a law unto themselves by simply rejecting God's law and making up their own. But these are merely other ways of saying, "I am going to be my own god. I am going to make my own law." This is a little like a man's trying to deny the existence of the law of gravity before jumping off a ten-story building. "I deny the law of gravity," he cries out. "I have my own law. I call it the 'new gravity,' and no one can impose his idea of gravity on me." But when he jumps, the result will be the same. God's law, like gravity, is beyond challenge. It simply *is*.

But what is the result of man's worship of himself? Levels of social dysfunction and emotional disability have never been greater. The American culture is in chaos, and society is destroying itself in violence and rage. Each year crime costs this nation in excess of one hundred billion, and we have more than 1.1 million men and women behind bars—the highest custody rate in the entire world. The rate of incarceration in the United States is ten times that of Japan, Sweden, Ireland, and the Netherlands. The government spends more than $250 billion per year in welfare subsidies, yet the rate of poverty is rising year by year and the number of the nation's homeless may be as high as a million people. In excess of fifty-six million Americans are suffering from some sort of venereal disease, with more than 1.4 million diagnosed cases of AIDS nationwide. Each case costs the taxpayers from $140,000 to $170,000. Is this the humanist utopia? Is this secular society's idea of peace on earth?

The things that Christian societies have legalized and passed laws about over the last ten centuries have been those things that are moral and ethical. Society has tried to defend those things that protect life and preserve the dignity of man and to punish things that degrade and destroy life. We have laws against killing because killing is immoral. We have laws against stealing, because the right to property and the pursuit of happiness are essential components of peace. We have laws against rape because our persons should be inviolable. And we have had laws against adultery, homosexuality, pornography, and sexual abuse because people have always believed that these are immoral, degrading, and cheapen the value of life. Now that these things are changing, we can see what they have done to the culture.

A survey by the Alan Guttmacher Institute, which has been widely publicized in recent months, reveals that fully twenty-five percent of Americans are currently infected with at least one of the twenty commonly transmitted venereal diseases (called "sexually transmitted diseases" or STDs). In 1992, one hundred-twenty thousand new cases of syphilis were reported, along with four million cases of chlamydia, 1.1 million cases of gonorrhea, and a half million cases of genital herpes. Yet government tells us this is not a moral issue—it's a matter of education—and "safe sex" is the answer.

Each year more than one hundred-sixty million dollars is spent by government to teach kids how to use condoms and to attack abstinence-based education, which they label "fear-and-shame based curricula" that "distort facts" and "hide the truth." The truth is that sex outside of marriage is dangerous, often deadly, and promiscuity leads to divorce, disease, abortion, broken families, and lives of misery and despair. But lest we forget, the secular solution is based on a "new morality." The secular solution has no place for God. And secular society, before the eyes of the entire world, is reaping the whirlwind of its own self-destruction.

FROM SMALL BEGINNINGS

It is easy to become depressed when we see such self-destructive behavior. And unless we keep our eyes on a higher standard, we can lose hope and assume that there are no solutions to these problems. But God is just, and there is hope. And throughout history we find examples where godly men and women have made a difference in the struggle to restore fallen cultures. One such man was the great Dutch statesman, Abraham Kuyper, who served as Prime Minister of Holland in the last half of the nineteenth century. When he became active in public affairs, the nation was in a state of religious apathy and deep moral decline. He said that his goal was to see that the holy ordinances of God were carved upon the conscience of the nation so that renewal and honor might be restored to his people and that God might receive honor once again in Holland. So effective were his efforts that the Netherlands were saved from the brink of disaster, and for the next thirty years they experienced a tremendous spiritual, intellectual, and economic resurgence. So great was his impact on the culture that near the end of his life, on his seventieth birthday, Kuyper's birthday was declared a national holiday.

A man or woman of vision can have a tremendous impact on a nation. An act of God can also influence what people believe. But how does that affect us? Can a few Christians do any good in times like these? Try these numbers for size. When Jesus walked down the dusty path to the Jordan River where John was baptizing—on what would be the first day of Christ's earthly ministry—He was one solitary man, called of God to redeem the world. Later, in the Upper Room when He appeared to His disciples after the resurrection, there were eleven who believed. On the morning of Pentecost, there were one hundred-twenty believers. But the Bible says that after Peter addressed the crowds, "Those who accepted his message were baptized, and about three thousand were added to their number that day" (Acts 2:41).

At another time five thousand were added, and those who believed reached out to others, until by the year 300 A.D., there were fully twelve million Christians in the ancient world. By the year 1000, there were more than fifty million Christians in the world. And by the time Martin Luther nailed his ninety-five theses to the door of the church at Wittenberg, there were one hundred million men and women who professed to be followers of Jesus Christ.

By 1800, there were two hundred million professing believers in the world, and in 1900, thanks largely to the explosion of missionary activity around the world, the number had grown to more than five hundred million. Today there are an estimated 1,900,000,000 professing Christians in the world. This is almost two billion people who name the name of Christ. In this century more people have come to Christ than in the previous nineteen hundred years combined. Surely these people can make a difference.

And think what it would mean if every one of the people who claim to follow the Savior were to win just one more person for Christ. What a day of rejoicing that would be!

In the 1970s there were an estimated thirty million born-again believers in the United States alone. In the 1980s the number was closer to forty million. Recent surveys suggest there may be as many as seventy million evangelicals in this country and another one hundred million people who claim to be Christians. At the present rate of growth, more than half this nation will be born-again evangelical Christians by the end of this century, and if that does come to pass, as I believe it will, we are going to see a spiritual revolution that will shake the world!

THE SECRET OF MULTIPLICATION

The New Testament's secret for reaching the world for Christ is the process of spiritual multiplication. In the Evangelism Explosion (EE) program that I developed and which is being spread around the world with the assistance of our team at Coral Ridge Ministries, we have trained ministers and laymen in some one hundred-sixty-five countries around the globe to take the Gospel to the ends of the earth. By the end of 1995, we anticipate having trained EE workers in every one of the two hundred-ten nations of the world. In this program, we try to teach people how to evangelize by engaging in on-the-job training with a person who has been trained.

The program combines two things in one action: first, doing the work of evangelizing, and second, training others to do the same thing. One of the principal concepts of EE is that it is more important to train soul-winners than to win a soul. The reason is simple. If a person is converted but never trained, more than likely he will never lead anyone else to the Lord; but if he is trained to reach others, then there is no limit to what he may be able to do. A man or woman who is properly trained to share the faith may reach hundreds, thousands, even tens of thousands of people for Christ. And God multiplies the harvest.

That is the main reason I feel so strongly about the Great Commission. We need to double the number of Christians in this country. If that were to happen, the cultural mandate would take care of itself. We also need to see the number of Christians worldwide double. If every Christian in America led just one more person to Christ this year, that would mean that from seventy-five to eighty percent of this nation would be followers of Jesus

Christ. Just imagine what would happen to this country and to the world if that were to really happen. And, you know, it *can*. There is no reason why something just as great could not happen here before the end of this decade.

Recently, a study by the International Social Survey Program (ISSP) reported that some sort of international religious awakening is already under way. In the former Soviet Union, tens of thousands of people are coming to Christ. In the United States, there is a spiritual reawakening among the men and women of the baby-boom generation, and the levels of "religious devotion" pollsters discovered in the United States, Ireland, Poland, and other East European countries may be at the greatest levels in recorded history.

In their survey of nineteen thousand people in more than a dozen countries, the ISSP notes a great increase in the number of people who believe in life after death. Commenting on the results, Father Andrew Greeley said, "God didn't die, even under socialism." And David Barrett, editor of the *World Christian Encyclopedia*, said, "Everybody thought secularism would keep on undermining religion, and nothing could prevent it." But, he said, "We've all been proved wrong." Truly, the hand of God is moving in the world.

More than ninety percent of survey respondents in the United States and Ireland and eighty percent in Italy and Poland said they believe in the reality of God. In Israel, England, and New Zealand, where religion had been ruled officially dead, more than two-thirds of respondents expressed belief in God. In this country, thirty-five percent of respondents to the survey said they consider themselves "extremely close" to God, prompting researchers to conclude that "The decline in religion that was predicted with the baby boomers simply didn't happen."

There is no doubt that a large part of this new expression of religious values is a direct result of the deterioration of culture. When society begins to crumble, only God has answers that satisfy. The challenge before us today is to transform this new awareness of religion into genuine spiritual commitment. Then, the next step is to reclaim the nation by introducing the people to Jesus Christ who offers ultimate hope and meaningful change.

As I have already said, my great passion for America is twofold: first, that every believer would be absolutely faithful to the Great Commission; and then, that every believer would take seriously the challenge to reclaim this nation for Christ. If we become engaged and if we carry out the "cultural mandate" of the church, then there is no reason that we cannot reclaim our heritage of faith and freedom and see this nation renewed.

In 1816, John Jay, the first Chief Justice of the United States Supreme Court, wrote, "Providence has given to our people the choice of their rulers. It is the duty, as well as the privilege and interest, of a Christian nation to select and prefer Christians for their rulers." In a similar vein, Noah Webster, the great scholar and university president who gave us the monumental Webster's dictionary, said, "Let it be impressed on your mind that God commands you to choose for rulers just men who will rule in the fear of God . . . if the citizens neglect their duty and place unprincipled men in office, the government will soon be corrupted . . . If a republican government fails to secure public prosperity and happiness, it must be because the citizens neglect the Divine commands and elect bad men to make and administer the laws."

The cultural mandate demands that we think and act Christianly. It requires that we become engaged in the ongoing cultural debate. It challenges each man, woman, and child to stand by our heritage of Christian values and deny any further victories to the enemy. It also tells us that we must require honor, integrity, and moral responsibility in our national leaders. As the great patriots of this nation attest, when the people of a nation neglect the divine commands and allow men of poor character to rule the land, then corruption and dishonor are sure to follow.

In the next section, we will take a look at some of the specific cultural challenges before us today, including many of the dogmas of politics and science that parade as truth in our public institutions. Before we can overcome the lies of the enemy, we must first recognize what is being said and who is saying it. From there, we will be in a better position to determine our strategy for victory.❦

Part II

The Secular Challenge

5

A Wall of Separation

After more than twenty years in exile, Aleksandr Solzhenitsyn is returning home to his native Russia. A recent wire-service report said that the great author and Christian thinker, winner of the 1970 Nobel Prize for literature, expects fierce opposition from the people of Moscow and possibly even physical threats, but he still wants to go home, to offer his services as "a moral compass" and to help in rebuilding the character and the emotional well-being of his disoriented countrymen.

In an interview in the *New Yorker* magazine, Solzhenitsyn said his literary work is now behind him, and for the remainder of his life he wants to serve his fellow Russians. He is not looking for a political role, he said, but wants to use his power of influence to help foster a renewal of ethical and moral values. "My role can only be moral," he said. "What other role can I have?" And he added that "Life will not be easy in any respect. But I am going because I must try to fulfill my duty to society to whatever extent I can. How it will turn out, I do not know."

Here we have the odd situation of a man, born and educated under the Communist system, who has become the most perceptive critic not only of communism but also of the sentimental liberalism of the West and an expert commentator on the dangers of the decadence in modern society. From his adopted home in the Vermont woods, Solzhenitsyn has continued to write extensively over the past two decades. He has called for democratic reforms in the former Communist nations, but he has also scolded and challenged the flaccid socialism of Western intellectuals and academics.

For most of his life, Solzhenitsyn has been a perennial gadfly, always demanding that people stop, look, and listen at the crossroads of conscience and culture. But for all his honesty, and for all his brilliant insight into the crises of our age, he remains a man with more enemies than friends, at home and abroad. No one wants to hear the words of the prophet.

There is no doubt that Aleksandr Solzhenitsyn ranks as one of the most formidable intellects of our time; yet, too often his words go unheeded. His challenges to the complacent socialist dogmas of East and West are painful and embarrassing, and those who most need to hear his warnings have shut their ears and their eyes. He said, "There are those who weep for communism and consider me its main destroyer, the main person at fault. Some fanatics are literally saying they want my neck." American universities no longer invite him to speak. The think tanks and research institutions of the West seldom seek his opinion. The writer suspects he will not be allowed to speak in public when he returns to Russia, and he will probably be barred from television as well. But he refuses to give up. He cares too much for the souls of his people. And he cares for the salvation of mankind.

IN THE FACE OF DISSENT

In his famous commencement address at Harvard University on June 6, 1978, the world gained a remarkable insight into the character of this great man. Knowing that he would likely be criticized by professors and media pundits for his conservative views, he said that it is time for the people of the West to wake up to the real dangers of their actions. We need to recognize that we are letting our heritage of freedom slip through our fingers. One sign of the loss of the individual initiative and moral responsibility that support democratic thought is the way that the governments of the United States and some European nations have encouraged the idea of "rights" and "entitlements."

"The defense of individual rights," he said, "has reached such extremes as to make society as a whole defenseless against certain individuals. It is time, in the West, to defend not so much human rights as human obligations."[1] He argued that it is time to demand that citizens take responsibility for their own behavior, and for people of all classes to stop looking to government for their salvation. The savior of man is not the state, as many seem to think. But we have allowed government to become our god, while at the same time we have turned our back on God, who is the source of strength. The result of this transfer of authority can be seen in society's descent into self-indulgence, permissiveness, and every kind of evil. And much more than the hypothetical "wall of separation" erected by the courts and the bureaucrats, the separation between God and man is the greatest danger to the future safety of this nation.

Solzhenitsyn told his Harvard audience that "This tilt of freedom toward evil has come about gradually, but it evidently stems from a humanistic and benevolent concept according to which man—the master of this world—does not bear any evil within himself, and all the defects of life are caused by misguided social systems, which must therefore be corrected. Yet strangely enough, though the best social conditions have been achieved in the West, there still remains a great deal of crime; there even is considerably more of it than in the destitute and lawless Soviet society."[2] This irony cannot be missed. While Russia is returning to God and the Bible, the American people seem to be running from their religious heritage as fast as they can. And while the crime rate in the Soviet Union was comparatively low, this nation is being devastated by lawlessness and crime.

But Solzhenitsyn went on to say that there are telltale symptoms in history that should warn us when a society is in danger of self-destruction. "Such are, for instance, a decline of the arts or a lack of great statesmen," he said. "Indeed, sometimes the warnings are quite explicit and concrete. The center of your democracy and of your culture is left without electric power for a few hours only, and all of a sudden crowds of American citizens start looting and creating havoc. The smooth surface film must be very thin, then, the social system quite unstable and unhealthy."

The author said we must realize that we are engaged in "a fight for our planet" between physical and spiritual forces of cosmic proportions. We are engaged in a warfare of good and evil, and the truth of that fact is visible in the streets of this nation, in our public schools, in the headlines, and on the nightly news. It is not merely some vague notion of future crisis. It is not some fantastic vision of science fiction designed to scare people into good behavior.

No, the writer warned, the spiritual battle has already started, and it is visible in every city and town. "The forces of Evil have begun their decisive offensive. You can feel their pressure, yet your screens and publications are full of prescribed smiles and raised glasses." But he asks, "What is the joy about?"[3] Like a scene from the fall of Rome, Americans stand by cheering and laughing and indulging their senses, while the nation and the entire world are going down to defeat.

TRUTH ABOUT FREEDOM

Americans often behave as if the word "freedom" were some sort of magical charm that protects us against evil. We use it like an incantation, but we have lost our focus on the true source of freedom. Many people seem to feel that freedom grants them some kind of immunity from the dangers that have befallen nations throughout history. But mere freedom, the Russian author advises, does not solve the problems of life. Rather, it creates new ones. Freedom demands even greater courage, greater concern and engagement, and greater moral responsibility. Freedom is not a panacea for the stresses of modern culture but a heritage that must be cherished and defended against a host of dangerous ideologies.

And most perceptive of all, Solzhenitsyn recognizes that America's birthright of freedom was founded upon an essential faith in God. The founders of this nation understood that individual rights were granted with the understanding that man is God's creation. Political and individual freedoms were granted to individuals conditionally, with the assumption that we would remain close to God and continue to seek His guidance and counsel. But we have not been faithful. "Two hundred or even fifty years ago," said Solzhenitsyn, "it would have seemed quite impossible, in America, that an individual be granted boundless freedom with no purpose, simply for the satisfaction of his whims. Subsequently, however, all such limitations were eroded everywhere in the West; a total emancipation occurred from the moral heritage of Christian centuries with their great reserves of mercy and sacrifice."

Governments in both East and West became more and more materialistic. American democracy fell victim to the "consumer" culture while Russia and the East bloc came under the false theology of "dialectical materialism"—and the godlessness of atheism. "The West has finally achieved the rights of man," said Solzhenitsyn, "and even to excess, but man's sense of responsibility to God and society has grown dimmer and dimmer." This, he says, is the real root of the spiritual crisis of our age. We have turned away from God, and we are reaping the whirlwind. The political turmoil we are undergoing is evidence of the moral poverty of this century, and all our magnificent achievements and technological successes cannot redeem us from our own impending self-destruction.[4]

FAITH AND FREEDOM

How can we help but be moved by such acute perceptions and such stirring sentiments? We need to pay close attention to the words of this great man. There are two vitally important lessons that we must learn if we expect to avoid the same sort of collapse that destroyed the Soviet Union. The first is that utter failure and disaster will come upon any nation that follows the path of socialism. As the Union of Soviet Socialist Republics discovered to their great dismay, socialism annihilates freedom. It takes away the right of self-determination and offers mediocrity and stifling sameness. The second important lesson is the absolute necessity of religious liberty to a free society. The values and beliefs that support the idea of "freedom" are from God. They are not man-made, and unless we remain faithful to our God, just as Solzhenitsyn observed, we have no guarantee of safety or sanctity or security from the forces of evil in the world.

In just the past two years we have seen Russian citizens by the millions, hungry for the Word of God, queuing up in lines many blocks long just to get a portion of Scripture. Our missionaries have described the enormous crowds at book fairs and displays where Bibles were being handed out. In some cases, traffic was stopped in all directions until the supply of Bibles was exhausted. When word was spread among the members of the Russian Parliament in the spring of 1990 that Bibles were being handed out in the foyer of the government building, the entire assembly jumped up from their seats during the middle of the proceedings to run to the hallway and get a personal copy of God's Word. More recently, we have seen the tremendous eagerness for the Word throughout the newly liberated Eastern European nations. Bibles cannot be printed or shipped fast enough to meet the demand.

But what a strange contrast this situation now creates. Russia and the United States have always been at odds. We are very different in very many ways, and we always have been. But just consider how the situation has changed in the past five years. In Russia and in all of Eastern Europe today there is religious freedom. The laws that established atheism and banned religious freedom have been struck from the books, and the people are seeking for truth in the Gospel of Jesus Christ. But on the political scene, the change is just as great. The Communist party no longer rules in the East anymore. Communism has been declared illegal in most places, and democratic rule is the law of the land.

Only in America is the ideology of communism still at large. Communist rhetoric and socialist idealism are the reigning orthodoxies of American intellectuals and political elites. The universities are the chief promoters of the socialist dogma, and the federal government seems to be doing everything in its power to encourage the growth of the socialist welfare state in this country, following the model of Germany and other East European nations. We no longer have complete religious freedom in this nation—the courts have ensured that religion must be banned from the public arena. Now all government organizations, the public schools, and other public institutions are being stripped of the symbols of our religious heritage. Every year, and with each passing day, more of our great treasures are being taken from us. The founders would be shocked to see what has been done to the religious liberties they dutifully enshrined in the Constitution, the Bill of Rights, and the foundational principles of this nation.

If these sound like empty charges, please observe the following rulings from the courts of the land. In the case of *Reed v. van Hoven*, in 1965, the court ruled that if a student in a public school prays over his lunch, it is unconstitutional for him to pray aloud. In the case of *DeSpain v. DeKalb County Community School District*, in 1967, the court ruled that it is unconstitutional for kindergarten students to recite the nonsectarian prayer, "We thank you for the flowers so sweet; / We thank you for the food we eat; / We thank you for the birds that sing; / We thank you for everything." If you remember this prayer from your youth, you will notice that the word "God" does not even appear in the verse. But that was still not acceptable to the courts of this nation. Someone might think of God!

But there is more. It is also unconstitutional for students to arrive at school early to hear a student volunteer read prayers. Even though the chaplains in both the United States House of Representatives and the Senate offer prayers at the start of each session, and even though those same prayers are printed in the *Congressional Record* each day, students and teachers in America's schools are prohibited from professing allegiance to their God. They may not pray, they may not have a moment of silence, they may not bring a Bible even in a plain brown wrapper.

It is unconstitutional for a board of education to use or refer to the word "God" in any of its official writings. It is unconstitutional for a kindergarten class to ask during a school assembly whose birthday is celebrated at Christmas. It is unconstitutional for a kindergarten class to recite: "God is great, / God is good. / Let us thank Him / For our food." And it is unconstitutional for the Ten Commandments to hang on the walls of a classroom in our public schools.

Furthermore, it is unconstitutional for a school graduation ceremony to contain an opening or closing prayer. In the Alaska public schools, students were told that they could not use the word "Christmas" in school because it had the word "Christ" in it. They were told that they could not even have the word in their notebooks, and they could not exchange Christmas cards or Christmas presents, or participate in any activity that acknowledged the important and historic place of this most sacred holiday of our Western tradition.

In many places, teachers have taken the spirit of these anti-Christian laws into their own hands and humiliated and punished students who somehow let it be known that they harbor religious sentiments. A kindergarten teacher in Michigan stopped a five-year-old from bowing her head and saying a silent prayer before lunch, telling the child that praying is against the law. In Selkirk, New York, a third-grade teacher stopped a child from reading the Bible in her free reading time. The child was threatened and, in tears, she was told never to bring the forbidden book to school again. A small boy in Texas was forbidden to read the story of Noah's Ark in school; and in California, children singing Christmas songs were told to hum or be silent if the words *Lord*, or *Savior*, or K*ing* appeared in their songs. The idea that religion might somehow enter the classroom was apparently horrifying to these teachers. What a sad and tragic day for America!

But these are only a tiny sample of the horrors taking place thousands of times every day in this nation, as both children and adults are being robbed of the rights guaranteed by the First Amendment. Instead of "freedom *of* religion," we now have "freedom *from* religion." Instead of ensuring that "Congress shall make no law respecting the establishment of religion," the courts render judgments that purge the nation of any expression of its faith in God.

Little by little, the message has been implanted that faith in God is a second-class activity not to be indulged or permitted by responsible organizations.

MORAL IMPERATIVES

In his book *1984*, George Orwell called the censors of language and belief "thought police." His somber vision was certainly perceptive, and it describes our situation perfectly. The courts, the legislatures, the public schools have become totalitarian thought police telling people what they can think, say, and believe. And the courts are zealous in censoring anything that might suggest that we still have faith in God—and they are succeeding. All these cases, and hundreds like them, flood the courts each year, and the battle is being waged in virtually every court system in the land. Every victory by the Left takes another bite out of the religious liberties we were once guaranteed by the founding documents of this nation.

Can we see what is happening under our very eyes? Is anyone outraged by all these examples of intolerance and secular bigotry? One has to wonder. When anti-Christian rulings are handed down by the courts and when such laws are passed in our national and state legislatures, we have to wonder if anyone is paying attention. Where is the outcry? Where is the dissent? Are we powerless to respond? It is true that there is a growing reaction from the so-called "religious right," but our victories to date are still small, and we have been largely ineffective in stopping the tide of judicial, political, and legislative activism.

In a very expressive article in the journal, *Foreign Affairs*, the brilliant author and political leader, Václav Havel, President of the Czech Republic, notes that the United States and Europe seem to be incapable of recognizing the moral dimensions of what has recently taken place in Eastern Europe. What happened there was a victory for freedom. It was a transformation of the soul brought about not only by the outcry for political liberty but by the demand for freedom of faith as well. Starved for spiritual meaning, the people of Eastern Europe attacked the institutions that held them in spiritual bondage. They were seeking the God who led the American patriots, but, ironically, once they were free, they found that the West has lost its way. Today it is we who are standing in the way of some sort of spiritual disaster.

In his article, Havel says that the hands-off approach being taken by the West is very dangerous. American statesmen seem to feel that everything is settled in the East, and there is nothing they can do. Havel says it is clear that we lack any sort of plan for dealing with the needs of the Eastern republics. He also observes that America's deep divisions over social and moral issues are signs of a weakness in the soul of the nation. He warns that we are in danger of losing our position of political and moral authority in the world.

An ardent Christian himself, Havel says, "The traditional values of Western civilization—such as democracy, respect for human rights and for the order of nature, the freedom of the individual and the inviolability of his property . . . all of these things become values with moral, and therefore metaphysical, underpinnings. Without intending to, the Communists taught us to understand the truth of the world not as mere information about it, but as an attitude, a commitment, a moral imperative."

Faced by inhuman isolation and restrictions, bound by a code of atheism and religious intolerance, the people of the East were driven to God. Almost by accident, they discovered that God is the true source of freedom. But, as Havel goes on to say, the loss of a sense of moral imperatives seems to be the source of America's problems today. He says, "I have the impression that precisely this awareness is sadly lacking in the present-day West." While the American people pay lip service to democracy, human rights, the order of nature, and responsibility for the world, they are not prepared to do anything that might threaten their comfortable lifestyle.

They are not willing to sacrifice for others. He says, "The pragmatism of politicians who want to win the next election, for whom the highest authority is therefore the will and the mood of a rather spoiled consumer society, makes it impossible for them to be aware of the moral, metaphysical, and tragic dimensions of their own program." In short, we have lost the ability to understand the eternal dimensions of our decisions. We have become addicted to our pleasures and our "rights."

The statesman wonders why the West has lost its ability to sacrifice. If the U.S. has won the Cold War, then it must face up to the more difficult task of winning the peace as well. But, sad to say, we suddenly seem terribly ill-prepared for that task. Then he says, "The economic advances of Euro-American civilization, based as they are on advances in scientific and technical knowledge, have gradually altered man's very value systems. Respect for the metaphysical horizons of his being is, to an increasing extent, pushed aside to make room for a new deity: the ideal of the perpetual growth of production and consumption."

Havel describes America as the prototypical "consumer society." Self-indulgence and greed have become our gods, and we have turned our backs on the God of heaven who is our true source of strength. "If [the United States] does not learn from our experience," the Czech leader warns, "about where human pride can lead, the hubris of people who invent a rational utopia for themselves and try to create a paradise on earth, if it persists in its anthropocentric understanding of the earth, it will bear the consequences itself, and so will the world. If its own consumer affluence remains more important for it than all the foundations of that affluence, it will soon forfeit that affluence."[5]

These ringing words are more than just an indictment by a man of courage and integrity who helped his people break the yoke of Communist oppression. They are one of the clearest predictions I have ever read of the impending judgment that will be brought down upon this land if we do not regain our moral priorities and return to faith in God. The focus on ourselves—which Havel calls the "anthropocentric" view—leads to self-destruction. Only a genuine "metaphysics" of faith, which recognizes the authority of the Creator, can save us from the hell of corruption and intolerance that will come upon any nation that loses touch with God.

A POOR TRADE, INDEED

When our politicians ignore these words, we must insist that they listen. And we must also ask ourselves some tough questions. Isn't it ironic that men like Solzhenitsyn and Havel, who have come through the crucible of political change in the past decades, should be the ones to raise these fundamental questions? To what are we committed, and what do we really believe? Did the founders of this nation set out to establish a secular government? Did they want to create a theocracy? Or did they even have a point of view concerning the "separation of church and state"? To answer these questions, let us look at the facts.

George Washington's first act as our nation's first president was to take his oath of office before God, and he did it with his hand on the Bible. After taking the oath, he bent down and kissed a page of the Bible. Anyone who believes this nation was conceived as a "secular society" will first have to explain the significance of that action. The next thing Washington did was to lead the entire Senate and House of Representatives to an Episcopal Church for a two-hour worship service. Are these the actions of a secular president? The true meaning of these actions by "the father of our country" ought to be enough to give the ACLU a case of collective apoplexy! But it gets even better. In his inaugural address to the Congress, the new president went on to say:

> It would be peculiarly improper to omit, in this first official act, my fervent supplication to that Almighty Being, who rules over the universe, who presides in the councils of nations, and whose providential aids can supply every human defect, that His benediction may consecrate to the liberties and happiness of the people of the United States . . . No people can be bound to acknowledge and adore the invisible hand which conducts the affairs of men more than the people of the United States. Every step by which they have advanced to the character of an independent nation seems to have been distinguished by some token of providential agency.

Again, are these the words of a "secular" man? Government keeps stressing the "secular" nature of American society, but where did the secularists come from? Who ordained this secular view of the state? The dictionary says a secularist is "one who rejects every form of religious faith and worship and undertakes to live accordingly; also, one who believes that education and other civil matters should be without the religious element." So the motivation of the secularist is to strip society of its relationship to and dependence upon God. It is the attempt to make religion—all religion—null and void.

From such a definition, it is clear that the secularists in our society do wield enormous power, but it is also clear that it was *not* that way in the beginning. At the same time that the first United States Congress was passing the First Amendment and the Bill of Rights, they also passed the Northwest Ordinance, a bill that has been called one of the four most important documents in American history. The other three are the Articles of Confederation, the Declaration of Independence, and the Constitution. In the Northwest Ordinance, the framers said, "Religion, morality, and knowledge, being necessary to good government and the happiness of mankind, schools and the means of education shall forever be encouraged."

Over the years, atheists like Madalyn Murray O'Hair have gone on radio and television to say that the American people don't want religion in their schools. This is a secular nation, she says, and people should get their religion in the churches. But isn't it odd that the same Congress that gave us the First Amendment also declared, in the Northwest Ordinance, that "schools and the means of education" must forever be encouraged to teach religion, morality, and knowledge, and thus help to develop character in our young people? Faith encourages those personal qualities that contribute to good government and responsible citizenship.

We have taken religion out of our schools by removing the Bible and prayers. We have taken morality out of our schools by removing the Ten Commandments, and now we have gotten rid of knowledge as well. After the *Engel v. Vitale* decision of 1962, which removed prayer from the schools, SAT scores plummeted downward for eighteen straight years. Student scores fell by more than eighty points between 1962 and 1980. Among the other landmark cases, *Abington v. Schempp* in 1963 declared that Bible reading could be "psychologically harmful" to children and would no longer be permitted in public schools. In 1980, the case of *Stone v. Gramm* prohibited schools from posting the Ten Commandments. Thanks to these and other rulings, our schools have become "de-moralized," and the disasters I described in previous chapters have come upon us because this nation is losing its soul.

Today, as high as eighty percent of all crimes in America are committed by school-age young people. For the most part, these are children who have never been to church; most haven't been taught morality or a code of ethics in their homes or schools. They have no concept of right and wrong, good or bad. They do things today as a matter of routine that earlier generations would have considered intolerable, immoral, and unnatural. Why? Because we have lost sight of the Light our founding fathers took for granted. We have taken the engines of democracy off the tracks that the founders laid down so carefully, and we have replaced faith with secularism.

A TALE OF TWO REVOLUTIONS

In 1776, the founders of this country had never heard of such a thing as a "secular nation." No secular nation had ever existed anywhere on the planet before our time. When one did come into existence in France, shortly after the founding of America, the founding fathers were appalled. They were horrified by what they saw in the French Enlightenment, and they wanted no part of it. The revolution in France was an unmitigated disaster that led to mass murder, the ruin of all the historic institutions of the nation, and the destruction of the Church and the Christian heritage of the French people. As attempts were made to throw off religion completely, a new theology of man—the roots of today's secular humanism—came into existence. Soon this false theology brought forth a river of blood, and then the tyranny of Napoleon. It gave birth to a tragedy from which Western society has never fully recovered.

For more than two hundred years, the nation of France has been trying to overcome the alienation and social dysfunction brought about by their revolution. But today, we are facing a similar crisis. The cover story of the December 9, 1991 issue of *Time* magazine, entitled "One Nation, Under God," asked the question: "Has the separation of church and state gone too far?" Looking at the ongoing debates over religious liberty and free expression, the writers conclude:

> For God to be kept out of the classroom or out of America's public debate by nervous school administrators or overcautious politicians serves no one's interests. That restriction prevents people from drawing on this country's rich and diverse religious heritage for guidance, and it degrades the nation's moral discourse by placing a whole realm of theological reasoning out of bounds. The price of that sort of quarantine, at a time of moral dislocation, is—and has been—far too high. The courts need to find a better balance between separation and accommodation—and Americans need to respect the new religious freedom they would gain as a result.[6]

Even *Time* magazine, not known for its excessive piety, recognizes that the so-called "separation" doctrine has gone too far. When we read about the court cases that stripped us of our religious freedoms, we have to ask, How could this have happened? Where did the train get derailed? When did we go wrong?

Consider the events we have witnessed in the last five years. We have seen the greatest experiment in socialism in the history of the world come to a disastrous end. Before our eyes, the Soviet Union crashed in flames and burned, bringing utter disaster, bankruptcy, and political chaos to that nation. But socialism is alive today in America. Why can't we see the simple fact that socialism doesn't work? It didn't work in the Soviet Union. It didn't work in Poland. It didn't work in East Germany or Cuba or China. It won't work in America, either. What is it going to take for our political leaders to wake up to this fact?

Of course, liberals don't use the name "socialism" openly. They use such terms as "progressive reform," "welfare assistance," "government subsidies," or "managed competition," but it's all the same thing—socialism by another name. Regardless what label they give it, it is "state socialism" that exalts government and the authority of bureaucracy over the lives of the people. All of the progressive programs being touted by Washington bureaucrats today are nothing but socialist schemes designed to keep people indebted to government.

At the time of the American Revolution, Alexis de Tocqueville stated that "The American republic will last until the populace discovers that it can vote for itself largesse out of the public treasury." We have certainly discovered the truth of those words. We even have television commercials that promise, "This little booklet will tell you everything you can get for free from the federal government." We can see now that the federal deficit, the national debt, the general insolvency of the government, and perhaps even the trade imbalance—which has made the United States the world's largest debtor nation—are due in large part to the fact that the citizens of this nation and their elected representatives have discovered only too well how to tap the till of the United States Treasury.

When we see the shakiness of business and industry, and especially the uncertainty of the New York Stock Exchange, we have to believe that the American people have lost faith in the free-enterprise economy. Instead, we are turning toward the socialist model and are being led there by government, by the members of the president's cabinet, and by policies designed by liberal think tanks and bureaucratic institutions. We are suffering the consequences of their socialist blind spot even now, but we have not begun to feel the repercussion that will be coming in the next few years. In fact, the Grace Commission Report, compiled by a blue ribbon panel of business and industry leaders, predicted that our national debt (which was about three trillion dollars at the time of the study) would grow to fourteen trillion dollars by the end of this century. Today we are already approaching five trillion dollars and growing at an outrageous pace.

GOVERNMENT OUT OF CONTROL

Sometimes we tend to forget that the government doesn't have any money. It doesn't earn money. Government does not create jobs or improve the economy. Government wastes money. It pours your tax dollars down the drain of waste and socialist programming. Government takes the hard-earned wealth of citizens and gives it to those with their hands out. That's something many people don't seem to understand.

Author Rus Walton[7] put it very well when he said, "Government is not a producer; it is a taker, a taxer, and a spender. Every dollar spent by the public sector is a dollar the government must take from the private sector, from the workers and earners and investors. The dollar taken by government cannot be spent or invested by that productive private sector."

That is why we are having problems. That $1.5 trillion that the government is taking this year will simply be the amount of the interest on the national debt by the end of the century. In just a few years, the interest on the national debt will consume the entire federal budget. And if we continue in the direction we are going at this moment, we may well see this nation self-destruct very much as the Soviet Union has already done. "America will last until the populace discovers that it can vote for itself largesse out of the public treasury." It seems we are well on the way to fulfilling that prophecy today.

Many of the schemes that come out of the federal government sound so benevolent, so humanitarian, so noble. "We're trying to help people," they tell us. They are "sincere." They have "good intentions." Nevertheless, the politicians and bureaucrats are leading us into disaster. What we must understand is that the federal government is extraordinarily wasteful and extraordinarily inefficient. Government creates far more problems than it solves, and to expect government to save us from disaster is like expecting the Titanic to sail us away to safety. The government's safe way is the surest way to self-destruction.

Professor Thomas Sowell of Stanford University, a brilliant black scholar who is one of America's leading economists, reports that waste, mismanagement, and lack of control have turned the so-called "welfare" system of this nation into a massive fraud. Government spending for welfare is already vastly greater than the people's actual physical needs, but government cannot solve the problem, and the problems are growing worse. Sowell writes, "The amount of money necessary to lift every man, woman, and child in America above the poverty line is one-third of what in fact is being spent on poverty programs. Clearly, much of the transfer ends up in the pockets of highly paid administrators, consultants, and staff."

Perhaps this is why the two "bedroom counties" of Washington, D.C. (one in Virginia and one in Maryland), have the highest per-capita income in America today. But it is also true that government is incredibly inefficient, and a cold, insensitive government bureaucracy can never expect to help people with real flesh and blood and real problems. There is no more obvious truism—government does not solve problems, it creates them. Not too long ago we heard a great deal about a well-meaning, benevolent-sounding program called CETA, the "Comprehensive Employment and Training Act." In this program, government was going to "create jobs" for people who needed to earn a living. Local agencies were excited. At last, here was a real leap forward for government involvement in community welfare.

But what happened? In Chicago a CETA program paid a young employee $750 a month to teach ghetto youths how to slap various parts of their bodies rhythmically in order to become "human drums." In Oregon, a CETA agency financed the construction of a steel-reinforced concrete rock thirty feet high and sixty feet across on a small island so people could practice rock climbing! In Ventura, California, a CETA agency paid one hundred-one people to count the dogs, cats, and horses in the county.

It has been estimated that the federal government spends twice as much money in creating a job as does the private sector. Sometimes they spend far more. For example, Stanford University received fifteen million dollars from the government for the purpose of creating jobs. They created a total of thirty-nine jobs. That averages out to $324,685 per job! The private sector produces jobs for twenty thousand dollars. But sadly, the more money we pour into these government projects, the less money is available in the private sector and the fewer real productive jobs will be created. The more taxes government takes out of the private sector, the less able private industry will be to create the jobs the nation depends upon.

Government is extraordinarily inefficient, and whenever the government gets involved in anything, the situation automatically gets worse. Whenever you find a serious problem in your community, you can be fairly certain that government had a hand in creating it. If you decide you have a problem only the government can solve, you will soon find that as soon as the government gets involved, the problem will become ten times worse.

Just consider what has happened in our urban ghettos. Time and time again we have seen government programs lead to disappointment and disaster. When government began giving money to women who had children out of wedlock, people soon discovered that they could get a lot more money if they stayed single and had even more children out of wedlock. So, where did government's solution take us? Today the rate of illegitimacy in the black urban community, as I have already described, is as high as eighty percent. That means that four out of every five black children born in our inner cities today have no father in the home and, in many cases, no male role models. Through socialistic welfare programs, the government has inadvertently destroyed the black family in America. Religious values and family ties used to be the bastion of black society. Prior to welfare, the illegitimacy rate among American blacks was just nineteen percent, but today government is destroying black families because the liberal giveaway schemes changed the balance of nature and created a "culture of dependency."

THE SEPARATION CLAUSE

What we need to realize is that the growth of big government, the escalating public debt, and the inefficiency of the federal bureaucracy are all symptoms of a nation that has been separated from its moral foundations. And the real danger of the so-called "separation" doctrine is not that religion has been put at arm's length from the government, but that this false concept has been used to install government as the sovereign power and benefactor of the nation. We have made an idol of government, and we have displaced the God of heaven from His rightful place as the Supreme Authority in our lives.

When Thomas Jefferson wrote his letter to the Baptist congregation in Danbury, Connecticut, in 1802, eleven years after the Bill of Rights had been ratified, he said that the First Amendment erected a "wall of separation" between Church and State. Even though Jefferson was a brilliant man and an important force in helping to establish many of our early laws and traditions, his statement was simply not true. I suspect it was a convenient excuse, perhaps a white lie to avoid some sort of lingering entanglement. But it was, nevertheless, a lie. The statement was immediately forgotten, and for one hundred-fifty years no one paid much attention to the idea. But in 1947, an ACLU lawyer came across the phrase and used it to help erect a barrier between church and state that had never before existed. And today the idea of a "wall of separation" is so common that many Americans have come to believe it is actually in the Constitution. But the only constitution in which the term ever appeared is that of the USSR—the collapsed Soviet Union.

I once asked a group of sixty people if they were familiar with that phrase. Every one of them raised his hand. I said, "Does anybody know the wording of the First Amendment regarding religion?" Nobody raised his hand. Then I said, "Do you know what the First Amendment actually says and what the difference between the First Amendment and the separation of Church and State really is?" They said they did not know. So I told them the Constitution of the United States *does not* include any reference to the "separation of church and state." But since Justice Hugo Black incorporated it into the Court's 1947 *Everson* ruling, the term has taken on the weight of law. No wonder so many people are confused.

Adolf Hitler said that if you tell a small lie, some people will believe it, but if you tell a big lie often enough and loud enough, everybody will believe it. That is precisely the place to which we have come regarding the separation doctrine. John Quincy Adams said, "The highest glory of the Revolution was that it united in one indissoluble bond the principles of Christianity and the principles of civil government." But in one stroke, the Everson Decision erected a wall severing that indissoluble bond.

Whereas the founders sought to restrain government from interfering in matters of faith, today the separation principle restrains matters of faith and belief from entering not only into government but into public view. Liberal jurists and legislators, then, have done their part to help take the shackles off of government and put them onto the people. This is precisely the opposite of what the founders intended the First Amendment to do.

In 1992, a friend sent me an article clipped from the newspaper in Richmond, Virginia, which described the effort of a group in the United States Treasury Department to slip a clause into the federal budget that would give the IRS authority to examine church records and even to confiscate them, to get the names and addresses of every person claiming a contribution of more than five hundred dollars a year to the church. This was not a legislative procedure, nor was it a matter brought before Congress. It was a subtle attempt to slip this into the budget unseen and, thus, to create a bureaucratic principle with the weight of law.

When I read the article, I immediately called Vice President Quayle about the matter. He said he had just learned of the documents and was already taking steps to halt passage of this element of the budget. He had spoken to the president about it, and neither of them was aware that such a statement had been included in that thousand-plus-page document. They discovered that the offending paragraph had been drafted by someone in the Treasury Department, and they were outraged. It was simply an attempt by unscrupulous bureaucrats to pass into law a measure that was clearly and historically unconstitutional.

As we have seen already, the founding fathers never intended for the United States to be considered a "secular" nation. They did not want the people of this country, nor their government, ever to become hostile to religion. Instead, government was to accommodate religious and moral values and to encourage a reverence for God. As Justice Joseph Story has written in his *Commentaries on the Constitution of the United States*: "Christianity ought to receive encouragement from the state." The intention of the Constitution and the First Amendment, said Story, was to encourage Christianity "so far as was not incompatible with the private rights of conscience and the freedom of religious worship."

The patriot Patrick Henry said, "It cannot be emphasized too strongly or too often that this great nation was founded, not by religionists, but by Christians; not on religions, but on the Gospel of Jesus Christ." Samuel Adams, the great orator of the Revolution, claimed that the victory of the patriots helped to ensure that God would be supreme in the New World. He said, "We have this day restored the Sovereign to whom all men ought to be obedient . . . let His kingdom come." Does that sound like a separation of church and state?

But today the ungodly are doing their best to destroy all of that, and the club they are using to beat back the idea of religious liberty is the "wall of separation between church and state," usually in the hands of the ACLU. Like Hitler's big lie, this false doctrine has been used to brainwash the American people and to attempt to drive Christians and the Christian faith into oblivion.

LIBERTY AND JUSTICE FOR ALL

Is there any hope that justice may yet prevail in this nation? One man put it this way: "There is simply no historical foundation for the proposition that the framers intended to build the 'wall of separation.'" Don't you wish that a man with such a belief could be in an influential position where he might do something about it? The man who made that statement is William Rehnquist, the Chief Justice of the United States Supreme Court. Justice Rehnquist went on to say, in the conclusion of one of the finest briefs I have ever read, "The 'wall of separation between church and state' is a metaphor based on bad history, a metaphor which has proved useless as a guide to judging. It should be frankly and explicitly abandoned."

Rehnquist also quotes Justice Joseph Story's statement that "at the time of the adoption of the Constitution, and of the amendment to it now under consideration [First Amendment], the general if not the universal sentiment in America was, that Christianity ought to receive encouragement from the State so far as was not incompatible with the private rights of conscience and the freedom of religious worship. An attempt to level all religions, and to make it a matter of state policy to hold all in utter indifference, would have created universal disapprobation, if not universal indignation.

"The real object of the First Amendment," said Justice Story, "was not to countenance, much less to advance, Mahometanism, or Judaism, or infidelity, by prostrating Christianity; but to exclude all rivalry among Christian sects, and to prevent any national ecclesiastical establishment."

At the same time that Justice Rehnquist handed down his opinion, Justice Byron White offered his concurrence, saying, "I appreciate Justice Rehnquist's explication of the history of the Religion Clauses of the First Amendment. Against that history, it would be quite understandable if we undertook to reassess our cases dealing with these cases, particularly those dealing with the establishment clause. Of course, I have been out of step with many of the Court's decisions dealing with this subject matter, and it is thus not surprising that I would support a basic reconsideration of our precedents." Even though the makeup of the Supreme Court has changed in the past three years, there is reason to believe that not all justices are blind. The High Court bench is lofty, and it changes people. But surely some of them can still see the truth, and we should pray that God will open the eyes of the Supreme Court and cause them all, once again, to take the side of liberty and justice for all—even for Christians.

As we have seen throughout these pages, we are facing dark times in this nation. Terror and catastrophe are all around us, compounded by the endlessly destructive machinations of the federal bureaucracy. But all is not lost. There is still hope. If we decide to get active in these matters and take our rightful roles as concerned Christian citizens and as activists in the cause of liberty, there is no reason that we cannot see some wonderful results in this country in the next few years. I believe we can put the train back on the tracks. We, the people, can restore religious liberty to this nation.

I also believe we can see the infamous *Roe v. Wade* decision, which has led to the slaughter of more than thirty million innocent lives over the past twenty-three years, overturned. If we are committed and involved in taking back the nation for Christian moral values, and if we are willing to risk the scorn of the secular media and the bureaucracy that stand against us, there is no doubt we can witness the dismantling of not just the Berlin Wall but the even more diabolical "wall of separation" that has led to increasing secularization, godlessness, immorality, and corruption in our country.

THE SMILES OF HEAVEN

When Francis Scott Key composed the stirring verse that eventually became our national anthem, he stood watching the bombardment of Fort McHenry by the British fleet. The shelling was so heavy, so fierce, and so long that there was no certainty the Americans isolated there could survive. His question was more than a poetic phrase. It had deep, heartfelt meaning. "Oh, say, can you see by the dawn's early light, / What so proudly we hailed at the twilight's last gleaming?" As the sun rose that fateful morning, he yearned to know if the fort, the flag, and the nation itself had survived.

The great joy of that anthem is that the American cause not only survived, but it triumphed. Today we know that our birthright of freedom could not be quelled by the bombardments of the enemy. It could not even be destroyed by the Civil War, the Spanish-American War, or the two World Wars that placed us at such great risk. But it has been fifty years since the last challenge of that magnitude. We have also endured Korea, Vietnam, the Persian Gulf War, and other conflicts around the globe, but can we survive the peace? Will this nation survive the systematic destruction of its liberties by the "wall of separation" that has purged us of faith and the free and open expression of our religious beliefs?

Aleksandr Solzhenitsyn recognized the peril in which we stand at this hour: "Even if we are spared destruction by war, life will have to change in order not to perish on its own. We cannot avoid reassessing the fundamental definitions of human life and human society. Is it true that man is above everything? Is there no Superior Spirit above him? Is it right that man's life and society's activities should be ruled by material expansion above all? Is it permissible to promote such expansion to the detriment of our integral spiritual life?"

This man who survived the gulag, torture, thought control, and all the other false ideologies of the Communists, offers a stern warning for American society. We must heed the perceptive words of this great friend of freedom when he says, "If the world has not approached its end, it has reached a major watershed in history, equal in importance to the turn from the Middle Ages to the Renaissance. It will demand from us a spiritual blaze; we shall have to rise to a new height of vision, to a new level of life, where our physical nature will not be cursed, as in the Middle Ages, but even more importantly, our spiritual nature will not be trampled upon, as in the Modern Era."[8]

If we are to survive, we must rise not just to a new vision but to the true vision of faith and freedom where God is sovereign once again. The challenge for us today, as we near the end of this momentous century, is to break down the artificial wall that separates us from God and work to restore a harmony of faith in every sphere of our lives. George Washington said that "the propitious smiles of Heaven can never be expected on a nation that disregards the eternal rules of order and right, which Heaven itself has ordained." Unless we can regain the favor of heaven by restoring religious liberties in this land, we can be assured that the smiles of heaven will soon turn to wrath.✟

NOTES

[1]Aleksandr Solzhenitsyn, *A World Split Apart: Commencement Address Delivered at Harvard University*, June 6, 1978 (New York: Harper & Row Publishers, 1978), 19, 21.

[2]Ibid., 21, 23.

[3]Ibid., 37.

[4]Ibid., 49, 51.

[5]Václav Havel, "A Call for Sacrifice: The Co-Responsibility of the West," *Foreign Affairs* (March/April 1994), 2–7.

[6]David Aikman and Richard N. Ostling, "America's Holy War," cover story in "One Nation, Under God" issue, *Time* (Dec. 9, 1991): 61–68.

[7]Rus Walton, *One Nation Under God* (Washington: Third Century Publishers, 1975).

[8]Solzhenitsyn, 59, 61.

6

The Repression of Religion

I sat stunned for more than an hour and a half as a man I had never met before told me about the horrors of his life under communism. He had been a political prisoner, he told me, and he was guilty of an egregious crime against the state. What was his crime? He had applied for a visa to come to America. After fifteen years in a disgusting and dehumanizing Soviet prison, he was now free, and his first act was to flee to the West to warn us about the dangers of the Communist lie. He came to challenge Americans to be strong and courageous and to resist the subtle traps of socialism.

Because he dared to request permission to visit the United States, this man was forced to spend fifteen years of his life in a foul and dangerous penitentiary. During all that time, he lived like an animal in a windowless cell. The water that seeped down the filthy stone walls immediately turned to ice. There was no light bulb, no opening of any kind, not even a slot in the door. He had no blankets, only an undershirt. Instead of a mattress, he slept on a board on the floor.

Needless to say, my visitor of nearly a decade ago opened my eyes to a number of things. He confirmed many of the reports we had all heard about life under the Communist system, but he also said something I will never forget.

He said that Marx and Lenin promised to give the world a "new man." The Communist super-man was supposed to be a new creation on the face of the earth. He was to be noble and selfless, concerned for others, and towering above the rest of humanity. Later, Friedrich Nietzsche would write about the *Übermensch*—the "overman" or "superman." The Communists were, in fact, out to create a whole race of supermen!

Under the brutal dictator, Joseph Stalin, the Soviet government took the theological dimensions of the Communist heresy to an even greater extreme as it tried to control every area of life and thought. Government bureaucracies controlled the affairs of workers, citizens, writers, artists, athletes, and merchants. They manipulated industry and agriculture and set the value of products, labor, and even human life. The state controlled the economy but also encouraged the rise of a "cult of praise" that took on many aspects of religion. It was a sort of deification of their evil leader. Policies handed down by Stalin were treated with all the solemnity and authority of papal edicts. His whims were enforced as law by the military and the secret police. While the excesses of Stalin caused his successors to become somewhat more moderate in their use and abuse of power, the totalitarian system in Moscow always had a strangely ecclesiastical character. The ruler was their god, and the people were to be the glorious creations of the state. These were communism's "new men."

My visitor told me that the Soviet idealists were correct—at least in part—for they had indeed given to the world a new man. But that new man, created by seventy years of atheism and repression, was not a noble and selfless paragon of virtue but a monster without heart or soul. The new man created by the Communist nightmare had been systematically deprived of his character and his conscience, along with his nobility, morality, and ethics. He had been reduced to little more than a wild beast in an urban jungle, with no compassion or compunction. Until finally freed from the grip of tyranny, the people of the Soviet Union were capable of committing atrocious acts of brutality. Anyone who has read even a portion of Aleksandr Solzhenitsyn's *Gulag Archipelago*, or any of the chronicles that have come out in the past three years, understands that these people were capable of doing things to other people that no civilized person could ever do, even in their worst nightmares.

THE FALSE EQUATION

What Marx and Lenin forgot in their theory of "dialectical materialism" was that only the Spirit of God can make people better. The Bible says,

"Where the Spirit of the Lord is, there is liberty." There is no other way to have freedom. It is only when the reality of God's Spirit is felt and acknowledged that true liberty can exist. And the power to exercise that liberty for the good of others and for godliness can only survive where there is an atmosphere of faith and religious conviction. Without the re-creation of man through faith in Christ, no "new man" will ever be created.

During the same week that I spoke to that former prisoner, I talked to another man from Eastern Europe who told me that a government bureaucrat had once come to him and said, "We know that you have a way . . . a method of making people good. We want you to use it." They said this to a Christian because they didn't have any idea how to reform people any other way. They had tried everything, and everything failed. Tyranny, repression, spying, threats, the false theology of the state, and all the other Communist methods failed abysmally. Having created those beasts of the jungle called "new men," they repressed them under the iron heel of tyranny for decades. Most of the citizens of those fifteen East Bloc nations had known no other life. But when the iron fist was suddenly lifted, they became wild men freed from their cages, roaming the streets and committing outrageous crimes against society.

Even today, nearly five years since the collapse of the autocratic power of the Kremlin, crime is still rising in Eastern Europe, and nobody knows what to do about it. They have observed the positive influence of the church in the West, so today they are saying, in effect, "You Christians have a way of making people good. We don't understand what it is or how it works. But, whatever it is, and whatever it involves, even if means bringing God and the Bible into our country, please do it now!" What they have now is moral chaos and social anarchy, and the leaders of the Commonwealth of Independent States say they are willing to try anything to bring about some sort of spiritual and moral reform.

A story told by Ernest Gordon in the book, *Through the Valley of the Kwai*, tells about a group of American soldiers taken prisoner of war by the Japanese in World War II. These men were humiliated, starved, and treated as savages by their captors. Torture and every sort of indignity were heaped on them, and as a result they became no better than animals. They were angry and violent, fighting among themselves and stealing food, and there was genuine doubt that any of these men would survive their captivity. When it looked as if things could not go on any longer, Ernest Gordon decided to read aloud from the New Testament, and little by little, just by hearing those life-changing words, almost all the men in the camp were converted to Christianity. Suddenly the beasts who had been snarling and fighting and stealing from each other began to live in peace, to endure their tribulations with a sense of composure and endurance, and many of them came through the experience as new creations in Christ. They were truly born again, all because they gave up everything and turned to the Savior.

This is such an important observation. When people are outside of Christ, there is chaos and anarchy. They become brutal and self-serving, and this will always be so. And if the personal and spiritual convictions that come through faith in Jesus Christ are removed, then a nation must either have harsh tyranny imposed upon them to control their destructive instincts or there will be anarchy, when the people are out of control. It is no secret that this is also the root of the social problems in the United States today. As Dr. W. C. Robinson has said, "Christ always has been and always will be crucified between two thieves: legalism and license." In the political realm, that amounts to either tyranny or anarchy, and in either extreme there will be chaos.

As sad as the tragedies of Russia, Bosnia, Poland, Slovenia, and Hungary have been over the last several years, it is easy to think, "Well, at least it is half a world away." But, the fact of the matter is that right here in our own country we have been following in those same footsteps, and we, too, have made the same fatal mistakes. We have forgotten that it is only by the Spirit of the Lord that there can ever be real liberty. *Only God gives liberty that does not degenerate into license.* Only the Spirit of God can give peace that is not corrupted by all manner of immorality and cruelty.

As we have seen, over the past twenty-five years the United States Supreme Court and many of the lower courts have done their best to strip this nation of its religious heritage. Through some misguided view of "fairness," they have taken the Bible from our young people, they have denied their freedom to pray in the schools, they have removed the Ten Commandments because those biblical values may contaminate the minds of the young with ideas of honor, fidelity, and respect for their elders. Now they want to deny the existence of a Creator and, before you realize it, they will be trying more and more to restrict the practice of Christian worship under any circumstance. Believe me, that is not an exaggerated statement. And I do not believe we are far from it today.

THE ASSAULT ON RELIGION

The assault on Christianity has been going on a very long time, and the attacks of atheists and agnostics seem to be escalating at this hour. In his book, *The Essence of Christianity*, published in 1841, the German philosopher, Ludwig Feuerbach, claimed that God is nothing but a human invention. The God of the Bible, he said, is merely a representation of all that is good and evil in the character of man. In reality, the skeptic argued, we have created God in our own image, and the very idea of a great and powerful being who controls the events of human existence is absurd. He said this belief has created an environment of isolation and disappointment. Our idea of God has alienated mankind from himself. By creating a "Supreme Being" with greater authority than man himself, man had reduced himself to a pathetic, evil being who can only be kept under control by a powerful church or a totalitarian government.

If only religion could be abolished, Feuerbach argued, then human beings would overcome their terrible disappointments and alienation. This was a concept ready-made for the likes of Karl Marx, who incorporated many of these same ideas in his theories about private property. The purpose of man, Marx said, is to advance not just himself but the human species. Man, he said, is a "species being." Religion and private property both encourage the worst kinds of behavior. They take away man's sense of responsibility for his fellowman. They allow him to become selfish and acquisitive, and this spells disaster for the human species. In a treatise published shortly before the release of the *Communist Manifesto*, Marx called for the elimination of private property, the creation of a new proletariat of workers guided by an elite cadre of socialist leaders, and the absolute abolition of religion.

All together, these revolutionary ideas from such nineteenth-century thinkers as Feuerbach, Marx, Nietzsche, and Arthur Schopenhauer, helped to make the basic premises of atheism a standard feature of both science and socialist thought from that time to this. The intellectuals were militant critics of religion in general, but they especially hated Christianity, since faith in Jesus Christ represented such a fundamental challenge to all their beliefs and practices. Today, anyone associated with movements such as state socialism, Marxism, existentialism, Freudianism, and logical positivism, is not just an enemy of the republican form of democracy but is almost certainly an atheist and an enemy of Jesus Christ.

As a philosophy, atheism is both theoretical and practical, but it offers no moral theory of its own. The principal argument of atheism is that there is no valid proof of the existence of God and no practical reason for believing in a Supreme Being. The concept of a personal deity, whether perceived as a spiritual being or as a God-Man, such as Jesus Christ, is simply irrational. When Christians say, as we often do, "I believe in God the Father Almighty, Maker of heaven and earth," these people claim we are babbling nonsense. In the name of science, sociology, and psychology, they claim that religious speech is incoherent and meaningless. Nietzsche said that belief in the supernatural devalues the significance of human life. Sigmund Freud claimed that Christianity and Judaism are merely superstitions that demonstrate the childishness and helplessness of those who hold such beliefs.

ADVOCATES OF ABOLITION

After Marx, Darwin, Freud, Huxley, and the philosophers had suggested the abolition of religion as a practical and scientifically plausible idea, others eagerly joined in the assault on the church. Ever since the eighteenth century, with the rise of rationalism and the spirit of the Enlightenment, there have been many challenges to the authority of the Bible and to the authority and purpose of the church. Evolutionism teaches that man is a random accident of nature, a creature who is neither the image of God nor of any lasting significance. With no tangible or even mathematical proof of their bizarre theory, biologists and other scientists immediately accepted the idea and used it to challenge the teachings of Scripture.

Ironically, the great universities of the United States had all been founded as Christian institutions of higher learning. Harvard, Yale, Princeton, Dartmouth, Columbia, Brown, Bryn Mawr, Amherst, and many others had been established to teach theology and religion, with the view that all earthly knowledge flows from the knowledge of God and the principles of His Word. The fact that these very schools have now become some of the most radical, anti-Christian institutions in the world, is evidence of just how great the shift away from God has been in this century.

The followers of the new science looked for "nontheistic" explanations for natural phenomena, wanting to prove that God had no part in creation and ultimately that God could not exist. Freedom from religion, they felt, would mean freedom to pursue their own passions and desires without guilt or fear of divine retribution. Life might be "solitary, poor, nasty, brutish, and short," as Thomas Hobbes had once suggested, but at least it would be over when it was over and there would be no God to judge them for their sin. At least, that was their pathetic hope.

Among the doctrines of the *Humanist Manifesto* by Paul Konrad Kurtz, first published in 1933 and revised in 1973, is the principle that humanists are socialists by nature. Like Karl Marx, they see private property as primitive and selfish, nationalism and pride of country as dangerous, and allegiance to any power other than the socialist state should be illegal. Ideas, ethics, and the means of production belong to the state, they claim. For supporters such as Paul Kurtz, B. F. Skinner, John Dewey, Francis Crick, Isaac Asimov, and the other signers of the manifesto, communism and state socialism were the only logical solutions to mankind's problems. In the first edition of that thin volume, they wrote, "A socialized and cooperative economic order must be established to the end that the equitable distribution of the means of life be possible . . . Humanists demand a shared life in a shared world."

From 1917 to 1989, humanistic atheism grew in league with communism, and the two forces supported each other. Advocates of atheist ideals included the American Association for the Advancement of Atheism (1925), the League of Militant Atheists (1929), and today, Madalyn Murray O'Hair's American Atheists. Atheist organizations have been the principal supporters of much of the anti-Christian and anti-religion litigation of the past thirty years, along with the legal and strategic assistance of their primary allies, the American Civil Liberties Union (ACLU).

CIVIL LIBERTIES, SO-CALLED

Under the benign sounding name of civil libertarians, the ACLU have been behind some of the most destructive and defamatory anti-religious litigation in history. Founded as the Bureau for Conscientious Objectors in the middle of World War I, the organization was the brainchild of Roger Baldwin, a pacifist, atheist, and anarchist. In the early days the group was part of the pacifist organization, American Union Against Militarism, but in October 1918 became independent under the name National Civil Liberties Bureau.

From the start, members of this group were involved in anti-American activities. In August 1918, FBI agents raided the Bureau and discovered subversive materials. Three months later, Baldwin began serving a one-year term for sedition. It was after his release from prison that the organizers changed the name of the organization to the American Civil Liberties Union.

Today, even though its aims, values, and objectives have hardly changed since those days, the ACLU now claims more than 250,000 dues-paying members, seventy staff lawyers, and as many as five thousand volunteer attorneys. Supreme Court Justice Ruth Bader Ginsburg served as an ACLU attorney, as have several other members of the Clinton Administration. The organization has an annual budget in excess of fourteen million dollars and is capable of handling as many as six thousand separate cases at any given time. Needless to say, they are one of the most formidable adversaries of conservative Christian values on earth.

Several of the ACLU's original executive board members were later prominent leaders in the Communist Party USA. Among them were William Foster, Elizabeth Gurley Flynn, and Louis Budenez. Baldwin himself once said, "I am for Socialism, disarmament, and ultimately for abolishing the state itself as an instrument of violence and compulsion. I seek social ownership of property . . . Communism is the goal." All this from a man who was an ardent defender and supporter of Joseph Stalin.

As I have said repeatedly, true liberty comes only through Jesus Christ. So, does the ACLU stand for liberty? In a few well-publicized cases, ACLU attorneys have defended cases of religious discrimination. In Boston, for example, ACLU lawyers helped the Jews for Jesus organization to gain the right to distribute literature in and around the subway stations in the city. But the overwhelming majority of their cases have been in support of leftist and radical causes, and their natural perspective is liberal and anti-authoritarian. They have defended, for example, the "free speech" rights of child pornographers, Satanists, Ku Klux Klan members, and American Nazis.

Each year, like clockwork, they sue cities and other organizations that wish to display Nativity scenes or Hanukkah symbols at Christmas. They have stopped carolers from singing "Silent Night" and "Away in a Manger" in public places. They have fought to deny tax-exempt status to churches while maintaining it for themselves and even occultic groups. They have been consistent opponents of prayer in the schools, at graduations, and at any public event. They have tried to force the armed forces to get rid of all chaplains and to remove the words "In God We Trust" from American coins. In short, this is one of the most prominent organizations in this nation, and they are sworn enemies of God and those who love Him.

THE ANTI-CHRISTIAN AGENDA

The battles we have seen in the schools, the workplace, and even in our homes are only an indication of the larger agenda of the anti-Christian forces in this nation. If the actions and beliefs of the newest member of the Supreme Court offer any insight into the position of the activist court, then we have good reason for alarm. In a review of the public record on Justice Ruth Bader Ginsburg's position on social issues, Focus on the Family compiled this disturbing list of the jurist's views:

1. The traditional family concept of the husband as a breadwinner and the wife as a homemaker must be eliminated.
2. The federal government must provide comprehensive child-care.
3. The Homestead Law must give twice as much benefit to couples who live apart from each other as to a husband and wife who live together.
4. In the military, women must be drafted when men are drafted, and women must be assigned to combat duty.
5. Affirmative action must be applied to equalize the number of men and women in the armed forces.
6. The age of consent for sexual acts must be lowered to twelve years of age.
7. Prostitution must be legalized. She wrote: "prostitution as a consensual act between adults is arguably within the zone of privacy protected by recent constitutional decisions."
8. All-boy and all-girl organizations must be sexually integrated, as must all fraternities and sororities. The Boy Scouts and the Girl Scouts must change their names and their purposes, to become sex-integrated.

The justice who was hailed as a moderate by the press, by the Clinton Administration, and even by a number of conservatives, clearly has a radical agenda that is counter to the interests, the welfare, or the history of this nation. If implemented, her objectives will destroy the already weakened foundations of the family in this country and create further division, hostility, and dissatisfaction between men and women. These are clearly the beliefs of a woman who has no fear of or respect for God.

Another presidential appointee, Kristine Gebbie, a liberal activist, is the Clinton Administration's AIDS czar. When she met the press on the White House lawn, she said that this nation has a repressed, Victorian view of sexuality, and she wants to change it. This is a society, she said, that "misrepresents information, denies sexuality early, denies homosexual sexuality particularly in teens, and leaves people abandoned with no place to go." And then as an obvious taunt in the face of God, she said, "I can help just a little bit in my job, standing on the White House lawn, talking about sex, with no lightning bolts falling on my head."

Churches, Christian ministries, and individual believers all over the nation are recognizing the intensity of the battle being waged against them. The Alliance Defense Fund, an organization founded to support legal defense and advocacy of cases involving religious freedom, the sanctity of life, and family values, monitors all cases currently in litigation and follows events that could threaten religious liberties and Christian values in this country. According to Alan Sears, the organization's executive director, the pressure from the Left is building at an unprecedented pace, placing those who hold traditional religious values in greater jeopardy than ever before.

In this decade, Sears warns, we can expect to see a concerted effort in Congress, the Justice Department, and the federal courts to "reevaluate" the tax-exempt status of religious organizations such as parachurch ministries, religious schools, and charitable organizations. Expect increased control over religious organizations to prevent them from participating in political activities —especially regarding abortion, homosexuality, or the distribution of condoms in public schools.

Sears believes we will see much stricter enforcement and harsher penalties on religious organizations based on "anti-discrimination" laws. The government's shock tactics will attempt to force churches and other Christian groups to hire homosexuals, atheists, and others whose beliefs and behavior are in conflict with biblical values. There will also be attempts to use building codes, and safety and health regulations, as weapons against resistant religious groups. And the court will likely pay much closer attention to "malpractice" suits against clergy and lay counselors.

Zoning restrictions will be harder on Christians; expansion of church facilities will be limited; restrictions on Sunday schools, church schools, and home schools will increase; and even greater (and more unconstitutional) limits will be placed on the rights of students to express their faith publicly. While non-Christian and anti-Christian groups will be given much greater freedom, and while unchristian beliefs and practices will be given special protection, the schools will most certainly become battlegrounds in the months and years ahead. And Christian legal groups expect the attacks on the traditional family, on would-be adoptive parents, and on many other rights and privileges that

Christians have taken for granted to become more numerous and more hostile. The lesson in these times should be that nothing is sacred to the state, and *nothing* can be taken for granted anymore.

ALTERNATIVE RELIGIONS

The attack on the church is not intended simply to destroy Christianity but to replace it with something else. According to John Naisbitt and Patricia Aburdene, in their updated bestseller, *Megatrends 2000*, that something else is the New Age movement and the various alternative and "nontraditional" religions. According to these authors, there were as many as twenty million New Agers in this country in 1990—compared to approximately sixty million evangelicals—and their numbers are still growing as the baby-boom generation, now reaching middle age, has discovered that they are spiritually empty. "New Agers represent the most affluent, well-educated, successful segment of the baby boom," they say, with an average household income of nearly fifty thousand dollars. Apparently, the real value of these people is not their faith but their affluence.

Quoting Dr. Harvey Cox of Harvard, Naisbitt and Aburdene report that the New Age revival in America is "a global phenomenon that has to do with the unraveling of modernity." The idea that science could solve all our problems, born out of the Enlightenment and the Industrial Revolution, has been disproved by the emotional and social crises of our day. "From Voltaire to Marx," writes sociologist Daniel Bell in *The End of Ideology*, "every Enlightenment thinker thought that religion would disappear in the twentieth century because religion was fetishism, animistic superstition." But instead, science and philosophy have come up empty, man is more adrift in the cosmos today than at any time in the history of the race, and a relationship with God is clearly the only hope for the future. But not everyone has come around to this view.

At the conclusion of their chapter on religion, the authors of *Megatrends* observe that the image of Apocalypse and some final conflict between good and evil seems unavoidable. The symbolism of the New Age and the end of the millennium are forcing society to address some essential questions. Are we facing the end of civilization? Should we expect a fire-and-brimstone millennium or a spaceship rescue? Or will the end come perhaps from a failed biotech experiment, a gene gone mad, finally destroying the human race? "The millennium is a two-sided metaphor of choice," they write. "On the one side, a man-made apocalypse represents the possibility that godlike technology in human hands could destroy the environment, create nuclear annihilation. But what if, in the language of symbolism, the Antichrist has already appeared in the form of the 'God is dead' philosophy, in the worship of only science, culminating in the creation of weapons of mass destruction and untold other ways to destroy ourselves and the earth?" In this final comment, Naisbitt and Aburdene are much closer than they may know to the truth.

But ultimately, these writers see the debates between church and state, and the emergence of new ideas about religious devotion, more as positive trends of interest primarily to marketers. They conclude that the emergence of a new epoch in history, based on the failure of our faith in science and the rise of all sorts of new religious ideologies, is a hopeful sign. It represents the acceptance of diversity, a healthy rise in tolerance and, alas, a process for healing the environment. The environment does not need healing; God's universe can take care of itself very well without our help, as it has always done. It is human souls and human lives that need healing, and that calls not for humanism but for faith in the Creator God who made us and gave His son as a sacrifice for our sins.

EVERYDAY ATHEISM

We all wonder—and we hear television commentators and newspapers columnists wondering, too—what has caused the dramatic rise in crime and evil in our country. Every group has a ready answer. Politicians say we need more policemen, more regulations, more laws. Sociologists and bureaucrats say we need to give the people better jobs, more money, newer homes, and greater self-esteem. University professors and many in the media say that democratic society is corrupt and needs to be reformed from the ground up. And the ACLU says Christians and religionists are the problem.

But none of these people has a clue what is really wrong. The truth is that we have forgotten what patriots like Ben Franklin knew when he said: "Only a virtuous people are capable of freedom. As nations become corrupt and vicious, they have need of masters." Thanks to the assault on religious values, the nation has indeed become lawless, corrupt, and sinful; and, short of some kind of divine intervention, only a stern master will be able to bring the lawless back into submission. But is that the best option?

John Adams said, "We have no government capable of dealing with an irreligious people." In other words, do away with religion and you do away with America. It is only through the religion of Christ that people can be free and be good at the same time; nevertheless, we hear the sophisticated pundits of modern morality arguing that this is not a Christian nation. But there was another group at another time that disagreed. Please note what they said:

Our laws and our institutions must necessarily be based upon and embody the teachings of The Redeemer of mankind. It is impossible that it should be otherwise; and in this sense and to this extent our civilization and our institutions are emphatically Christian . . . This is a religious people. This is historically true. From the discovery of this continent to the present hour, there is a single voice making this affirmation . . . we find everywhere a clear recognition of the same truth . . . These, and many other matters which might be noticed, add a volume of unofficial declarations to the mass of organic utterances that *this is a Christian nation.*
—CHURCH OF THE HOLY TRINITY V. UNITED STATES, 1892

This, of course, was the conclusion of the Supreme Court of the United States. But how far we have fallen from that great judicial insight. How blind have become the new leaders of the blind in this nation. "The highest glory of the American Revolution," said John Quincy Adams, was this: "It connected in one indissoluble bond the principles of civil government with the principles of Christianity." And yet today too many people have little or no understanding of this fundamental principle.

When we see how the courts have trampled religious liberties in this century, it is hard to reconcile the past, present, and future of the nation. Men and women in places of authority have a vendetta against the Christian church. Almost all references to Christianity have been expunged from the textbooks in our schools, said the blue-ribbon panel appointed by the president to examine the history and social-studies books in our public schools. It is as if some paranoia is driving writers and publishers to do away with every reference to Christianity, said the chairman of that committee. Yet it is only when the Spirit of Christ dwells within us, and changes our hearts and minds and renews us from within, that godliness, morality, and freedom can exist. How odd that the leaders of Russia have no difficulty accepting this proposition today, while the leaders of this nation find the mere suggestion of "Christian virtue" so intolerable.

James Madison, who has been called the "Father" of the Constitution, summed it up well when he said, "We have staked the whole future of American civilization, not upon the power of government, far from it. We have staked the future of all of our political institutions upon the capacity of each and all of us to govern ourselves, to control ourselves, to sustain ourselves according to the Ten Commandments of God." Such words are not hidden. They are not obscure. They are readily available to all students of history; yet our modern Supreme Court rules regularly against religion in every situation and continually seeks to alter the traditions and laws of this land. This is the practical, everyday atheism of America.

LOSING OUR WAY

Aleksandr Solzhenitsyn said that when he was just a young boy, while the Communist revolution was still going on, millions of Russian people were being slaughtered. The streets ran red with blood, and fear stalked the land. One time he overheard two peasants arguing about why all this was happening. He said he would never forget what one of the peasants said: "It is because we have forgotten God! That is why all this is happening to us. We have forgotten God!" The great author said that in spite of all of the education and all of the experience he has gained, including the eight long years he spent as a political prisoner in the gulag, he never forgot the wisdom of that simple peasant: "It is because we have forgotten God. That is why all this is happening to us."

With those words, that simple peasant demonstrated a far greater wisdom than that of the leaders of this nation today. He understood a truth that our schools, courts, and public institutions all seem to have forgotten. The incisive British broadcaster and social critic, Malcolm Muggeridge, put his finger on the problem when he said:

> Since the beginning of the Second World War, Western Society has experienced a complete abandonment of its sense of good and evil. The true crisis of our time has nothing to do with monetary troubles, unemployment, or nuclear weapons. The true crisis has to do with the fact that Western man has lost his way.

We have come to a place where we call evil good and good evil, which, Isaiah tells us, is disastrous. There is only one sin left in modern culture, and that is intolerance of sin. The key words in liberal society are "diversity" and "tolerance." The only unforgivable sin among American sophisticates is the sin of being "judgmental" or "absolutist." Woe to the person who asks what the Bible says about promiscuity or sensuality. Such a person will be mocked and scorned. And yet, it is only upon this solid Rock, the Gibraltar of faith in a living God, that there is any hope for lasting freedom. The Lord God has spelled out very clearly what He expects of us. He wants men and women to live godly and moral lives, apart from what any police or police state have to say about them. That is an aspect of our freedom in Christ. The decision to flee from sin is not a legal issue but an issue between mankind and God.

The Israelites in the Old Testament went through exactly the same experience. God redeemed them from the hand of Pharaoh and set them free, and with a mighty outstretched arm He brought them into the land of Palestine. The pagan peoples who lived around them rose up and conquered them and reduced them to slavery and misery until, at last, when they had suffered for many years, God raised up a deliverer, a judge, who threw off the yoke of bondage and set the people free. But just a few years later, they once again turned their backs upon the living God, and then another group of pagans who lived in their midst rose up and conquered them once more. Finally, after years of servitude and slavery, God mercifully sent another deliverer and set them free. This happened over and over and over again—*fourteen* times.

But sadly, we who have the entire historical perspective upon civilization still haven't learned that lesson! We are warned by historians that as soon as a nation forgets God, then destruction comes upon it. But we continue in our folly. Today America is making the same mistakes, and we suppose that somehow our Constitution, our nation, our institutions of freedom will continue forever despite all the wickedness in the land. That simply is not so.

A LIGHT IN DARKNESS

President George Bush talked about "a thousand points of light"— a thousand instances of thoughtfulness and caring exhibited by men and women whose godliness and goodliness have caused them to reach out to help other people. It is a wonderful idea to radiate the love of God and to bring blessings to others. But the reality of our time is that men and women in this society are seeking for "self-fulfillment," "self-esteem," "self-motivation," "self-actualization," and a thousand other selfish ideals. They are looking for "self-gratification" and "self-realization," and they slide easily into sin and "self-indulgence" because they have been told, "You're worth it." Television commercials tell us, "You deserve the very best," and "Get all the gusto you can get." These are the roots of pride, lust, greed, avarice, and sensuality. This is, at least in part, the darkness of our age. Malcolm Muggeridge has written:

> The darkness falling on our civilization is like-
> wise due to a transposition of good and evil. In other words,
> what we are suffering from is not an energy crisis, nor an
> overpopulation crisis, nor a monetary crisis, nor a balance of
> payments crisis, nor an unemployment crisis—from none of
> these ills that are commonly pointed out—but from the loss
> of a sense of a moral order in the universe.[1]

Good and evil provide the theme of the drama of our moral existence. When we lose sight of that fact, and when we call evil good and good evil, then destruction is not far away. Not only did Israel and every other nation discover this truth, but it is true also for each individual man, woman, and child in America. The price of everything has changed. Inflation, deflation, wage-and-price escalation, and the cost of living have all changed. But one price has remained the same throughout the history of man: The wages of sin is *still* death (Rom. 6:23).

King David said, "The nation that forgets God shall be turned into hell," but consider what sin cost even the saints of the Old Testament:

- ❏ Adam and Eve lost their lease in Paradise because they ignored God's instructions.
- ❏ Moses was denied entrance into the Promised Land because he disobeyed.
- ❏ Samson was made a Philistine slave and lost his life because of his sin.
- ❏ Saul was stripped of his kingdom because he defied the words of God.
- ❏ David forfeited peace in his own family because he committed sexual sin.
- ❏ Solomon sacrificed the most glorious reputation of all because of his pride.
- ❏ Elisha's greedy servant lost his health because of greed, and
- ❏ Jonah was sentenced to the belly of a whale because he refused to obey God.

In the New Testament, the same truth is taught over and over again. Those "thousand points of light" can only come forth where godliness prevails. We will have to shake off the lethargy that often exists in the church; we will have to overcome the spirit of selfishness and complacency throughout this nation if we are going to reach out and touch the world. For too many of us, affiliating with the church has become just another spectator sport. I often feel that there are more spectators in the churches than there are in the sports arenas and stadiums of this country.

But Christianity cannot be a spectator sport. It has to involve us twenty-four hours a day, seven days a week. To serve Christ means that our hearts must constantly be committed to advancing the kingdom of God. Recall the words of the Pilgrims at Plymouth Rock. Or the New England Confederation of May 19, 1643, which says, "Whereas we all came into these parts of America with one and the same end, and aim, namely, to advance the Kingdom of our Lord Jesus Christ . . ."

That has to be our commitment as well, and we don't have to cross four thousand miles of ocean in the dead of winter to do it. If those men and women could undertake all they did to bring forth this Christian nation, can we do less?

Is that your motivation? Is the compelling motive and purpose of your life to serve the Lord, your God? Do you devote your thoughts, prayers, and energies to advancing the kingdom of our Lord Jesus Christ? Or is your heart set on something else? Most Americans today don't have the faintest notion of the motivations of the founders of this country. We have allowed the secular state to strip away our foundations and tell us that religion has no place in public life. We have accepted the subtle atheism of the state and lost our allegiance to God.

WAITING FOR PAYDAY

The wheels of God's righteous judgment often seem to grind very slowly, and sometimes people suppose that because they do, God will not deal with their sin. That is a very dangerous mistake. God will indeed deal with sin. That is absolutely, positively certain. Even though He may be merciful and gracious to us, there comes a time when His patience is expended. Then there is nothing left but destruction.

Samson discovered this too late. Time after time he sinned against God, and God gave him amazing strength to preserve him from the just consequences of his sin. But finally, at long last, there came a time when God's patience was used up. Samson's strength was depleted, and destruction came upon him. First it was the red-hot iron with which the Philistines put out his eyes. In the end, he brought down God's wrath upon the servants of the alien gods, but he brought down the temple upon his own head as well. The Bible says, "Be sure your sins will find you out." That word is as true for us as it was for the ancient strongman.

The whole story of our existence is a drama of good and evil, and behind it all is God. There are many people who have never experienced the liberty in their own hearts that Jesus Christ can give. There are many who accept the view that religion is a threat to modern society and that the Christian religion belongs behind the closed doors of the church. We must see before it is too late that only Christ can set us free. Only Christ can give us hope. Where the Spirit of the Lord is, there is liberty. Doesn't even reason tell us these words are true?

The Greek word *eleutheros* means "free," or "at liberty." Martin Luther called himself Martin Eleutheros—Martin-the-Free. He said, "Christ's bondslave is the freest man." When we attempt to become autonomous, self-centered, and self-directed men and women, we degenerate into a bondage so dark and bitter that only the love of God can save us from self-destruction. The skeptical poet W. E. Henley wrote, "I am the captain of my fate; I am the master of my soul." But those who have experienced the loneliness of such self-deception know the spiritual isolation that overcomes the man or woman who turns inward and away from God.

Do you want to be truly free? Then my advice is that you become the bondslave of Christ, who made you, and who offers you ultimate freedom. You were designed by God for a specific task, and if you try to pursue some other task with your life, you're going to be very disappointed. Nothing will go right until you find God's unique purpose for you. We were created to have fellowship with God, to walk with Him, to love Him with all of our heart, soul, and mind. Now you may do a lot of things very well, but until you do that for which God has created you, everything in your life will seem like failure.

I hope and pray that you will make a decision to stop being a spectator in the great drama of life and start being a participant. There is a struggle of cosmic proportions between good and evil in this world, and God has given each of us the honor and privilege of being His emissaries. We are all called to be Christian soldiers. I challenge you, from this very hour, to commit yourself to serving Christ, to living for Him, to doing His will, to making Him known, to being a part of the solution instead of part of the problem.

I especially urge those who are living with one foot in the church and the other in the world—those of you who go to church once a week and feel you have done all that the Christian life expects from you—to realize that the walk of faith demands every hour of every day of your life. There is a war against true believers. Atheists, agnostics, and even well-meaning advocates of diversity and tolerance are trying to stop the Word of God from going forth. We cannot allow that to happen.

You should strive, through the power of the Holy Spirit, to bring every thought and action into subjection to Jesus Christ. If you have not yet come to that place, I urge you with all my heart to do so now. In this very hour and in this minute, yield your life to Jesus Christ. The hour is late; the day is far spent. Payday is coming, and this is one decision you cannot afford to put off another minute.❦

NOTES

[1]Malcolm Muggeridge, *The End of Christendom* (Grand Rapids: Wm. B. Eerdmans, 1980), 17–18.

7

Relativity and Truth

There are no absolutes, everything is relative, and you have no right to force your idea of right and wrong on anyone else. Every child in America's public schools knows these three concepts by heart, even if not by name. The principles of relativism have been indoctrinated as liturgy and impressed upon the hearts of the young in the name of science, tolerance, diversity, and relativism. These are the great truths of our day, the holy trinity of modern secularism.

There was a time when science was considered the companion of true religion. When the first principles of physics and astronomy were cataloged in the sixteenth and seventeenth centuries, men such as Copernicus, Galileo, and Newton felt as if they were looking into the laboratory of God. They were astonished by their own discoveries. They had tapped into the secrets of the cosmos. Sir Isaac Newton said, "God in the beginning formed matter . . . in such proportion to space, as most conduced to the end for which he formed them." And, in accounting for his own gifted insights into nature, Newton wrote to Sir Robert Hooke, "If I have seen further (than you and Descartes), it is by standing upon the shoulders of Giants."

There was a sense of humility in these great men because they knew that the ideas and concepts they discovered were not new. They were as old as the universe. But, thanks to the "new learning" and advances in mathematics and physics, they had been privileged to live at a time when such phenomena might at last be observed and recorded. They felt honored and gratified. Nature was not a puzzle to be solved but a textbook to be studied. The world around them was infinitely rich and loaded with detail, and to know science was to know something of the nature of God. This was not mysticism or magic, it was true science. As Albert Einstein said, "God is a scientist not a magician." The early scientists had no problem with the reality or the authority of God.

But what has happened to the objectivity of science in our own time? The attitudes of scientists have changed enormously since those days. In the nineteenth century, the great men of science concluded that they had surpassed the ancients. They had invaded the laboratory of God and taken it over. Friedrich Nietzsche declared, "God is dead, and we have killed him." There was certainly no place for religion now, no hope of heaven, and it remained only to prove that there was no longer any need for God in their theories.

THE GREAT COMPROMISE

The sacred talisman of the scientists in the nineteenth century was the "scientific method." Based upon empirical research—which meant conducting physical experiments under various conditions and observing the results—countless new discoveries were made. The study of optics, thermodynamics, gravity, chemical properties, and basic biology opened up wonderful new surprises. But as the amount of learning in each of these areas began to multiply beyond all expectations, a new pride and arrogance began to appear.

Little by little all reverence for God disappeared. What had once seemed mysterious now seemed clear. No more divine interpretations were needed. Scholars were convinced that science made God superfluous. Thomas Henry Huxley, companion of Charles Darwin and grandfather of Sir Julian, claimed that skepticism is the heart and soul of science. He said, "skepticism is the highest of duties, blind faith the one unpardonable sin."

But, for all their boasts and their high-flown rhetoric, the great men of science have been compromised by their own methodology. The discovery of new concepts—including, relativity, nuclear physics, and quantum mechanics —forced a reevaluation of all their pet theories and perfect structures. The new science of the twentieth century said that there was no final and ultimate truth. Just as the observations of Copernicus and Galileo had changed all our basic beliefs about the movement of the earth and stars, new observations were showing that the universe is not what science had assumed.

Atoms were not solid, the movement of light in space was not linear, and even time was jerky and irregular. By the time of the stock market crash of 1929, the secure environment of science had imploded along with everything else Americans treasured, and the smug certainty of scholars was transformed first into abstraction and then to chaos.

How would scientists reconcile all these new dilemmas? The great Austrian philosopher of science, Karl Popper, argued that the knowledge discovered by science can never be absolute or even probable. At best, the scientist can only make educated guesses about the world of natural phenomena. In other words, the idea that science gives truth could no longer be taken for granted. At best, the scientist may seize a piece of the truth for an instant. As Richard Tarnas says, "Even the basic facts are relative, always potentially subject to a radical reinterpretation in a new framework. Man can never claim to know the real essences of things. Before the virtual infinitude of the world's phenomena, human ignorance itself is infinite. The wisest strategy is to learn from one's inevitable mistakes."[1]

All of the landmark research and the great discoveries of the past century have clouded and complicated the issue. The work of Maxwell in electromagnetics, Michelson-Morley on light and ether in space, Becquerel's discovery of radioactivity, the work of Bohr and Heisenberg in quantum mechanics, and Einstein's study of relativity theory changed the entire equation. Nature was once so simple. What happened? Had God's laboratory grown more complex? Science, once the source of ultimate meaning and certainty, was adrift in a world of seemingly incomprehensible speculations. What had become of truth?

The natural philosophers of the eighteenth century were replaced by the specialists of the twentieth. Mathematics, astronomy, physics, and biology were no longer general areas within the field of science but specific and esoteric disciplines that required highly specialized scientific knowledge. The private study of science in the nineteenth century gave way to entire departments in the universities. Government and industry became participants in the search for new applications and new extensions of the research. At the same time, expense became a factor, which meant that financial support and patronage was needed, and suddenly, endowments, support agencies, industrial clients, and paying students became essential.

In 1900, the German physicist Max Planck published his theory that energy is emitted in discrete packets, or quanta, proportional to the frequency of radiation. This new concept was to be very important in atomic theory, but it was not until Albert Einstein published his papers on the special theory of relativity five years later that the elements of a new physics of nuclear particles could come into being. However, when that happened, all previous theories of space and time were thrown out the window. Even after Einstein published his general theory of relativity in 1915, the sciences remained in a state of tremendous uncertainty. And Werner Heisenberg's new concept, the "uncertainty principle," published in 1927, simply confirmed what everyone already knew. Science is a learning process, and the scientist could no longer boast of any special access to truth.

The fragmentation of science has accelerated enormously in the twentieth century. Competition between laboratories and individual scientists and scholars added intellectual intensity as well as emotional disturbances to the process. Some have called the last half of the nineteenth and the first half of the twentieth centuries the "golden age of science." Much-publicized studies reported that the productivity of new research was doubling every fifteen years or so and that fully ninety percent of all the scientists who have ever lived were alive and engaged in ongoing study and research. But all the excitement could not disguise the fact that there had been a radical shift in understanding of the origins and destiny of the universe.

When telemetry and space exploration were added to the mix, a new vision of the planet began to emerge that proved that we are very far from understanding the true complexity and the magnitude of our world. The amount yet to be known is so much greater than the sum of current knowledge that the specialist often seems helpless and confused. Scientists of the past had boasted that they had no need of God, but suddenly science was lost in a cosmic flux that only God could comprehend, let alone create.

IT'S ALL RELATIVE

The idea that ethical decisions could be made on the basis of practical matters without regard for right and wrong has a long history that dates back at least to the ancient Greeks. However, in the 1870s men such as C. S. Peirce and William James conceived a new idea, a new attitude called "pragmatism," which holds that the value of any idea is to be found in its "conceivable sensible effects." Belief, they said, comes through "habits of action." William James went even further, describing pragmatism as the means of discovering genuine Truth. True ideas, he said, are consistent, orderly, and predictable. In concert with such prominent "new thinkers" as Peirce, John Dewey, George Herbert Mead, and Clarence Irving Lewis, James insisted the pragmatic approach was the only valid approach to truth.

Pragmatism found its natural companion in Darwin's theory of evolution, built on the concepts of "natural selection" and "the survival of the fittest." Good ideas, like good breeding stock, would survive the challenge of time and chance. Truth was that which survived. The pragmatism of James and Peirce stressed action and creativity, but they refused to define truth or to claim they had discovered a specific set of norms.

Like evolution, the pragmatic approach was always relative and changeable. What is true for one time or place may not be true for another, James said. Reality, like human knowledge, is constantly evolving. Morality is constantly changing. Good and evil, true and false, he said, are never absolute. The important thing is the practical outcome. Does it make the situation better or worse? Does it make you happy or sad? Does it contribute to or reduce the common good?

Oddly enough, those who subscribed to the ideas put forth by James and the others did not see these concepts as arbitrary or subjective. No, they said that relative and situational evaluation of ethical and moral issues was absolutely valid. And the principal test of truth for the pragmatists was how everything comes out in the end. In other words, true ideas are those ideas that the people will accept. False ideas are the ones they reject. And in one great sweep of the hand, our nineteen hundred-year heritage of faith, judgment, Christian moral values, and biblical revelation was tossed into the philosopher's wastebasket.

These are the roots of the moral relativism of our own time. While science had gone through a crisis of uncertainty, and while philosophy had gradually evolved into a bizarre and imponderable jumble of academic gibberish, scholars were now putting forth the notion that moral values cannot be proved, but they are true if they are palatable. There may be no moral absolutes, but common behavior is absolutely right, true, and good.

The old ideas of right and wrong are simply matters of personal opinion or of public acceptability. Thus, the skeptics and social scientists set out to challenge the beliefs and customs of mankind, to debunk the authority of Scripture, and to establish a new hierarchy of values based on their own subjective and cognitive rejection of revealed truth.

Moral and ethical relativism, also known as "situational ethics," says that there is no correct moral code for all times and people. Each group has its own morality relative to its local customs and values, and ultimately all moral values are equal. But there are many obvious risks in such theories. For example, even scholars recognize that, by this view, cannibalism must be completely moral and ethical. If you happen to come from a tribe in which eating human flesh is a commonly accepted practice, then who am I to force my idea of right and wrong on you? Just because it is not acceptable in Western culture and could really challenge some long-standing ideas about meal time does not mean it is wrong! What *would* be wrong, the new thinking holds, would be to say that Western values are superior to the values of cannibals. Perish the thought!

The problems of such a viewpoint are obvious. If there is no absolute standard of right and wrong outside the standards of the local culture, then what happens when different cultures with conflicting views and values come together? Whose standards ought to prevail? Whose standard is right? Suddenly, somebody has to make an ethical choice, but who will be so bold? The old saying, "When in Rome, do as the Romans do," comes to mind. If you happen to be visiting in a cannibal village, are you expected to do as the cannibals do? Or should you insist that the cannibals conduct themselves by the standards of your culture?

What the modern pundits wish us to believe is that sin is also relative. Right and wrong are relative. The intellectuals will not accept the possibility that they could be guilty of sin and living under condemnation. Behaviors that would be considered sinful in one culture might be perfectly acceptable somewhere else, they say. Anthropologists—those who study the nature and behaviors of the human species—prefer to view all civilizations in terms of cultural relativism.

Such anthropologists will not say that slavery, head-hunting, and cannibalism are wrong, but that they are not productive or widely acceptable practices. But there are more who simply observe these things without offering any sort of judgment. They occasionally express concern about Hindu, Islamic, and African tribal practices that mutilate women and children; they worry about genocide; and they worry about punitive maiming and ritual sacrifices, but they say very little about the ethical issues. They are more likely today to see these things from the "environmental" perspective. If it harms the environment, they say, then it is clearly wrong! But if it harms only humans, then that's another matter. After all, who are they to force their idea of right and wrong on anybody else?

DOES ANYTHING MATTER?

The degeneration of philosophy and science into relativism is just one more indication of the moral poverty of American society. It is evidence that we have become corrupt. The esteemed scholar Russell Kirk said, "Without Authority vested somewhere, without regular moral principles that may be consulted confidently, Justice cannot long endure anywhere. Yet modern liberalism and democracy are contemptuous of the whole concept of moral authority; if not checked in their assaults upon habitual reverence and prescriptive morality, the liberals and democrats will destroy Justice not only for their enemies, but for themselves."[2] In their fierce determination to deny their own guilt, and to deny any possibility that a divine Judge may be a witness against them, the modern scholar denies all moral authority. The only truth for science and philosophy is that there is no truth.

We used to have an idea what values were right and acceptable in this nation. We used to know what America is and what we stand for. President Theodore Roosevelt once said, "Americanism means the virtues of courage, honor, justice, truth, sincerity, and hardihood—the virtues that made America. The things that will destroy America are prosperity-at-any-price, peace-at-any-price, safety-first instead of duty-first, the love of soft living, and the get-rich-quick theory of life."

These first values were the values of a disciplined, dedicated, and caring people. While Americans of that day were reasonably tolerant of individual differences, they were not blind to careless, stupid, and irresponsible behavior. Justice meant swift and certain judgment, not moral blindness. Sad to say, we have come a long way since the muscular Americanism and the fortitude of Teddy Roosevelt and the Rough Riders.

But make no mistake: When relativity becomes the prevailing orthodoxy of a culture, the character of the people will wither and die. Both the individual and the nation as a whole will be reduced to selfishness and expediency. Pragmatism becomes the new law of life, and moral discretion will have no power to restrain evil. Albert Einstein, the father of the science of relativity, was shocked by the tendency of intellectuals and social pundits to confuse his mathematical models with moral behavior. He saw this as a deadly mistake, and he said so.

He understood many things about the nature of matter, space, and time. But Einstein said repeatedly that ethical behavior depends on the existence of an inner moral strength that is fixed and permanent. Good and evil are never relative; right and wrong are never arbitrary. "The real problem," he said, "is in the hearts and minds of men. It is not a problem of physics but of ethics. It is easier to denature plutonium than to denature the evil spirit of man." The prophet Jeremiah had said, "The heart is deceitful above all things, and desperately wicked. Who can know it?" The father of relativity knew this to be true. Remember: Relativity applies to physics, not ethics!

As we observed in the previous chapter, atheism has never been able to come up with a moral code. Anybody can sit down and write out his own moral code and come up with twelve commandments or twenty or six. But the problem is getting other people to live by them. Who is going to enforce your morality? And how are you going to get people to live by it voluntarily? A few years ago, Ted Turner, the founder and Chairman of CNN and the Turner Broadcasting Network in Atlanta, said he would pay a million dollars to anybody who could come up with a workable, practical moral code to replace the "outdated and unrealistic" Ten Commandments. That's a lot of money, yet nobody has been able to come up with an acceptable set of rules.

But that is a large part of our problem today. For three-and-one-half-thousand years we have had a practical, reliable, proven, and authorized set of rules from the hand of God Himself. But man, in his pride and arrogance, refuses to acknowledge or live by them. But without the support of biblical values and the principles of Scripture, we have no other moral foundation. If you ask the average college student what he believes in, he will probably shrug his shoulders and say, "Whatever." He has never thought about it. Unless people have been brought up in the church, they are conditioned by their culture not to think about such things.

But if you ask if they believe that everything is relative, they'll they, "Sure!" And if you ask them, "Who says so?" very likely they will say, "Einstein." They are convinced that Einstein proved that everything is relative—space, time, morals, everything. But that is simply not true. Einstein never said anything about moral or cultural values in his studies of physics. He said that time and space are relative, under certain circumstances, at the limits of physics theory, but he spent the last years of his life trying to tell people that his ideas applied only to physics and not to ethics or morals. He was horrified by the atomic bomb, and he would certainly be horrified by what liberals have done with his theory of relativity.

In his book of the same name, Francis Schaeffer asked, "How should we then live?" That is still a fundamental question. Given the history of science and the arts, of ideas and ethical concepts, whose morality are you going to follow? If not God's, then whose? Stanford professor, James Q. Wilson, writes in his book, *The Moral Sense*, that, "Over the course of the last hundred years the world has experienced a shift from an era in which crime chiefly responded to material circumstances to one in which it responds in large measure to cultural ones. That shift had many causes, but one is the collapse in the legitimacy of what once was respectfully called middle-class morality but today is sneeringly referred to as 'middle-class values.'

"The moral relativism of the modern age," he says, "has probably contributed to the increase in crime rates, especially the increases that occur during prosperous times. It has done so by replacing the belief in personal responsibility with the notion of social causation and by supplying to those marginal persons at risk for crime a justification for doing what they might have done anyway. If you are tempted to take the criminal route to the easy life, you may go further along that route if everywhere you turn you hear educated people saying—indeed 'proving'—that life is meaningless and moral standards arbitrary."[3] What a profound description of the easy, morally ambivalent values of our day. And what a condemnation of the failures of cultural relativity.

THE CRISIS OF FAITH

Peter Marshall, former chaplain of the Senate, made an interesting statement. He said that in the time of the apostles, whenever they went out to preach there were either riots or regeneration. In our time, we generally get a pat on the hand and, "Nice sermon, pastor," and that's about all. But the Scripture says that if we are really standing for the truth, and if we are convicting men of sin and their need of repentance, then we are going to be persecuted.

I have been threatened and attacked, and many, many people in this world have suffered much more than I have. But a number of people have come into our church with malice in their hearts. There have been many death threats, and on occasion people have come to carry them out. Fortunately God has stayed their hand. I have been threatened with guns, knives, explosives, and even AIDS-infected blood. It is risky business to preach against sin these days, but we are called to do it. In a world of moral relativism, it is risky business even to believe in Jesus Christ.

But look how far modern science and moral relativity have brought us. Today, it is *illegal* to put a crèche on public property or to erect a cross in a public place. Yet, the National Endowment for the Arts, with public tax money, supports radical demonstrations, "art shows" they call them, and displays that have, among other things, such blasphemy as a crucifix— Christ upon a cross—immersed in urine! The moral lesson is quite clear: In America today we can put up a cross with public money, only in urine. That is how far this society has degenerated.

But that is to be expected, isn't it? How many people these days, because of their lack of faith, will turn away from the risks involved in standing up for their beliefs, saying, "No, it's too risky. The threat is too great. I'm not called to face those kinds of threats." But consider what happened to the disciples and apostles. As recounted by Frank S. Mead in *The March of Eleven Men*, James the brother of Jesus and James the son of Zebedee were killed by the mobs in Jerusalem. Matthew was run through with a sword in Ethiopia. Philip was hanged in Greece. Bartholomew was flayed alive in Armenia; Andrew was crucified in Achaia, and Thomas was killed with a lance in East India. Thaddeus was shot with arrows, Simon the Zealot was crucified by the Persians, and Peter was crucified upside down by the Romans. Only John, the author of the fourth Gospel and the book of Revelation, escaped a martyr's grave. And, need I say, Jesus Himself was beaten, humiliated, spat upon, and crucified between thieves. I pray that such a thing may never happen again, but Christians must be willing to take the risks whether or not it may ever come to that.

The basic beliefs and opinions about the things that matter most to Americans are changing radically. Research organizations that examine such changes periodically publish their findings, and the results can be eye-opening. One such group, the Barna Research Group in California, made an intensive study of the changing religious views of Americans, and the study reveals some disturbing trends we need to be aware of if we are going to discern the signs of the times in which we live.

This dominant religious belief of the majority of Americans is a witch's brew made up of one-part traditional Christianity, one-part secular humanism, and one-part New-Age theology. This poisonous concoction will no doubt be spiritually fatal to everyone who imbibes it, but there is no doubt it will be destructive of American society as a whole if we continue to move in the direction that this trend is leading us. When a culture finds it easier to bow to false gods and graven images—for that is what the New Age and the false teachings of our day actually amount to—then they must expect retribution.

Barna's survey of American beliefs says that the most common myths of modern culture are these: "There are no absolutes. All truth is relative. And you have no right to force your idea of right and wrong on anyone else." Where have we heard this before? Currently sixty-two percent of American adults believe these statements to be true. And if young people between the ages of eighteen and twenty-five are included, the figure rises from sixty-two to sixty-four percent. That would have been absolutely unthinkable a hundred years ago, or even fifty years ago. A hundred years ago ninety-nine percent of Americans believed that there are moral absolutes and that truth is certainly not relative. Even if they did not live faithful Christian lives, they nevertheless believed that there are eternal standards of right and wrong and that God will judge sin.

ABSOLUTELY NO ABSOLUTES

As Allan Bloom has said, even if today's high school and university students haven't learned anything else in twelve years of school, the one thing that has been impressed upon their minds with indelible pressure is, "All truth is relative, and there are no absolutes." I heard about one student who may not have quite gotten the message. When his professor said, "We can know nothing for certain," the young man raised his hand asked, "Professor, are you sure of that?" and the teacher answered, "I'm certain." Now, that may be a joke, but it actually points out the underlying inconsistency and contradiction of this whole concept. To say that there are no absolutes is a contradiction in terms because the statement itself is an absolute statement. And to say there absolutely are no absolutes, by the principles of the most basic logic, is self-contradictory.

This reminds me of a problem philosophers were having a few years ago with the philosophy of logical positivism, which was popularized by Sir Alfred Ayers and the Vienna Circle. This whole philosophy was derived from one simple statement: "The only statements which are true are those which can be proved by empirical science." The claim, then, was that observable reality is the only truth. The philosophy spread across the world until somebody woke up one day and pointed out that their basic defining statement could not be proved by empirical science!

Furthermore, if the truth of science depends upon empirical evidence, then practically everything that science has touched in the past half-century is unreliable and false. As we have just seen, scientific research today has come to the point where the vast majority of its postulates and principles are theoretical and incapable of empirical proof. I would like to say that the whole façade of logical positivism promptly fell to the ground; but, like most of the bizarre philosophies of our day, it still exists. There are many people for whom truth and falsehood, logic and self-consistency, don't mean very much anymore.

Consider what is meant by the statement that there are no absolutes. Why do people hold that view? If you were to talk to an average person and suggest that something is absolutely true, that person's reaction would probably be one of amazement. He would say, "Don't you know that we live in a relativistic universe? Where have you been for the last fifty years? Haven't you heard about Einstein and the theory of relativity? Don't you know everything is relative?"

Now, I suspect this massive indoctrination in moral and cultural relativity involves duplicity and sleight of hand on the part of some of our cultural "elites" and intellectuals. They know exactly what they are doing, but on the part of most of our students and the general public, the unquestioning acceptance of these strange and contradictory beliefs is more a demonstration of their ignorance. Maybe Christians need to point out their ignorance to them, to put a little pin in their bubble. Remind them, for example, that Einstein made one thing very clear: Relativity deals with matter, mass, speed, light, and motion. Period! Even children know the formula: $E = mc^2$. Energy equals mass times the speed of light squared. There is no symbol for morality in that equation. There is nothing there about culture. The great scientist said, "Relativity refers only to the realm of physics—not ethics." And with that the whole bubble bursts. But ignoring Einstein's own statements, the pundits and cultural czars have tried to make ethics, morals, religion, culture, and everything else relative.

Some people will respond, "Well, things are changing, and what was true ten years ago and certainly a hundred years ago is no longer true." They believe in progress. But there is something these people desperately need to understand. There are two kinds of knowledge in our world today.

One is discovery, which is the foundation of science and empirical research. Science is man's attempt to wrest from nature whatever truths he can discover about its manner of operation. It started with very little and has been growing over the centuries until we have come to the place where we are today. We will never learn everything, and when the world ends there will still be volumes and volumes that scientists, scholars, and explorers never understood and never even suspected.

But the other source of knowledge is revelation, where God reveals Himself and His nature to us in certain and absolute truths. These truths are revealed to us in Scripture and ultimately in God's only begotten Son, Jesus Christ. When these truths were revealed, and when these revelations were complete, all things necessary for our salvation were *perfectly* revealed. That revelation has not increased one iota over the centuries since its completion in the first century. God gave us a perfect revelation and it continues to be valid, just as He declared it through the prophets, the disciples, and the apostles, from the very beginning.

But please make the essential distinction between these two forms of knowledge. One—the process of discovery—is changeable, expandable, and it is infinitely variable. The other—divine revelation—is perfect, unchangeable, and infinitely reliable. Relativity applies only to discovery and scientific knowledge. Ethics, morals, and religion come through revelation, and we have been given this revelation from Christ. He tells us, "Then you will know the truth, and the truth will set you free" (John 8:32).

THE HEART OF THE PROBLEM

But let me take this one step further. If you were to check the word "absolute" in the dictionary, you would discover that it comes from two Latin words, *ab* meaning "from," and *solvere,* meaning "to set free." But what does the word "absolute"—to set free from—set us free *from*? I will offer these suggestions:

- ❏ Free from any imperfection. It is pure.
- ❏ Free from any admixture. It is perfect.
- ❏ Free from any limit, restriction, or qualification, as an *absolute* monarch.
- ❏ It is positive, certain, authoritative.

That is what absolutes are, whether we are talking about persons or about truth. If something is absolute, it is free from any kind of error, admixture, imperfection, or limit. And to say there are no absolutes is, in the final analysis, to say there is no God. By saying there are no absolutes and covering that denial over with some kind of scientific mumbo-jumbo about Einstein's theory of relativity, men want to create a false impression. It is simply fraud. What they are actually doing is masking the fact that they are teaching atheism, and this is the heart of the theory that is being pumped into you and your children by modern educators and the secular society.

If there are no absolutes, then there is no God, because God is the ultimate absolute. His omnipotence is without limit, restraint, or qualification. His omniscience is unlimited. His omnipresence is without restriction. God is the altogether absolute One. He is the absolute Monarch, the absolute God. And whenever you hear someone claiming with the voice of authority that there are no absolutes, you should perceive their sleight of hand, and you should object! To accept or even to go along with their lies makes you a dupe and a stooge to their deceit and hypocrisy. Perhaps they are merely parroting the "smelly little orthodoxies" of the age. Do not be taken in by the deception.

When you speak for traditional moral values or Christian principles, some people will say, "Well, that may be true for you, but it's not true for me." Or perhaps you have heard it put this way: "Well, that's your truth; not mine." Remember the cultural anthropologist? The modern educator will say, "What's true for one culture need not be true for another." But those who espouse cultural relativism must admit that there are many times when they run into difficulty. What they fail to acknowledge is that when moral and cultural values become relative, and when laws become unenforceable because "no one can force their idea of right and wrong on me," it is then that the very foundations of civilization are in greatest danger. Taken to their logical and unavoidable conclusion, these views will dissolve the bands of society and civilization, and they will eat away our hearts and destroy the soul of a nation.

At the famous Nuremberg War trials after World War II, Nazi criminals were tried for "war crimes" by representatives of the Allied military forces. Cultural relativism was already being taught in the great universities of the world by that time—including America. The trial lawyers had all been taught the so-called "modern" values, and some of them were teaching them themselves.

In order to carry out the mass murder of the Jews in the Nazi concentration camps, the Supreme Court of Germany had declared the Jews to be "nonpersons." If a race of people ceased to be persons, then to murder them could not be considered a crime. Sadly, this is precisely the way the United States Supreme Court has dealt with its own conscience in their decision to permit the massacre of thirty million babies in their mother's wombs. They declared infants in the womb "nonpersons," so that the carnage, murder, and destruction of life can be ignored. To kill a child is against the law; but to kill "a blob of fetal tissue" is no problem.[4]

The Nazi criminals were very clever men. So what did they do? They stood up and said, "We have done nothing wrong. We acted according to our own culture, according to our own *mores*. There was nothing wrong in our killing six million Jews." Eichmann himself protested, "I had to obey the laws of war and my flag." This created an intense ethical debate, and for a long time the judges were stymied. The defense attorneys cried out, "Who are you to come over here from an alien culture, another society, and impose your morals on us? Don't you know, all truth is relative and morals are culturally relative?"

The American and British lawyers were thrown for a loop. What could they do? They got together and studied the impasse and finally they decided that they would have to appeal to—believe it or not—natural law. If you recall the firestorm that erupted in the congressional hearings when the (then) Supreme Court nominee Clarence Thomas claimed to believe in something called "natural law," then you will understand the anxiety this decision must have caused the court. The attorneys were not willing to appeal to the revelation of God in Scripture, so they appealed to natural law, which is far more vague and less precise.

But they claimed there is a law above human law, which is eternal, and it is a part of the general understanding of decency and civil order within every one of us. Certain things, they said, are simply right and wrong, and everybody knows what they are. But we know that such a law is not *culturally relative*—it is *absolute*. Whatever they may have called it in Nuremberg, they were of course describing the moral law—the Law of God. Cultural relativism would not work!

THE WORD OF TRUTH

The words of Christ are the repudiation of the relativism and moral equivocation of our day. "Then you will know the truth, and the truth will set you free." There are three precious jewels embedded in this text. The first jewel is that there is real truth. Jesus didn't say, "You will know *a* truth." He said *the* truth. It is absolute truth. It exists. It is real. It has been revealed to us by the absolute God. And where is that truth found? It is found in His Word. In His passionate prayer in the Upper Room, Jesus prayed to the Father, "Sanctify them by the truth; your word is truth" (John 17:17).

He had told His followers in the Sermon on the Mount, "I tell you the truth, until heaven and earth disappear, not the smallest letter, not the least stroke of a pen, will by any means disappear from the Law until everything is accomplished" (Matt. 5:18). The Word of God is truth. The Scriptures are the revelation of the perfect and absolute truth of God.

These truths are seen in many, many ways. All of the statements of Scripture are absolutely true because they come to us by divine revelation. For example; "You [absolutely] must be born again" (John 3:7). That does not apply to some people and not others, to some cultures and not others. Every human being who would ever live in the presence of a Holy God must be regenerated; there must be a new birth from above. "Do not be deceived: God cannot be mocked. A man reaps what he sows. The one who sows to please his sinful nature, from that nature will reap destruction; the one who sows to please the Spirit, from the Spirit will reap eternal life." (Gal. 6:7–8). That is a great truth of God.

"So then [absolutely], each of us will give an account of himself to God" (Rom. 14:12). That is absolutely certain for every human being on this earth. God's promise does not apply to you and not to others. Every human being, regardless of his culture, his background, his race, or anything else, will give an account of himself to God. The Bible says, "for [absolutely] all have sinned and fall short of the glory of God" (Rom. 3:23). "Salvation is found in no one else, for there is [absolutely] no other name under heaven given to men by which we must be saved" (Acts 4:12). No other name but Jesus Christ. And that is an absolute truth.

The Bible constantly deals with absolutes; life and death, heaven and hell, obedience and disobedience, righteousness and sin, saved and lost, light and darkness, God and Satan, good and evil, faith and unbelief, judgment and salvation. Therefore, when someone says there are no absolutes, they are saying not only that there is no God but there is no inspired Word of God, there are no Scriptures. That sleight of hand is going on constantly. But there is real truth. It is found in the written Word. It is found also in the Living Word. Christ Jesus said, "I am the way and the truth and the life. No one

163

comes to the Father except through me" (John 14:6). He is the absolute incarnation of Truth.

How ironic that Pontius Pilate said, "What is truth?" when standing right before him, right in his presence, was Jesus Christ, the incarnation of Truth itself. The ruler of the Roman province of Judea was blind to see the truth before his very eyes. And how many millions are just as blind today? Pilate's descendants fill the world, blind to see the absolute truth of Jesus Christ. But please understand these affirmations of Christ's truth:

❏ Christ is the One who is free from any admixture of sin. He is therefore absolute.
❏ As St. Peter stated, "He is the one who did no sin."
❏ Paul echoes, "The one who knew no sin."
❏ John declares, "In him is no sin."
❏ "Without sin," the writer to the Hebrews affirms.

No sin! Those words rang from the hills of Galilee and rumbled through the streets of Jerusalem, and they have resounded down the corridors of time until this day. No sham of modern science and revisionist ideology can deny that Jesus Christ is the altogether lovely One, the well-beloved Son, the crystal Christ, the One in whom there is no admixture of sin or impurity or error. He is the absolute God-man.

Those who say there are no absolutes want us to believe that there is no God, there is no Word of God, and there is no Christ! But no thin veneer of scientific mumbo-jumbo can sustain that challenge. Relativity, Einstein proclaimed, applies to physics, not to ethics. Absolute truth applies to God. Those who say there are no absolutes are saying that there is no God; that the Bible is not the Word of God; and that Jesus Christ is not the Son of God. But they can prove none of these things!

KNOWING THE TRUTH

Jesus said, "You will know the truth, and the truth will set you free." And the second great jewel in the text of John 8:32 is that truth can be known—we can have absolute knowledge. In science we can never be absolutely certain. Science tells you that you can know nothing for certain—all you have is probabilities, possibilities, and potentialities. Anything that you may think is true now may be shown to be false in five, ten, or twenty years. But that does not mean that there aren't some things of which you can be absolutely certain. We can have certain knowledge because the God who created us is omniscient. The One who knows all things has given us the ability to know the truth, and He has given us the truth we can know. The Bible says, "I write these things to you who believe in the name of the Son of God so that you may know that you have eternal life" (1 John 5:13). We can know the truth—the truth of God's Word, the truth of the written Word, and the truth of the Living Word, Jesus Christ.

This is the great hope we have as Christians. This is what indeed lifts us up to a level that the unbeliever can never know. This is why unbelievers are always in ignorance, always in disbelief, always uncertain. They are always fearful about the future. They don't know what is going to happen to them when they die. Yet God has revealed those things to us. We can know the written Word and we can know the Living Word, Jesus Christ. "Now this is eternal life," said Jesus, "that they may know you, the only true God, and Jesus Christ, whom you have sent" (John 17:3). We may know. We may know Christ personally and intimately as Savior and Lord of our lives.

The third jewel in Christ's statement is that not only is there truth and not only can we know the truth but that the truth will set us free. The response of the Pharisees to that statement was, "We are Abraham's descendants and have never been slaves of anyone. How can you say that we shall be set free?" (John 8:33). What a ludicrous statement! Throughout the history of the Jews, they were in bondage to the Egyptians, the Assyrians, the Babylonians, the Philistines, and the Canaanites. Later they were under the Greco-Syrians under Antiochus, the Macedonians, and the Romans. There was a Roman governor in the palace at that very moment, Roman flags at their seaport, Roman soldiers in their midst, Roman tax collectors, and a Roman coin with the image of Caesar stamped on it! They were blind to their bondage (as are people today) and they missed the one hope of freedom, who had come as their Messiah—Jesus Christ, the King of the Jews.

We need to understand not only what is happening today and what people are believing, but we need to understand why they believe the way they do. What is really at the bottom of all of this? It is a perverted sense of the very thing that Christ was talking about. Those people, as all people everywhere, wanted freedom. People today want liberty; they want freedom. But they want a freedom that has degenerated into license. The "free thinkers" and the "new thinkers" of our day are like the Prodigal Son, and they end up in the same way—in the pen with the pigs.

Every living creature has been given God-ordained limits. God has given us an ordained element in which we are to live, both physically and morally. The fish who decides he doesn't like the restrictions of the water and wants to expand his horizons—to visit new places and do new things—may take an adventuresome leap onto the shore, but his expected liberty will soon turn into gasping as he flops his life away there in the deadly air. What he thought was going to be his pleasure and joy becomes his sure destruction.

Relative values, moral ambivalence, cultural relativism: These are the dangers that confront us and our children today. This is the slippery slope America is sliding down, bringing about its own ruin and self-destruction. Can anyone read the headlines and deny that fact? Moral relativity is nothing less than immorality, and immorality leads to lawlessness, deceit, corruption, and anarchy. And the tragedy of our time arises from a common and thinly disguised atheism spread by our cultural elites.

But be warned, that way leads to perdition. Erwin Lutzer says, "No moral theory can arise out of atheism. Those who wish to create a secular state in which religion has no influence will of necessity bring about meaninglessness, lawlessness, and despair. Such conditions often spawn a totalitarian state, instituted to restore order by brute force. When a nation loses its moral roots, a dictator often arises who takes away personal freedoms to restore order. In his own perverse way, a dictator also indirectly affirms the existence of God, but because his atheism does not allow him to give his subjects dignity, he can justify his brutality."[5]

What those who do not believe in absolutes tend to ignore is that when they go beyond the moral boundaries that God has established, they put their own welfare in jeopardy. Having absolute moral limits is no crueler than having restrictions on fish to make sure that they stay in the water, where they can live and thrive. Moral boundaries are for our good, and when we break through the fences, we do not find liberty—we find slavery. Sin is degrading, it is addictive, it is destructive, and it imperils the souls of men and women who slide into it. Freedom cannot be found in bondage to sin; it can only be found through service to Jesus Christ and His Truth.

THE TRUTH OF FREEDOM

The lesson of "relativity" is that only Christ can give real freedom. He can break the shackles that bind, whether they be gambling, or alcohol, or drugs, or sex, or licentious material, or food and gluttony, or even intellectual self-indulgence—whatever they may be. Sin binds people in slavery, but Jesus Christ can set them free. He breaks the chains that bind you. They are dissolved by the blood He shed at the cross of Calvary.

One of the great tragedies of the slavery of sin is that so often those who are most in bondage are the most blinded by their sin. For such people it is not until their life is utterly destroyed that their eyes are opened to see what they have done through arrogant denial of the truth. There is such profound agony in the destruction that is brought about by sin. There can be no sound more chilling than the cries and laments of those who finally realize that their lives have been destroyed by their addiction to sin. If we really knew sin for what it is, we would hate it as we ought and we would flee from its clutches into the arms of Christ. Have you turned away from the clutches of sin? Have you warned those around you of its insidious dangers?

C. S. Lewis said that it was his disappointment with the injustice of life that finally convinced him that there must be a God. Injustice is obvious. It is everywhere. In fact, it was the one thing he could see that was not relative or uncertain. But if life makes no sense and all is chaos—as atheists and agnostics believe—then, Lewis wondered, why was it so apparent that injustice is a fact of life? After all, if man is a part of nature, and if nature is senseless and has no higher purpose, then a man should not be concerned with "right and wrong" or "justice and injustice." Everything simply *is*.

Thus, in the very act of trying to prove that God does not exist, Lewis was eventually forced to see that at least one part of reality—the idea of injustice—is logical and makes perfect sense. And if this is the case, then atheism is illogical and untrue, for if the universe has no meaning, then he could never have discovered that it has no meaning. As an example of this concept, he said: If there were no light in the universe, then the creatures would have no eyes. They would never know that it was dark, because darkness would have no meaning for them. Atheism says the world is pointless. But if a man can recognize that he is in the dark intellectually, and that he can perceive injustice, then he must have the equipment to judge justice and injustice—light and dark—and for him that must be proof of a cosmic order and purpose in the universe. By this line of reasoning, Lewis concluded that he was indeed a part of an orderly whole. And, furthermore, only God could have conceived and created a world that made such perfect sense.

Ultimately, belief in God is a leap of faith. It is a moral and intellectual risk. The person who makes such a leap suspends judgment even as he calls upon God to save him. He says, "God, I don't know You, and I don't know much about You. But if You're there, please save me. Reveal Yourself to me and I will believe." This submission of the will, whether spoken aloud or only spoken in the heart, is a part of every true conversion. The next step is to confess before God that you have sinned, that you know you have done wrong in your life, and to ask Jesus Christ to come into your life and make your heart His home.

Prayed sincerely and with genuine repentance, that simple request will change even the most darkened heart into a new creation. Those who have lived a good and decent life, who may feel they have no sin in their heart, are no more virtuous in the eyes of God than the worst felon in the darkest cell on the planet. Short of honest repentance and faith in Christ, no one will ever be acceptable in God's eyes. But when you take that leap of faith, you will be eternally secure in the loving arms of the Lord and Creator of all, who will make you "free, indeed."

If you prefer to take the easy way, to live according to an easy immorality that will never make demands upon you, and if you prefer the modern idea of relativity and ethical uncertainty, then stay away from God's Word; for Christ's truth will convict your heart of sin and make you feel terribly uncomfortable. But if you are concerned about character and destiny, and if you want to have a commitment to values that are eternal, then Jesus Christ is the only answer.

The nineteenth-century American scholar F. W. Robertson once said that, "Truth lies in character. Christ did not simply speak the truth; He was Truth—Truth through and through, for truth is a thing not of words but a life and being." Whatever the cost, come to Christ and let Him be Lord of your life. And if you already know the Savior, then begin seeking how He can use you as an instrument to help stop the slide into immorality, and to resist the subtle doctrines of the relativists that are destroying this nation. Let the Source of all Truth, who is the Light of the world, reign in your heart and you will never need to fear the darkness again. And that is an *absolute* fact!

NOTES

[1] Richard Tarnas, *The Passion of the Western Mind* (New York: Ballantine, 1993), 360.

[2] Russell Kirk, *The Roots of American Order* (Washington, D.C.: Regnery Gateway, 1992), 462.

[3]James Q. Wilson, *The Moral Sense* (New York: Macmillan Free Press, 1993), 10.

[4] cf. Joseph P. Witherspoon, "Representative Government, the Federal Judicial and Administrative Bureaucracy, and the Right to Life," *Texas Tech Law Review* 6 (1975): VI, 1975. 363ff.

[5]Erwin Lutzer, *Exploding the Myths that Could Destroy America* (Chicago: Moody, 1986), 47.

8

Origins and Destiny

Do you remember the old college questions? They're questions that perennially come to the mind of young people long before Philosophy 101. When young men and women begin to step out into the world on their own for the first time, they are often confronted by such very basic questions as, Who am I? Where did I come from? Why am I here? How should I live? and Where am I going? Those are some of the most important questions any person will ever have to answer—in or out of college. Maybe you haven't thought of it just this way; or maybe you dealt with these questions in some other way. If a person doesn't examine the fundamental hopes and fears expressed in these questions, then we have to wonder if he's alive at all! Over the years, the questions have never changed. But today there are basically two different sets of answers, and they are diametrically opposed to one another. The answers normally given by the person who believes in God and His creation will reflect the basic dignity of man. For example:

Who am I? I am a child of the King, a prince of the royal realm.

Where did I come from? I came from the heart and mind of the almighty and omniscient God. I have been made a little lower than the angels.

Why am I here? I am here to serve and glorify the Almighty and to enjoy Him forever.

How should I live? I should live according to the commandments that God has given to me in His Word, which are designed for my good and my advancement.

Where am I going? I am going to a paradise that is magnificent beyond my comprehension.

The apostle Paul, who had been taken into the presence of Christ in a vision, referred to the words of the prophet Isaiah when he reported, "'No eye has seen, no ear has heard, no mind has conceived what God has prepared for those who love him'—but God has revealed it to us by his Spirit. The Spirit searches all things, even the deep things of God. For who among men knows the thoughts of a man except the man's spirit within him? In the same way no one knows the thoughts of God except the Spirit of God" (1 Cor. 2:9–11). For the Christian, we can be assured that we have a noble origin and destiny. And in between our origin and our destiny, our lives are crammed full of meaning, value, significance, and purpose. That is the plan of God concerning us, if we hold to the Word of God.

But there is also another set of answers that is often given by those who believe in the theory of evolution—those who trust in the system that is taught in virtually every public school in this country, and in virtually every nation in the world today. These answers are being systematically drummed into almost all our children, from kindergarten through graduate school. They say:

Who am I? I am a product of blind chance, descended from the apes.

Where did I come from? I come from a cell composed of matter and energy procreated by a male and female of my species.

Why am I here? This is not a valid question. There is no purpose for my life. I merely exist, and when I die I will merely cease to exist.

How should I live? I may live as I please because everything is relative. There are no right or wrong answers, there are only "choices." I must find my own reality.

Where am I going? I only go around once, so I must get all the gusto I can get.

For at least three generations, young Americans have gone out into the world with these answers, and the statistics of stress, depression, divorce, domestic violence, suicide, and frustration tell the story of their journey. It is a sad tale.

EVOLUTIONARY FAITH

Life in a warm little pond is the notion that Charles Darwin conceived. After his trip to the Galapagos Islands, which set him thinking about the possibilities of species development, he had to come up with a scenario by which life could have evolved spontaneously without the aid of God. After considering dozens of possible options, he finally wrote in a letter, "We could conceive in some warm little pond, with all sorts of ammonia and phosphoric salts, light, heat and electricity, etc., that a protein compound was chemically formed ready to undergo still more complex changes."

Isn't that a reassuring image? But you may want to ask for a little more detail. For example, where does the warm little pond come from? And what about the ammonia and the salts? Who brought those things in? And I seem to recall reading somewhere that, in the beginning, God said, "Let there be light." If Mr. Darwin does not wish to consider the "theistic" consequences of that statement, then let him explain where the light did come from. And the electricity and the heat and the primordial soup itself. But evolution has no answers, only a hypothesis, a theory, a notion that God had no hand in the affair.

Some time ago I spoke to a student who was attending a university in Minnesota. He told me that his biology teacher had informed the students from the very first day of class that his purpose in teaching biology was to show students that evolution is the only valid answer. The theories of Darwin are the way things are to be understood, and no other conclusion would be considered valid. Throughout the semester, said the professor, he was going to do his best to persuade Christians to abandon their faith and to adopt the faith of evolution.

The faith of evolution? Yes, and that is the correct way to phrase it. Make no mistake, evolution is a faith. Dr. L. Harrison Matthews, a noted evolutionist who wrote the introduction to the 1971 edition of Darwin's *Origin of the Species*, said, "The fact of evolution is the backbone of biology, and biology is thus in the peculiar position of being a science founded on an unproved theory—is it then a science or faith? Belief in the theory of evolution is thus exactly parallel to belief in special creation—both are concepts which believers know to be true but neither, up to the present, has been capable of proof."

The German scientist, Max Planck, who won the Nobel Prize for physics in 1918, said it even more graphically in his book, *Where Is Science Going?*: "Anybody who has been seriously engaged in scientific work of any kind realizes that over the entrance to the gates of the temple of science are written the words: *Ye must have faith*. It is a quality that the scientist cannot dispense with."

Obviously, scientists and evolutionists will have a very different set of answers to the old college questions. Bertrand Russell, one of this century's leading philosophers, was among many other things a skeptic, an atheist, an unbeliever, an evolutionist, and a radical. When he wrote his book, *Why I Am Not a Christian*, he failed to mention his multiple adulteries, his countless fornications, his seduction of the daughters of his hosts, and many other sins too numerous to mention. No doubt these were the real reason he wasn't a Christian. But he told us what life is all about. These are his answers to the basic questions. He said: "We started somewhere, we don't know where; we are here, we don't know why; we are going to some great oblivion, we know not whither." Those are the answers to the basic questions of life that Bertrand Russell has given to us. Yet, in spite of the fact that evolutionists offer no hope, no vision of human potential, or even scientific proof for their assertions, their ideology has completely dominated modern education.

But the battle between the supporters of evolution and those who believe the Genesis account of creation is just one skirmish line in the war of conscience and values. Is evolution just some sort of silly theory taught in biology classes? No. It has influenced every aspect of our lives. I am often shocked and saddened that so few Christians seem to be able to grasp the significance of the debate between evolution and the creationist view.

FUNDAMENTAL DIFFERENCES

Is the doctrine of Creation as opposed to evolution important? Well, the very first phrase in the first sentence of the first chapter of the first book of the Bible says that it is: "In the beginning, God created the heavens and the earth." That is where God began the story, and that is where all of life and theology and action ultimately has its beginning.

Ernst Mayr, professor at Harvard and a leading evolutionists has written: "Man's worldview today is dominated by the knowledge that the universe, the stars, the earth and all living things have evolved through a long history that was not foreordained or programmed."

René Dubós, in *American Scientist* magazine says, "Most enlightened persons now accept as a fact that everything in the cosmos—from heavenly bodies to human beings—has developed and continues to develop through evolutionary processes." Huxley said, "evolution is the totality of reality." Well, the totality of reality is God, but for such adherents as these, evolution has become their God. Charles Darwin wrote in the conclusion to the *Origin of the Species* that "Man with all his noble qualities . . . with his godlike intellect which has penetrated into the movements and constitution of the solar system . . . still bears in his bodily frame the indelible stamp of his lowly origin."

What kind of a view of man is this? Is the human species godlike or apelike? Is man a noble creature with a noble origin and destiny, or a base creature destined to dissolve into a barren and empty eternity of dust? Consider the appraisals of man given by some of the leading proponents of the evolutionary theory:

- ❏ "A hairless ape" (Schoenberg)
- ❏ "A fungus on the surface of one of the minor planets" (Du Maurier)
- ❏ "A rope stretched over an abyss" (Nietzsche)
- ❏ "Small potatoes and few" (Kipling)
- ❏ "A jest, a dream, a show, bubble, air" (Thornbury)
- ❏ "A mere insect, an ant" (Church)

This is the value of mankind to the evolutionist. Next to nothing at all! Yet, this is what students are being indoctrinated with from kindergarten all the way through graduate school. I am reminded of the child whose kindergarten teacher told him on the first day of class that no one could prove the existence of Jesus Christ. They don't wait one day to get started on tearing apart the faith of our little ones! As Dr. Paul Blanshard, a leading humanist, evolutionist, and a vigorous critic of religious education, has said: "Our schools may not teach Johnny to read properly, but the fact that Johnny is in school until he is sixteen tends to lead toward the elimination of religious superstition."

The "religious superstition" Blanshard is talking about is the faith that Christians hold dear. He is not referring to paganism, mysticism, New Age pantheism, or even Devil worship. No, he means Christianity. But this is typical of the value system of those who want to convince our children that we are just slightly above the apes.

THE GREAT COLLAPSE

A man by the name of Potter started a Humanist church. Where one might expect to find a cross or crucifix, he has erected a statue entitled *The Chrysalis*. A chrysalis is the silken case from which the butterfly emerges. But here the statue consists of a naked man emerging from an ape-skin. That tells a lot about the theology and philosophy of evolution, in spite of the fact that the whole thing has crumbled. All of the major pillars upon which evolution has rested have fallen apart in the last decade. As recently as 1992 it was announced that pictures taken by the infrared astronomical satellite launched in the mid-eighties, which has been traveling around the earth for the last five or six years, have given us the best view of the universe we have ever had. And now that those pictures have been analyzed, the results are shocking. As one writer put it: "It would appear that the Big Bang has gone bust."

One of the final pillars of their evolutionary views has just been dealt what many feel to be a mortal blow. The Big Bang theory proposed that some particle smaller than an atom contained all the matter in the universe and at one point, fifteen billion years or so ago, and it exploded and sent everything out into space.

If that were so, you would expect to find would be a homogenous distribution of matter in the universe. Debris should be spread evenly in every direction from the source of the explosion. But now that we have the best pictures of the cosmos that has ever been taken, we discover that "it ain't necessarily so!" There are not only clusters of galaxies in space, there are structures of galaxies, and there are superstructures of galaxies and, worst of all, right across the middle of the universe, a great wall of galaxies—billions of them. Billions of galaxies in the most complex structures, five hundred billion light-years long and twenty billion light-years high, of such complexity that there is no way it could ever have been formed by a "big bang."

If that isn't bad enough, the paleo-anthropologists, sometimes called the "stones and bones boys," have been lining up bones for us for a hundred years or more. They have three-and-a-half-million years of human ancestry (supposedly) all set up! Then along come a couple of geneticists who do some research. They conclude that "the slow changes that have taken place in human

DNA over the millennia indicate that *everyone alive today may be a descendant of a single female ancestor!"* What? Shades of Eve!

The astonishing thing to me is to see the way the stones-and-bones boys just capitulated right and left. Oh, a few are holding out. But what about all of the assured results of modern science, all of these things that our students were told were "facts"—that have now been chucked out the window!

If that isn't bad enough, recently scholars at the Massachusetts Institute of Technology gave us another shocker. There, meteorologist Dr. Hyman Hartman said that life did not emerge from amino acids in a primordial slime getting together to form proteins and then cells and all of the rest. Millions of people have been taught that as fact over the past century, but Dr. Hartman reports that the crucial reaction was between carbon dioxide and a substance called montmorillonite. In other words, *common clay*. Shades of Genesis 1 again! Not only have they gone back to one woman, but now they've gone back even beyond that and found the beginnings of the man himself.

Dr. Francis Crick, the co-discoverer of DNA, received the Nobel Prize for that discovery. He decided later to apply probability analysis to the possibility of just one DNA molecule's coming into existence by random chance in the entire history of the earth—that supposititious history, which according to the evolutionists is 4.6 billion years. What were the probabilities? Just that one DNA molecule—not a cell, not a monkey, not a man, but just a single molecule—albeit the most complex molecule that we know anything about. It is so tiny that it fits inside of the microscopic nucleus of a microscopic invisible cell. He discovered that there is *no possibility* that the DNA molecule could ever in the entire history of the earth have originated by chance.

Crick was and is an atheist. So what did he do? He came up with a new theory of evolution that he calls "directed panspermia." The idea is very simple. Since life could never have arisen here naturally, and since he assumes there is no God, therefore, some advanced race living on some other star, revolving around some other sun, somewhere out there in space, sent space ships out into the cosmos containing sperm cells and *voilà*! Here we are! And that is being taught in many schools in this country today. This, of course, is not science; it is science fiction. It has played well on *Star Trek*!

FROM FACT TO FICTION

A person who still has something operating between his ears is going to ask the question: But Doctor, where did that advanced race come from? "Well, you see, they had been seeded by a more advanced race that lived on another planet, around another star, maybe in another galaxy." That, of course, is called in logic an "infinite regress." One thing it does is to place it totally out of the realm of science and completely in the realm of science fiction.

Across the ocean in England, however, perhaps an even more prestigious scientist, Sir Fred Hoyle, former professor at Cambridge University, discoverer of the Steady State cosmogony, one of the two major cosmogonies of the twentieth century, a great mathematician, along with Chandra Wickramasinghe, a mathematician from India, performed a fascinating study. They decided to find out what were the probabilities of an entire cell—the simplest living cell—coming into existence anywhere—not merely on the earth—not merely in 4.6 billion years, but in the entire history of the universe (which figure, by the way, keeps changing from year to year and is now estimated to be roughly 15–20 billion years).

What did they (neither of whom was a Christian, by the way) discover? They concluded that the chances of a living cell's coming into existence spontaneously anywhere in the cosmos would take ten to the forty thousandth power years. Anything with less probability (which means a higher number) than ten to the fiftieth power is never going to happen in the entire universe, we are told by probability experts. "The chances," he said, "of a tornado blowing through a junkyard and creating a 747 are vastly greater."

Let me tell you what ten to the forty thousandth power years would be. We talk about twenty billion years. How about if we say, two hundred billion? Two million billion years? Two thousand, trillion, quadrillion, billion years? Multiply that by a hundred, a million, ten million, billions, trillions, you haven't even come close to ten to the forty thousandth power. It never happened. The chance evolution of a cell never happened at all, anywhere, anyplace, anytime, period. End of the story!

"Where did we come from?" asked former atheist Sir Fred Hoyle. There is no other universe to appeal to. He concluded that the only explanation for the existence of any life anywhere in this universe is that there must be some sort of gigantic mind that has eternally existed and which, if we wish, we may call God. Science forced him reluctantly to that conclusion, for which he has received an enormous amount of persecution and threats of various kinds.

No, God is not dead. That has never been proved. But those who have come to know Him have come to know that He is very much alive. The reason so many college students commit suicide today is because they believe that life has no meaning. They believe life has been robbed of all of its meaning and significance, that all there is at the end is a pile of ashes and a skull. That is just not going to suffice, because the soul is going to peek out around the day after tomorrow and desire some assurance of a continuing existence that is better and finer. God has placed immortality within the heart of man, and we can't get around it. There are those who have denied it, but what do they have? What are their lives like?

Every new advance and every step taken by science confirm not evolution but the Genesis account of creation. Yet evolution still continues to be taught as fact. It is no wonder our students today are filled with so many problems and doubts. It is no wonder self-worth has gone right down the tubes. Millions of students are running around trying to discover some sort of acceptable self-image, but they are told they are the long-lost cousins of apes with no more value than an animal, a tree, or an environmental oddity. Believing you are nothing but an accidental happening in the chaos of eternity doesn't create a great deal of self-worth. Yet, this is exactly the kind of idea being taught to our students from kindergarten on. Thus, the honorable place that had been given to human beings by God is surreptitiously aborted, and they are dragged down into the slime.

THE TOTAL SYSTEM

One writer said, "An evolutionary view of man leads to frightening conclusions." If you think this is just a theory in a biology classroom, let me say that it applies not only to every academic discipline today but also to everything else, including international relations, as well. Only the most benighted in our time do not know that

- ❏ Marx thought that evolution had given him a pseudoscientific foundation for communism . . . so much so that he wanted to dedicate his book, *Das Kapital*, to Charles Darwin—who at least had the good sense (at the urging of his wife) to decline that dubious honor.
- ❏ Hitler was a zealous follower of Nietzsche, who was a devoted evolutionist.
- ❏ The idea of the "super race" grew out of Nietzsche's concept of the "superman."

178

❏ Mussolini quoted evolutionary catch-phrases and believed that peace was anti-evolutionary, and that war is what drives the race on to new heights.

❏ Mao Zedong was also an evolutionist and killed fifty-five million Chinese in the process of evolving his own socialist doctrines.

Two young men born with silver spoons in their mouths—both the sons of millionaires—were students at the University of Chicago. Thanks to their extensive reading and the encouragement of their philosophy professors, they had become thoroughgoing Nietzscheans. They believed the words and works of Friedrich Nietzsche, which means they were also devoted evolutionists. They especially believed in Nietzsche's concept of the superman. In fact, they believed they were supermen themselves. At least, one of them thought the other one was the superman.

So, to prove their intellectual superiority, they decided to do some of the things Nietzsche had described in his books. They were not common men who had to obey laws made for the common crowd. They were above the law. They were free. Like Raskolnikov, the murderer in Dostoevsky's *Crime and Punishment*, they believed they could take human life with no remorse and no consequences. Raskolnikov reasoned, "If God does not exist, everything is permitted." Thus these two young men believed that, for them, everything was indeed permitted. What they did was to murder a fourteen-year-old boy. After all, what is life? But when they were taken into court to face the penalty of their crime, Leopold and Loeb discovered that they were not supermen. Richard Loeb was not Nietzsche's superman, as he had thought himself to be. He was a common criminal who had let false doctrines lead him astray. Now he had to pay the price.

THE DISPOSABLE CREATION

What is human life worth? Wolf Larsen, an evolutionist, says life is nothing but junk. "Life? Bah! It has no value. Of the cheap things it is the cheapest." It is disposable. But what we believe about life and about the value of our fellowman will determine how we act toward others. I think of the exterminations of Jews in Germany, the massacres in Cambodia under Pol Pot, the massacres in South America under the Sandinistas, and genocide taking place today in many parts of Africa.

All these are the result of extremist ideologies, either extreme Right or extreme Left causes, motivated by the revolutionary beliefs of Nietzsche, Marx, and others influenced by the evolutionary hypothesis of Darwin. We also have to wonder about many decisions of the United States Supreme Court in this century. One of this nation's most esteemed Supreme Court justices, Oliver Wendell Holmes, said: " I see no reason for attributing to man a significant difference in kind from that which belongs to a grain of sand."

Is this the "sanctity of human life"? Is human life worth anything at all? A justice of the United States Supreme Court who passes judgment upon law and order and has the power of life and death once expressed the belief that your life is no more valuable than a grain of sand that can be taken up by the handfuls and thrown away. And that is precisely what evolutionists have been doing throughout the twentieth century—just taking human life by the handfuls and throwing it away because it supposedly has no real value at all. From such a view we understand how the Court could dispassionately allow the *Roe v. Wade* decision to change the balance of life in this nation.

C. S. Lewis said that modern secularism has taken the heart out of the chest of man and then expected him to act as if he still has one. And so today we have people in this nation, and around the world, who are acting like animals, and we can't believe that they could do the things that they do to other human beings. But is it really all that different from life under Hitler, or Stalin, or Pol Pot?

What you believe about the sanctity of life and what you believe about the origins of man, will absolutely determine how you treat other people. Remember: Hitler was a devotee of Nietzsche, who was a follower of Darwin, who was an atheist and had no respect for the reality of God. Hitler's concept of a "master race" was simply an extrapolation from Nietzsche's theory of the "superman." And we should note that the subtitle of Darwin's book was *The Preservation of Favored Races*. The concept of evolution, from Darwin to Hitler, enabled men to do things to other people that would be unthinkable to Christians. The inhuman and barbaric beliefs of the Nazis allowed them to annihilate six million Jews, Gypsies, Poles, and evangelical Christians in the ovens of Auschwitz, Treblinka, Buchenwald, Belsen, and other horrible places.

They treated human beings like vermin, like rats. Scientists do terrible things to rats in laboratories. So if man is simply a complicated rat, why not do such things to people? Clearly this was the belief of Joseph Mengele, the butcher of Auschwitz, known as "Dr. Death." I have read the statements of evolutionists saying what they believe people to be. They say we are nothing at all, we are no more than a fungus on this planet. On the MacNeil-Lehrer news program, I once debated Stephen J. Gould—the Harvard professor who is probably the best-known evolutionist today. What Gould says in one of his writings is that man is just a twig. Not a branch, not a tree, not a forest but a dry twig. That's all that man is to this great man of science.

You don't really care a whole lot about human life if you consider it to be no more than a twig. You can throw it in the fire, break it up, stomp on it, cut it up, and do with it whatever you wish. And if we are just grains of sand, some will feel free to toss us around and do whatever they please to us. But when children are taught that they are animals, or less than animals—fungi, grains of sand, twigs—then their sense of self-worth will be destroyed, and at that point the door has been opened for the most ghastly kinds of behavior.

Erwin Lutzer has observed that there are approximately thirty trillion cells in the human body. Each cell contains forty-six chromosomes—twenty-three from the father, twenty-three from the mother. The activity within each cell is equivalent to that which takes place in a large city, such as New York, Los Angeles, or Miami. Each cell is outfitted with a unique program that allows it to integrate and interact with the brain and all the other parts of the body. Walter T. Brown has said that the information programmed into one cell is equivalent to a four thousand-volume library. Now when you multiply four thousand volumes times thirty trillion cells, you begin to understand the complexity of a living human being. But for the evolutionist, this body has only the value of a grain of sand or a twig!

THE DIGNITY OF MAN

The human brain, which, as one writer has pointed out, is capable of containing more information than the twenty-three millions of volumes in the Library of Congress, is of no value. If a team of scientists and computer programmers were to try to assemble a brain of comparable intelligence and complexity, using the most sophisticated digital and electronic technology known today, it would require a structure the size of the Empire State Building to house it, and it would require more electricity to run than it takes to power a city the size of New York. Yet, for the evolutionist, this brain has no value. And even if scientists and programmers were able to create a brain with the complexity of the human mind, that brain could not, even at the expense of billions of dollars, produce one single original thought. It is a physical impossibility.

That is not hyperbole; it is an absolute fact of science. Machines can process information, and they can calculate and offer options. They can retrieve data and apply it to solving problems, but they cannot think as even the dullest humans think. The processes of the mind are beyond all science and all human comprehension, yet we originate magnificent thoughts every day, in the blink of an eye! No heat, no wiring, no strain. Only God could have conceived such a creature.

Dr. Myron Augsburger points out that the mind is a faculty of the human spirit. The brain may be the physical part, but the mind itself contains the spirit, or the greater life force, which is merely housed in the body. "We do not understand all the dynamics of the mind," he says, "or the differences between persons in the realm of intellectual ability. Observation of human achievement shows that intellectual development is determined by more than the IQ; there are the elements of the spirit of discipline, of inquiry, of creativity, of imagination, and of conscience. When the spirit of the mind is set free to engage the meanings of the truth of God, we frequently see 'average' persons outstripping the 'intellectuals' in various aspects of life."[1]

But the evolutionist's view is like that of Thomas Huxley, who said that the action of the mind is merely a by-product of spontaneous chemical interactions within the brain. Just as the sound of a babbling brook is merely the result of water rushing against stone, so the intricacies of thought are merely the inadvertent accidents of chemicals reacting with brain tissue. The former Harvard psychologist, B. F. Skinner, said that the concept of evolution dictates that there can be no moral pretext in human behavior. Rather, we simply make "choices" that are convenient and acceptable to human society. For the renowned behaviorist, there are no principles or standards by which acceptable behavior should be judged, for we are merely creatures of chance bound by laws of social obligation. Surely this explains the title of his best-selling book, *Beyond Freedom and Dignity*. As creatures of evolution, we can have neither freedom nor dignity. If we are but grains of sand we can have no freedom, and without freedom there is no dignity.

For the proponents of the evolutionary theory, we are merely ciphers—empty digits, numbers on an indecipherable scale—and meaningless biological tissue to be exploited. We may be programmed and exploited. We may be used and abused. We are but tissue with a brain. Dr. Francis

Schaeffer summed up it up very well when he said: "The concept of man's dignity is gone. We are in the post-Christian world. Man is junk. If the embryo is in the way, ditch him . . . if the old person is in the way, ditch him. If you're in the way . . . ." You know the rest.

Evolution can only create an environment of meaninglessness for life and worthlessness for man. Life has no purpose. It is just an accident that took place in the slime or in the clay. You are not worth much of anything at all. But how different this view of evolution is from what God offers. Fortunately, there have been those who have been honest enough to admit how they feel about all of that. Skeptic W. O. Saunders, an evolutionist and unbeliever, said this about the materialists and the unbelievers:

> For him there is only the grave and the persistence of matter. All he can see beyond the grave is the disintegration of the protoplasm and psychoplasm of which his body and its personality are composed . . . But in this material view I find no ecstasy nor happiness. Is this the end and all of human life and endeavor? . . . Therefore would I try to convey to your mind and heart something of the wistfulness and loneliness of the man who does not believe in God.

The study of evolution is so pervasive in our schools and throughout society that many Christians have tried to unite faith and science by saying that God gave things a push, then the process of evolution took over. This view, called "theistic evolution," is not only a direct contradiction of Scripture but a fundamental challenge to God's authority. And it is inconsistent with both belief systems: it is neither Christian nor scientific.

As Erwin Lutzer says, "After all, if evolution can do what it claims, God is unnecessary. And if God is needed at the beginning of the process, then it is just as easy to let Him be responsible for the initial creation and the species as we essentially know them today. The crucial debate is atheistic evolution versus the creative power of a personal God." In short, you cannot have it both ways. If nothing else, God will not allow it. You may choose God, or you may choose Mammon. The decision is yours. Whom will you serve?

LIFE WITHOUT HOPE

What do unbelievers have to offer? Theirs is the way of depression and suicide. Surely the destructive psychology of evolutionism has contributed to the epidemic of hopelessness and violence on our campuses. Surely it is one of the principal causes of death of our college students. The existential writer, Albert Camus, a companion of Jean-Paul Sartre who was lionized by the young radicals of the sixties, began his famous book, *The Myth of Sisyphus*, with the words, "There is but one truly serious philosophical problem . . . ." Only one? There's only one serious philosophical problem, only one question that you should be directing your mind toward? Would you like to understand what is at the pinnacle of this evolutionary, existentialist, and atheistic view of life? There's only one question worthy of consideration, we are told. Not merely the most important, but the *only* significant question of our time: "It is," said Albert Camus, "suicide."

Have you been studying "the only significant question" as you should? Let me assure you that students in many of our public schools and universities are giving it a lot of attention. In some of our public schools, students are being taught how to write suicide notes. They are being shown a variety of methods of committing suicide and given recommendations about which ways are to be preferred. They are told about and taught and do, indeed, build models of their coffins. The Bible says that those that hate God love death, and that is what all of this is: death and more death—the death of human aspirations, the death of human dignity, the death of human meaning and significance, the death of all future hopes.

Major studies suggest that teenage suicide is rising at an alarming rate. According to a report in *USA Today*, as many as one in seven teens may have attempted suicide. According to the American Academy of Child and Adolescent Psychiatry, suicide is the third leading cause of death among teens. Specialists cite the "breakdown of the nuclear family" as a major cause, along with the increase in substance abuse and clinical depression arising from a general loss of hope. From sixty to eighty percent of teen suicides involve depressive illness, and the *New England Journal of Medicine* reports that there are at least thirty thousand suicides in this country each year. Suicide is the option for those who have lost hope. When life is meaningless, why prolong the pain?

But with the help of authors such as Derek Humphry, the former head of the Hemlock Society, you don't need to prolong the pain or agonize over how to do it anymore. His book, *Final Exit*, raced to the top of the best-seller lists and sold in the hundreds of thousands of copies. The book is just one-hundred-ninety-two pages long, set in large type for the benefit of people with poor eyesight. It tells all about committing suicide, with chapters such as "How Do You Get the Magic Pills?" "Self-Deliverance Via the Plastic Bag," and for couples, "Going Together?" One chapter, called "Bizarre Ways to Die" includes a list of methods the author doesn't necessarily endorse, not because they're not good ways but because they sometimes fail.

Death. The final release. The final exit. But when life has no meaning, the cold-hearted rationalist will argue, why romanticize it? Perhaps this attitude has never been more eloquently expressed than by one of the great unbelievers of the early part of this century, Robert Ingersoll, a leading atheist, evolutionist, and skeptic in his day. A brother whom Ingersoll loved very much died suddenly. The brother was also an unbeliever, so there were no clergymen to call. How does an atheist have a funeral? What is the point? Ingersoll conducted the graveside funeral himself. I hope you will never forget his words. They are some of the saddest I have ever read:

> Whether in mid-sea or among the breakers of the farther shore, a wreck must mark at last the end of each and all. And every life, no matter if its every hour is rich with love and every moment jeweled with joy, will, at its close, become a tragedy, as sad, and deep, and dark as can be woven of the warp and woof of mystery and death. . . . Life is a narrow vale between the cold and barren peaks of two eternities. We strive in vain to look beyond the heights. We cry aloud, and the only answer is the echo of our wailing cry.

This is what unbelief offers to man. I thank God that in His Word we read: "What is man that thou art mindful of him? . . . For thou hast made him a little lower than the angels . . . Thou madest him to have dominion over the works of thy hands; thou hast put all things under his feet" (Ps. 8:4–6 KJV). What is man? He is a prince or princess in a royal realm. His origin comes from the heart and mind of God and his destiny is paradise forever and ever. "No eye has seen, no ear has heard, no mind has conceived what God has prepared for those who love him" (1 Cor. 2:9). This is the glorious origin and destiny of all who trust in Christ.

A DOUBLE DIAGNOSIS

If you are one of those still standing in the valley of the shadow of death—one who has no hope, who has no meaning or significance, who sees no value to life; if you have no more expectations beyond the grave; if your final companion is not to be the Christ of God but rather the conqueror worm in the grave, then I would urge you to lift up your eyes unto the Cross, to the One who will provide meaning and value to your life. There you will find your origin and destiny.

"Through him all things were made; without him nothing was made that has been made" (John 1:3). This is the One who has gone to prepare a place for us in paradise. This is the One who is the Creator of the galaxies. This is God the Son, who came and died, and by His death gives such value and such meaning and such purpose and transcendent worth to human beings as could not even be conceived in any other way. If you would know of your origin, if you would know of your destiny, then open your heart and invite Him to come in. Carl Wallace Miller said, "Belief of God is acceptance of the basic principle that the universe makes sense, that there is behind it an ultimate purpose." If there is no purpose or meaning to life, then why go on in pain and sorrow? But if God gives life meaning, then "we are more than conquerors through him who loved us" (Rom. 8:37).

In some medical conditions, I understand, doctors will give what they call a double prognosis. At the Tulane University Medical Center in New Orleans, a very highly recognized surgeon had a patient who had gangrene in his legs. The patient was a heavy smoker and over a period of time the lack of oxygen in his system had reduced circulation in his legs so badly that the doctor gave him a double prognosis. The first prognosis was that if he continued to smoke, the patient would most certainly lose both his legs. But the surgeon said that if the man would stop smoking right away, then he was confident he could be successfully treated and his legs could be saved. What would any rational person do under such a prognosis? Well, this man refused to stop smoking, and within a matter of months he lost both his legs.

How could anyone be so addicted to something that he would be willing to give up his legs for it? There was a clear-cut prognosis for his dilemma. On one hand, he was going to lose his legs if he didn't change his behavior. But if he did change, he could have full use of his legs restored. I cannot help feeling that this is precisely what is likely to happen to America sometime in the next decade if we continue to live and behave as we have been doing in this second half of the twentieth century. We have witnessed the rise in immorality, godless secularism, and promiscuous lifestyles that contribute to venereal disease, AIDS, and death. All these things are disastrous. They are literally killing us.

What will happen when the financial collapse of this country comes upon us and when all the problems brought about by moral relativism are allowed to exact their toll upon the nation? If the people of this country will repent of their sins and fall on their knees and call upon God and seek His face, as we learn in 2 Chronicles 7:14; and if we learn the importance of being obedient to God and to His Great Commission, then there can yet be a glorious future and a hope for this nation.

The church has failed to evangelize the nation as it should, and the church has failed to fulfill the Great Commission. Consequently, there are more and more unregenerate people in this country. And Christians, by vacating the public square, have provided a vacuum for those unregenerate people to move into, so that all the positions of influence are being filled by pagans who subscribe to all the unchristian teachings and relative values of the age. It is vitally important that Christians be obedient both to the Great Commission and to the "cultural mandate"—that they evangelize the lost and endeavor to become involved in the political system. We must encourage our children to get into careers and professions in which they can have an influence on the world. If we are to be spared a prognosis of doom, then God's people must share their world- and lifeviews with all men and nations.

George Washington Carver once said, "I love to think of nature as an unlimited broadcasting station through which God speaks to us every hour, if we only will tune in." God is speaking to us today, calling us to resist the alien doctrines of this world. Will we do that? If so, then there is hope. We know that our origin is of God, and through faith in Jesus Christ we have a glorious destiny. Let us resolve to share that good news with the world and avoid the double prognosis that will otherwise condemn this nation to destruction.

Notes

[1]Myron Augsburger, *The Christ-Shaped Conscience* (Wheaton: Victor Books, 1990), 99.

Part III

The Victory of Faith

9

A Test of Character

In the first decade of this century, Britain's Viscount Morley remarked that, "No man can climb out beyond the limitations of his own character." High office, noble ambitions, even great success cannot long disguise the true nature of the soul within. When the thirty-one-year CIA veteran, Aldrich Ames, was arrested in February 1994 on charges of spying for Moscow, the world witnessed yet another example of weak character corrupted by greed. The fifty-two-year-old career intelligence specialist had been the head of the counterintelligence section, the group that keeps an eye on cheaters and double agents. But in 1985, Ames and his wife had begun accepting payoffs from the KGB, and over nearly ten years they pocketed at least $1.5 million. There is no telling what damage may have been done to this nation because of the Ameses' acts of selfishness. We do know that the reports this American couple supplied to the Russians led to the deaths of at least ten American agents in Eastern Europe, but they may also have compromised many other aspects of United States security and caused problems that will handicap our intelligence service for years to come.

Even more troubling for many people is the fact that the concern expressed by our diplomats and public officials in Washington when the

Ameses were apprehended was not what we might have expected. Yes, there was some verbal hand-wringing, a few charges and protests, but the official response expressed more irritation than outrage. Moscow's chief intelligence officer in the United States was expelled—which is standard procedure in such cases. But with the exception of a handful of angry congressmen, the Administration seemed more concerned that these events might disrupt friendly relations with Boris Yeltsin and the government of Russia than that vital personnel and resources had been compromised. There was hardly any mention of the ten lives that had been lost.

What is the value of a human life? Can life be measured in dollars and cents? By the implications of their actions, Mr. and Mrs. Ames contributed directly to the assassination of ten men. Is $150,000 enough for the life of a human being? That's how much blood money they collected. Just a few years ago their act would have been considered treason. Both of them would have been executed for their crime. But today the case appears to be merely another temporary annoyance for diplomacy as usual. The designers of the new world order have bigger fish to fry.

THE MARKS OF CHARACTER

As Dr. Os Guinness points out in *The American Hour*, until recently if you asked any American what he or she considers the greatest danger to this nation, the answer would have been "national security." For two hundred years Americans believed in themselves, their strength, their rugged individualism, and their historic values. The greatest dangers to the nation were from outside our borders. But all that has changed. If you ask Americans today what they consider to be the greatest threats to the nation, they will most likely mention one of the dozens of moral or social problems that plague the nation—crime, lawlessness, racial violence, political polarization, AIDS, falling educational standards, moral decline, the breakup of the family, or the general loss of respect for human life.

What a sad commentary on the soul of the nation. Instead of concern for external dangers, today our greatest fears concern the internal decay and the moral deterioration taking place within our own borders. What should trouble us most is the general loss of character that spells even greater danger for this country in coming years than the possibility of foreign aggression.

But what is character? It is not an easy quality to describe. By definition, character is a distinctive mark or stamp. In a person, character includes those habits and personality traits that distinguish us as individuals, especially with regard to personal integrity, courage, moral fiber, and individual initiative. Character is like an engraving; it is an image stamped on the soul. The marks of character are deep and indelible, but they can be read by the people around us from the way we live, behave, and speak.

Character is intimately related to our moral values and our deepest beliefs about who we are as people, but it is visible in the pattern of behavior a person exhibits when only God sees what really happens. Character also involves matters of choice. Sometimes it means choosing to do or say something even when it may cost you great suffering and pain, yet you do it because it is "the right thing to do." Character means making hard choices.

Other times it may mean *not* doing something—the exam you could easily have cheated on because you were on the honor system, but you didn't. The money you found that no one would have known about if you had pocketed it, but you decided to turn in. The confidential information about someone that others were dying to learn, you decided not to tell because you cared too much for that other person's feelings. Character is a matter of integrity, self-respect, an inner sense of right and wrong, and a sense that things have eternal consequences. Character is that inner sense that cares.

Sometimes character takes a more active role, however, such as doing something exceptional when it is not expected—sacrificing your own comfort, time, safety, even your life for a greater good. You may recall that at the end of Charles Dickens' novel, *A Tale of Two Cities*, the self-indulgent Englishman, Sydney Carton, sacrifices his life so a Frenchman he believed to be more worthy could escape to freedom. As Carton takes the place of the French aristocrat, Charles Darnay, he is taken away to the guillotine, but he says to himself in the last line of the story, "It is a far, far better thing that I do, than I have ever done; it is a far, far better rest that I go to than I have ever known." Putting others first, regardless of what it may cost, demonstrates the deepest virtues of the human character.

Sometimes the strong moral character of one person can light a flame and help mold the will and the resolve of many others. I think particularly of Winston Churchill during the bleak days of World War II when the fate of the world seemed awfully grim. Out-manned and out-gunned by the hugely superior Axis forces, England was expected to surrender quickly, as most of Europe had already done. But Churchill said that he and his countrymen would rather die than give in to Nazi tyranny. In a speech before the House of Commons, he said, "We shall defend our island, whatever the cost may be; we shall fight on the beaches, we shall fight on the landing grounds, we shall fight in the fields and in the streets, we shall fight in the hills; we shall never surrender." While virtually every other leader of the nation was calling for capitulation, the strong moral character of this one man rallied the British people to, as Churchill said, "their finest hour." And tiny England fought alone against overwhelming odds for a year, finally turning the tide of battle by virtue of their moral fortitude alone.

I think also of the citizens who risked their own lives for others during those dark days. One was the family of Corrie ten Boom in Holland, who, for years, along with many other courageous Dutch families, hid Jews in their homes, trying to save them from the Nazis. Knowing that they could be executed or imprisoned for the rest of their lives, they chose to put their own safety at risk simply because they believed it was "the right thing to do." It was what their Christian faith and their good character demanded. As you know, Corrie's family was taken prisoner by the Nazis and almost all of them perished in the concentration camps—but there were no regrets. Putting self last, doing the right thing, even when it is not expeditious, even if no one expects or even understands, and even when no one else will ever know. That is the test of character.

FALSE FAITHS

But do we still have the capacity in this nation for character like that? And if we do, is it common or just occasional? Are the American people still willing to risk their own safety and comfort for the good of others? Os Guinness writes, "Americans with a purely secular view of life have too much to live with and too little to live for. Everything is permitted and nothing is important." Thanks to the secularization of our age—and the degree to which Christians willingly hide the fact of their faith in order to avoid possible embarrassment— the deeper marks of character have grown soft or invisible.

Too many people today have traded their faith in the "eternal verities" for the cheap substitute of "material possessions," and, as a consequence, the citizens of this nation have compromised both their character and their soul. "But," Dr. Guinness warns, the secular answer is hollow and unfulfilling, and, "once growth and prosperity cease to be their reason for existence, they are bound to ask questions about the purpose and meaning of their lives: Whence? Whither? Why? And to such questions secularism has no answers that have yet proved widely satisfying in practice."[1]

Materialism has failed us. The false faiths of our age have failed us. Freudianism, Marxism, deconstructionism, and social permissiveness have all failed to render the great social order or the peace of mind their adherents promised. None of these seductions have added anything to the meaning of life or accounted for the growing poverty in the soul of this nation. "Even secular humanism," says Guinness, "turns out to be, not the bogey its enemies feared, but an oxymoron its supporters regret—for secularism does not produce humanism; humanism requires, not secularism, but supernaturalism."[2]

The human spirit requires more than merely physical food for its deepest hunger. It needs spiritual food. And character cannot survive when greed, lust, selfishness, and ambition are the only criteria of value. Whether in Europe, in Soviet Russia, or in modern America, materialism is a destructive disease that destroys character. It is only too clear that this nation has already contracted the disease and is in an advanced state of decline. The only cure for our illness is a return to the moral values that help build strong character and a good conscience. And such values only come through a return to faith in God. Guinness says:

> The lesson is clear. When morality is strong, laws need not be. So if the scope of freedom is to widen, that of law should not. There is therefore great folly in the current notion that, because morality is a private affair, anything is right in public "so long as it does not break the law." Under the guise of this maxim, liberals seasoned in crusades against environmental irresponsibility have presided carelessly over a massive moral erosion of their own. Moral principles have been hacked down, special proprieties bulldozed to the ground. All that is not legally prohibited is socially allowed. Someday these radical rule-breakers will wake up to a world without rules. Then they will lament either the moral dust-bowl they have created or the dense underbrush of laws they have had to grow hastily in its place.[3]

Please understand the importance of what is being said here. The secular notion that you can have virtue or integrity or strong character without a framework of moral values is a lie. When morality is bulldozed by society in order to free people up, as Bertrand Russell said, to their erotic desires, then nothing can live in that soil. But please understand this fact also: The character of an individual or a group can only be built on a foundation of moral values, and there can be no morality without religion. This belief, which is so much a part of the history and tradition of this nation, suddenly seems alien to many people today. "What?" they ask. "No morality without religion? Why, that's absurd!" But history proves that this is true.

The founders of the nation understood this fact, and that's why George Washington left these sentiments for you to read today. In his Farewell Address, the Father of Our Country made these insightful remarks as "the disinterested warning of a parting friend":

> . . . Of all the dispositions and habits that lead to political prosperity, religion and morality are indispensable supports. In vain would that man claim the tribute of patriotism who should labor to subvert these great pillars of human happiness . . . And let us with caution indulge the supposition that morality can be maintained without religion.

At the very beginnings of this nation, the founders warned us to avoid the myth that morality can be maintained without religion. They knew that morality forms the soul and the character of mankind, and without the inner strength that comes through strong faith, the nation and every man, woman, and child within it will grow morally frail. You recall that the novelist, Fyodor Dostoevsky, once said that if there is no God, everything is permitted. And if everything is permissible, then nothing is impermissible! In other words, without God and the absolute standards of the Bible, there is no right or wrong. But this is the lesson of modern secular society: In their haste to get rid of God, the people have lost the essential values that come only through faith.

THE PAYOFF OF IMMORALITY

The existentialist writer, Jean-Paul Sartre, saw very clearly what would happen if we got rid of God as he had done. He said, "[Without God] all activities are equivalent . . . Thus it amounts to the same thing whether one gets drunk alone, or is a leader of nations." In other words, if you see an old woman trying to cross the street, it doesn't matter whether you stop your car and help her across, or whether you simply run over her. It doesn't matter whether you give or whether you take. If everything is permitted, Mother Theresa and Jeffrey Dahmer have precisely the same moral consequence and value. Without God, all activities are equivalent. Without God, fraud and integrity are the same, and honor is of no more value than dishonor.

The sad fact is that society has not, as a whole, condemned such destructive sentiments. Why not? Because too many of us have accepted the popular notion of "moral relativism" that is being promoted by the universities and by modern liberalism in general. Would that some of our modern thinkers would realize the truth of Sartre's statement. One of them certainly has. Ludwig Wittgenstein, one of the founders and leaders of the modern analytical philosophy of deconstructionism, said that if there are any ethical absolutes, they would have to come to man from *outside* the human situation. He writes, "If a man could write a book on ethics which really was a book on ethics, this book would, with an explosion, destroy all the other books in the world."

But Wittgenstein did not believe there could be such a book because, like Sartre, he had rejected God and His Word. But, unlike many of us today, these people knew what the result would be. For the last twenty-five years, God has been banished from the public square to an incredible degree. As we have seen throughout this book, the courts, the schools, the colleges and universities, and many other public institutions have done their best to strip away all evidence of religious faith. They have created "God-Free Zones" throughout the nation, and what have been the results? Have we maintained morality in the absence of religion? Have we found that religion doesn't matter and that we are as well-off today as we were three decades ago?

Pollster George M. Gallup, Jr., who has appraised the situation better than most, says, "The United States is facing a 'moral and ethical crisis of the first dimension' and needs to find spiritual answers to deal with the situation." At least the analysts who have seen the evidence of moral carnage are discovering where the solution is to be found.

For twenty-five years children in our public schools have been taught that there are no moral absolutes; no one can tell them what to do. They are simply to choose their own values, their own ethics. In the last verse of the book of Judges, we read that "Every man did that which was right in his own eyes" (Judg. 21:25 KJV). Unfortunately, that is exactly what we have today in our country, and I fear the consequences will also be the same. In his analysis of what the moral degeneracy and relativism of the age have done to us, James Driscoll reports that the nation has never been so demoralized. And in describing the character of the young people who have undergone this amoral reconditioning, he says:

At the core there is nothing. At the moral center
of many young Americans aged 18 to 30 there is a vacuum,

and it's nearly perfect. It contains none of the bedrock ethical values long considered essential to living a decent life: Honesty, personal responsibility, respect for others, civic duty. Instead, this self-indulgent generation believes passionately only in this: It is entitled.

This is a sad commentary on the character of our nation. But the results of the social conditioning taking place in the schools are overwhelming. Committees of the United States Senate and the House of Representatives studying the moral condition of the nation came up with these appalling results: "Suicide is now the second leading cause of death among adolescents, increasing 300 percent since 1950."

At the same time, they have discovered that teen pregnancy has risen 621 percent since 1940. More than a million teenage girls get pregnant each year. Eighty-five percent of the teenage boys who impregnate teenage girls eventually abandon them. And every year substance abuse claims younger and younger victims with harder and harder drugs. The average age for first-time drug use is now thirteen.

FACING THE FACTS

Why do I insist that we can't have morality without religion? First, let me make several things clear. There are some people who are irreligious who live reasonably decent sort of lives, but that is not because they are pursuing their own morality. It is not because they have discovered some new secular ethical standard that allows them to live virtuous and honorable lives. No, they are in fact simply agreeing to abide by principles as old as the Christian church, principles of respect, honor, and duty that have been handed down for a hundred generations in Western society. As Erwin Lutzer says, "they piggyback on the Judeo-Christian ethic. When they believe in human dignity, freedom, and peace, they are assuming a theistic view of the world," but without giving credit where it is due.[4]

James Michener, who was featured on the cover of *Parade Magazine* a few years ago, says in the accompanying article: "I am a humanist." And he adds, "If you want to charge me with being the most virulent kind, a secular humanist, I accept the accusation." And then he says, "I am a humanist, because I think humanity can, with constant moral guidance, create reasonably decent societies."

That is a very interesting comment. We have to wonder where that constant moral guidance is going to come from? Will it come from Sartre or Wittgenstein? Will it come from MTV or CBS News? Surely it won't come from Michener's books, we hope. Where will the people of the world find the "constant moral guidance" this great humanist assumes to be so readily available? Typically, he gives no examples of any of these "reasonably decent societies." It only requires a glimpse at the headlines to see that, wherever you look around this globe, where God is in disfavor there are *no decent societies*. The world is in chaos precisely because we have accepted the false theology that man can be good without God.

A much better perspective comes from the historian, Will Durant. Even though Durant was also a humanist and no particular friend of religion, at least he was more honest. Writing in the February 1977 issue of the *Humanist* magazine, Durant says that "We shall find it no easy task to mold a natural ethic strong enough to maintain moral restraint and social order without the support of supernatural consolations, hopes, and fears." And he adds that "There is no significant example in history, before our time, of a society successfully maintaining moral life without the aid of religion."

Even Napoleon Bonaparte, a product of the French Enlightenment, said that he understood the nature of men without God. He saw them in the French Revolution, and he said, "One does not govern such men; he shoots them down." When men have descended to the level of the beasts, they are of no value to a just society. Again, the point should be clear. There is no significant example in all of history of any people ever maintaining morality without religion. Therefore our modern secularists and humanists who maintain that we can have morality without religion are either totally ignorant or they are trying to pull the wool over our eyes.

There are at least three good reasons why you can't have morality without religion. The first is that you can't create any standard of right and wrong to which people are going to adhere voluntarily. This is a page from the humanists' own handbook. Yes, they can draw up some list or code of ethics. They can even set policies and standards and make all kinds of rules. But they cannot make people follow their code of ethics. When no one claimed the million-dollar prize he offered, Ted Turner drew up his own set of ten commandments. But who could name even two of them today?

I will grant that the humanists have tried to create ethical codes. They even offered a set of principles in the *Humanist Manifesto*, but what they have done is to turn all the Christian moral values upside down. They have taken all the behaviors and beliefs that have been considered sins for centuries and declared that they are suddenly moral. So their "ethics" condones gambling, divorce, suicide, free love, fornication, adultery, incest, euthanasia, and a number of other things—all of which have been considered immoral acts in Christian society for nearly two thousand years. No doubt they can entice some people to follow their list of immoral acts and call it morality! It has never been difficult to get people to wander down the path of self-destruction. But, in the end, the atheists and immoralists cannot force people to live by their code of ethics. The fate of the Soviet Empire offers adequate proof of that fact.

The second reason you can't maintain morality without religion is because you cannot impose your standard of behavior on others. Isn't that what the humanists have been telling us for so long? When Christians speak of the Bible or our view of God, we are immediately silenced and told we cannot impose our standards on anyone else. But, ignoring their own rule, the humanists have come up with their own set of "moral" principles, and they are determined to impose their idea of right and wrong on the rest of us. Using the ACLU as the storm troops of their atheistic assault upon American values, they have come up with *their* set of ethics and values, and they have been extremely successful in imposing their pagan ideologies on this nation by law. But the only way they have succeeded in doing it is by legal enforcement, and by the complicity of the courts. And today we see the secular state acting as a moral despot, enforcing godless laws and penalties on everyone else.

This fact was brought home very clearly to Dr. Frank Rhodes of Cornell University in a meeting of university professors and educators. He made the comment that we need a renaissance of education and morality in American colleges and universities. In the face of all the evidence showing how far morality and ethics have fallen, you would think such a remark would have been applauded. But no, he was loudly booed. Faculty members and visitors actually hissed at him. They yelled, "Whose morality, Professor, are you going to impose upon them?" Ungracious, undignified, wild, and disrespectful? Yes, but they were right. Whose morality did he have in mind? Schmidt couldn't answer the question because he, too, had abandoned the ethic of traditional Christian values. He had nothing else to offer.

ETHICS BY THE BOOK

The idea of ethics is a very fundamental issue. In its rightful context, it is often astonishing. We read in Scripture: "When Jesus ended these sayings, the people were astonished" (Matt. 7:28 KJV). The word in Greek means "knocked out." The Scripture tells us, "He taught them as one having authority." Here Jesus is declaring an ethical code. Not only is He declaring an ethical code, He is saying that everybody must live this way. And not only is He saying that everybody must live by an ethical code, but He is going to enforce it. He said:

> Many will say to me on that day, "Lord, Lord, did we not prophesy in your name, and in your name drive out demons and perform many miracles?" Then I will tell them plainly, "I never knew you. Away from me, you evildoers!"
> — MATTHEW 7:22–23

We also learn that any person who builds his life upon Christ's words is like the man who builds his house upon a rock, and it stands because the foundation is secure. But the person who does not build on that secure foundation is like the man who builds his house upon sand. When the winds blow and the rains come down, the floods will wash it away, and great will be the fall of it. Why do the secular humanists deny the truth of Scripture? Because they cannot bear the fact that their sins will be judged. They cannot bear the idea of ethics or moral integrity, but someday they will have to answer to the Judge of judges for their crimes. Jesus Christ is the Judge, the Creator, and the King of kings.

Scripture leaves no doubt of that fact. He is Judge, and all men and women who have ever lived will be called to account for the life they have lived. They will stand before the bar of God's justice, and they will be required to give an account of whether or not they have lived according to His Word. I may not be able to impose my idea of morality on anyone; but rest assured, God can and will impose His morality on everyone.

The third reason you cannot have morality without religion is because as soon as you get rid of the Word of God and the absolute standards of the Bible, you are left without any reliable guidelines. You can look around and imitate the behavior of other people, but that is not morality. The *Humanist Manifesto* says that all human ethics are experiential; they are based upon human experience. But the authors of that document have overlooked something that every modern philosopher and every teacher of ethics can tell you. As far back as the Scottish philosopher, David Hume, who lived in the seventeenth century, we have understood that "You cannot get an *ought* from an *is*." Simply because something happens one way does not mean that it "ought" to be that way.

For example, George Gallup may survey the entire population of America and find that 99.9 percent of the people are stealing from their employers. But that does not mean the people *ought* to be doing those things. In fact, if you were to take a survey you could determine that one hundred percent of the American people are sinning. But that certainly does not mean we *ought* to sin. One recent survey says that fully ninety-one percent of Americans admit to lying to other people, but that doesn't mean they *ought* to lie. As Hume said, you can never obtain an "ought" from an "is." And once you get rid of divine revelation of God and the secure structure of religion, there is no way that you will ever have a strong enough foundation to tell people what they *ought* to do by simply relying upon some rational standard.

In a recent survey of five hundred families conducted by the Roper Organization, for *Family Circle* magazine, respondents were asked whether they followed basic rules of behavior—what the reporters described as The Ten Commandments put into everyday language—and also whether they thought other people regularly followed them. Nine out of ten respondents said that their families didn't steal, but only half believed that other people do not steal. Three out of four said that they do not envy other people's belongings; but an equal number said they thought other people do envy others. Approximately ninety percent of married respondents said they do not cheat on their spouses; but only half thought that other people are faithful. Surprisingly, sixty-four percent said they do not curse; but only fifteen percent said they believed that other people do not curse.

According to the *Wall Street Journal*, where I read this story, the results of the survey show that most people tend to be self-righteous about their own behavior and critical of the behavior of others. But I wonder if there isn't another interpretation. Namely, that most Americans do try to be wholesome and responsible in their behavior, but the dominant media culture has convinced us that most moral standards are arbitrary and irrelevant. Even those who try to abide by basic principles of right and wrong have come to believe that they are the only ones doing it. They are out of touch with the culture. They may be faithful to their wife or husband, but they think most people are not. What this says is that they are being encouraged to "get in on the action" because "everybody's doing it."

THE FAILURE OF REASON

Professor Allan Bloom told us in *The Closing of the American Mind* that "Reason cannot establish values." Let us keep in mind that in our schools, children are taught that they should simply sit down and rationally and reasonably decide what their values should be. Then those values will become *their values*, and therefore they can decide what is right and wrong for them in any situation. They don't have to worry about absolute standards of right and wrong. After all, thanks to secular humanism, they can have their own private morals. They have been taught "Values Clarification," which says that everything is permitted so long as you "feel good" about your decision. But Dr. Bloom begs to disagree. He says, "Reason cannot establish values," and the suggestion that it can is the stupidest and most pernicious illusion.

So today our children are being taught the height of stupidity, because it doesn't matter how much you look at what people do. The behavior of other people is no standard. Even if the entire world happens to behave in a certain way, that does not mean it is moral or acceptable behavior. You cannot even say, "Well, it's the end result that matters." This is the pretext of today's so-called "outcome-based education," which says it doesn't matter what a child learns so long as the "outcome" is acceptable.

The NEA and other liberal teachers groups say, "We're going to decide if something is right by whether or not it produces a good end." But that is a bad policy. Sure, there are times when telling a lie will produce a more beneficial result—at least for the short run. Based on that "outcome," we might conclude that lying would be right because it produced a "good end." But that is a dangerous principle, and sooner or later a person who subscribes to that policy will end up in serious trouble, in jail, or possibly even dead. The "end" doesn't justify the "means."

Materialism, which underlies communism, socialism, and even capitalism when it is divorced from Christian principles, is the idea that man can do quite well in the world without any need for God or divine revelation. But materialism alone cannot support reason, much less morality. Without God, rationality cannot be established. Without God's ordinances and His law of right and wrong, there is no foundation for human reason. Even Charles Darwin knew this fact. He said it was a horrid thought to realize that all of his speech may have no more significance or meaning than the babbling of a monkey. "And who would put much stock," he said, "in the conviction in the mind of a monkey —if indeed such a mind has any convictions at all." Darwin recognized that, without an eternal standard, the day-to-day affairs of humanity were absolutely insignificant; but he could not accept the reality of God, and his views have led millions of people in our day into acceptance of a godless existence.

Another materialist expressed the distinctive view of the humanist perspective when he said, "The brain secretes thought as the liver secretes bile." You have no control over the bile that your liver secretes, and you have no control over the thoughts that your brain secretes. Materialists and evolutionists believe that matter, without soul or spirit or any indwelling presence of a divine nature, can think.

But don't be too astounded at that, because they're not sure that those thoughts have any more significance than the babbling of a monkey. Darwin once said, "The horrid doubt always arises whether the convictions of a man's mind, which has developed from the mind of lower animals, are of any value or at all trust-worthy." The father of evolution had serious doubts about his own worth, as well as that of other people.

So, by their own standards, the evolutionists tell us that what you think depends simply upon the chemical reaction of the calcium, phosphate, and sugars currently operating in your brain. This reminds me of the "Twinky" defense. This case became famous after a California lawyer, defending a man accused of murder, said that his client was hopped-up on sugar from an overdose of snack foods. This has become known, not as a miscarriage of justice or an example of the ridiculous extremes that lawyers will go to in defending criminals, but the now-famous "Twinky" defense. "Why, your honor," the lawyer pleaded, "my client here is not guilty of any crime because he couldn't help himself. He had eaten so many Twinkies, and he had so much sugar in his brain that he lost control." In other words, his brain secreted the thought to kill another person, and for this defense the lawyer expected absolute clemency for his client.

In fact, the lawyer's case was entirely consistent with the materialistic evolutionary thinking of our day that says that man is not responsible for what he thinks. You can neither control your thoughts any more than you can control your bile, nor are you responsible for anything that you think. This is simply the inevitable conclusion that must be drawn from the materialistic, evolutionist view of man. When you take God and the Bible out of the equation, this is all that is left. And furthermore, it is not possible for such a creature to develop a moral code. The very idea is absurd!

THE MISSING LINK

But the missing link that the scientists have overlooked over the past hundred-fifty years is not to be found through DNA or paleontology or geology. The missing link in the history of man is the Creator who made us and who ordained every aspect of our being and every element of our emotions—our minds, our souls, our beings. In short, God is the Creator of all the ingredients of life that make "character" possible. The ancient Scripture known as the Shema, which dates back fourteen-hundred years before Christ, declares, "Hear, O Israel: The LORD our God, the LORD is one" (Deut. 6:4). There is but one God, who is righteous enough, who is powerful enough, and who is wise and loving enough to be able to create not only all of mankind, but the moral code by which we must live.

But wonder of wonders! Not only has God created such a moral code, but He has also revealed that law to us through divine revelation, through the words of the prophets, and through the revelations of Scripture. Furthermore, He has even made a way of redemption and forgiveness for those who have broken His laws—even to those who have despised and rejected Him. He has condescended to send His own Son into the world to be the only One who has ever lived perfectly by His moral code. But this righteous and holy Creator is also the just and holy God who demands that the price of sin must be paid. There is no exception. Sin must exact a penalty under God's law, just as the law of man demands a penalty.

But most awesome of all, this same God was also willing to send His own Son to the cross to endure capital punishment for the crimes that you and I have committed against Him. There, upon the cross of ancient Judea, all our transgressions, all our sins, all our iniquities, and all our violations of His moral code were heaped upon Jesus Christ. And the Savior of mankind endured in His body and within His soul the infinite wrath of God Almighty, paying the penalty for our sins, and He endured hell and was separated from God the Father until, as He had promised, He rose again after three days and declared victory over sin.

God declared through the prophets for thousands of years that any person who would believe in His Son, who would accept His gift of salvation, would also find forgiveness for his sins. The man, woman, and boy, or girl who says Yes to God's offer of forgiveness will hear the Savior's declaration, "Pardoned from all of your sins." And the new child of God will be clothed in the perfect righteousness of Jesus Christ, faultless, to stand before the very throne of God.

Does all this sound too fantastic to be true? Does it sound too far out for the humanist perspective of the modern age? The modern humanist says we are slime—meaningless tissue that somehow thinks and acts and breeds by some unfathomable chain of meaningless events. Or does the good news of God's plan for mankind, in fact, sound like the only way this terror-filled and self-destructive world can ever hope to survive?

As we have seen, character is behavior that demands inner strength, integrity, and moral fiber. But God is the only one who can create a moral code, and God is the only one who can forgive those who violate it. But what we must understand is that every one of us has violated God's moral code. In the end, no amount of personal integrity is adequate to pay for the sins we have committed. There is no exception. We are all guilty. The entire world is guilty and beyond hope in the eyes of a perfectly righteous Creator God.

The apostle Paul said, "There is no one righteous, not even one" (Rom. 3:10). Therefore, how marvelous that, by the grace of God, He would show us His unmerited favor. How incomprehensible that God would invite us to come to the cross of Christ and find forgiveness and mercy in a time such as this. How awesome that He would fill us with the strength of clear judgment and moral fortitude that allows us to overcome our sinful natures and become the children of God. My friend, this is the cure for America's dis-ease. In the warfare for the soul of this nation, this is the only medication that can heal our wounds.

FROM THE BOTTOM UP

No other means of addressing the crying problems of our age will suffice. There are no other means to touch the intangible corners of the human soul with all its intricacies of emotion, heredity, and experience. Until we come back to some fundamental understanding of the moral dimensions of human nature, the hope of restoring personal responsibility and virtuous character in the men, women, and children of this nation will be in vain. Yet character remains a major issue of concern today, and it is a concern that reaches from the bottom to the top of this nation.

Contrary to the suggestion of the moral relativists who insist that character is individual and not universal, the management specialist and sociologist

James Q. Wilson writes in his book, *The Moral Sense*, that character is a universal quality that does not change from place to place. People may change and circumstances may change, but character is consistent. It is never a matter of purely local custom, as the sociologists have said. In fact, Wilson suggests that if you doubt this fact, then go to any distant and exotic land of your choice and seek to employ a craftsman of some kind—gardener, carpenter, tailor, or anything else—and inquire about the person's suitability for the job.

"You will discover," the author says, "general agreement in those places as to who is and who is not excellent at these crafts, and their qualities of excellence will not be limited to technical skill but also embrace dependability, fair dealing, and an interest in your wishes." Echoing the words of Aristotle, Wilson says that, "A good character arises from the repetition of many small acts and begins early in youth." And because the traits of a good character are universal, reaching from the bottom to the top of all social strata, these key characteristics are just as visible in children as in adults. In making the relationship between character and morals in young people, Wilson adds:

> A moral life is perfected by practice more than by precept; children are not taught so much as habituated. In this sense the schools inevitably teach morality, whether they intend to or not, by such behavior as they reward or punish. A school reinforces the better moral nature of a pupil to the extent it insists on the habitual performance of duties, including the duty to deal fairly with others, to discharge one's own responsibilities, and to defer the satisfaction of immediate and base motives in favor of more distant and nobler ones.[5]

Almost universally, parents and educators recognize the truth of these statements, yet the teachers' unions and the liberal establishment in this country resist the idea of moral education. The result is only too clear, as we have seen throughout this study. Children deprived of character education become the animals that the evolutionists and atheists have programmed them to be.

In his important book, *Educating for Character*, author Thomas Lickona says that education in morality and good character are essential concerns of a democratic society. From the foundations of this country, our great leaders have understood that only a citizenry educated with moral standards will be capable of exercising their rights and demanding excellence in all things. Lickona says the reasoning of the founders was that Democracy is government by the people; the people themselves are responsible for ensuring a free and just society. That means the people must, at least in some minimal sense, be good. They must understand and be committed to the moral foundations of democracy: respect for the rights of individuals, regard for law, voluntary participation in public life, and concern for the common good. Loyalty to these democratic virtues, Thomas Jefferson argued, must be instilled at an early age.[6]

Based on that belief and a general moral sense embodied by the Protestant work ethic, previous generations tackled "character education" head-on. Strict discipline, the good example of teachers and other leaders, a curriculum that focused on moral behavior, and through their insistence on patriotism, hard work, honesty, thrift, altruism, and courage, young men and women were fully prepared to tackle any challenge by the time they finished the eighth grade. And many, in earlier days, made it no further. But even those who left school early were not handicapped by a lack of character. The system had already seen to that.

THE DEATH OF VIRTUE

When children read aloud in class or when they practiced on their own time, they read from *McGuffey's Reader*. Chock-full of tales of virtue, heroism, and noble sacrifice, this classic volume taught our parents and grandparents what it really meant to be honorable American citizens. By 1919, Lickona says, *McGuffey's Reader* was second in sales only to the Bible. Children disciplined in this book understood virtue, moral convictions, and the importance of making right choices. But moral education throughout all those years was never limited to the church. It was not something that mothers and fathers had to teach in their spare time. It was, by intention, a part of the public school curriculum, as it should be again today.

It was not until public education "experts" such as John Dewey, of Columbia University Teachers College, began to respond to "social forces" such as Darwinism, Einstein's theory of relativity, and the psychotechnics of Freud that things began to change for the worse. Dewey, Horace Mann, and their disciples taught that "right and wrong are also relative." They trotted out the old axiom that said, "One man's meat is another man's poison." And gradually the flood of moral relativism in the schools submerged and drowned the noble institutions that had been the mainstays of character education.

In the 1920s, Lickona tells us, two Yale University psychologists, Hugh Hartshorne and Mark May, conducted a study of 10,000 children who were put into situations in which they had the option of lying, cheating, or stealing instead of doing what they had been instructed to do. Based on their findings, the two men produced what they called the "doctrine of specificity," which said that honest behavior is highly variable and always depends on the situation in which people find themselves. This was a foreshadowing of what would come to be known as "situational ethics." The theory had many flaws and was, in fact, inconclusive. But when the headlines hit the newspapers of the day, what was most often reported was that *character is relative* and moral behavior varies from child to child. This was to become one of the most destructive weapons in the arsenal leveled against character education in this country. And today, except for New Age curricula and trendy pop psychology such as "Values Clarification," which is amoral in context, character education is no longer offered.

What has been the result of this situation? A study at the University of Southern California reports that employee theft today costs department stores and specialty chains a minimum of sixteen million dollars a day. In a survey conducted by *Psychology Today* magazine of twenty-four thousand readers in the early 1980s, forty-one percent admitted to having driven their car while drunk; thirty-three percent had lied to their best friends; thirty-eight percent had cheated on their income tax returns; and forty-five percent had committed adultery.

But there were two other findings of this study that should be mentioned. The researchers also asked the respondents to indicate whether or not they held any religious convictions. What they found was that the more religious the respondents were, the less likely they were to engage in bad behavior. And secondly, they found that the older the respondents were the less likely they were to engage in such activities. The analysts attributed the tendency to steal, lie, or cheat to the influence of the "new morality" in the schools. As religious instruction declined—especially among the younger respondents who had not grown up in churches—the likelihood that the person would participate in antisocial behavior increased. Those who had been taught Christian values were the most honest.

Among the social problems that concern us most today, Lickona offers an insightful analysis that demonstrates just how pervasive these ten symptoms have become:

1. Violence and vandalism
2. Stealing

3. Cheating
4. Disrespect for authority
5. Peer cruelty
6. Bigotry
7. Bad language
8. Sexual precocity and abuse
9. Increasing self-centeredness and declining civic responsibility
10. Self-destructive behavior[7]

The author details each of these behaviors with statistics and examples that reveal just how much the legacy of modern "value-neutral education" has impoverished the souls of the young. This is the inevitable fallout of the devaluation of character and moral behavior that follows the liberal doctrines of Dewey, Mann, and their ideological successors who have taken over control of the nation's public schools. When any nation expels God from the schools, every manner of evil will come right in. The evidence is only too clear.

IMPLICATIONS OF CHARACTER

Where does such character deficiency lead? In a column in *Time* magazine, Hugh Sidey observed that one reason the Clinton presidential campaign took to the highways in its bus caravan in the fall of 1992 was to reach out to the common people. As Sidey said, "to see and be seen, to talk about 'putting people first,' to point out idled steel mills and troubled coal mines." Already mired in charges about the candidate's moral values, the Gennifer Flowers episode, and suggestions of marital infidelity, the Democratic Party had hoped that after a good long tour of the farmers' markets, watermelon stands, and feedlots of America's heartland, they might emerge "at least partly cleansed of the dread questions about Bill Clinton's character."

But, the journalist adds, "The ringing convention testimony to Clinton's strength of character seemed a little too orchestrated for comfort." If there was nothing to hide, then why did the Democrats protest so often and so loudly? "Like it or not," said Sidey, "we are launched on a season of character analysis. Certainly in this business of judging a potential President there is a general standard, though vague, of decency, intelligence, honesty and courage that the person must have. But watch out after that. There is a portion of the character of any President, never glimpsed before, that emerges under the pressures of his office."

As the nation and the world have observed the bizarre sequence of events surrounding the death of Vincent Foster and the related Whitewater investigation, Sidey's comments now seem prophetic. Indeed, the pressures of high office brought forth a side of the new president that most of the nation found startling and unsettling. Only time will tell how these issues will pan out, but I predict that it will come down to an issue of character. It always does.

And Sidey's point, like mine, is that character must be a critical concern of every great nation, and there is absolutely nothing "relative" about right and wrong. If lying, cheating, adultery, and drunkenness are wrong in one situation, they are wrong in all situations. And if honesty, fidelity, chastity, and sobriety are expected from one member of society, they should be expected from every member—from the bottom to the top of the system. No one is exempt from the need to behave in a socially and morally responsible manner—especially when that person attains high public office.

In their best-selling book, *Teaching Your Children Values*, Linda and Richard Eyre offer a wonderful suggestion to parents for helping their children understand the moral implications of their decisions. This technique was common when my daughter was small, but it has been lost over the years. They suggest that parents teach their children to memorize the letters *W.W.J.D.* And whenever children do something especially nice, the members of the family may want to give them a "W.W.J.D. Award" to recognize their good behavior. W.W.J.D. stands for "What Would Jesus Do?" And the idea is that, in any ethical situation where you're not sure which way to turn, just ask yourself, "What would Jesus do?"

If your children know about Jesus and the things He taught during his life on earth, chances are they'll know what the right thing to do should be. But I add that, if Jesus is in the life of your child and you encourage him or her to live as Jesus would expect, then that child will already be a long way down the road to developing a good character.

As we turn now to further consideration of the battle for America's soul, we must not forget the role that character plays in our choices. The Greek philosopher, Heraclitus, said, "Character is destiny." Until this nation renews its concern for character and the moral values upon which character depends, the warfare for our souls will be desperate indeed.

NOTES

[1]Os Guinness, *The American Hour: A Time of Reckoning and the Once and Future Role of Faith* (New York: Macmillan Free Press, 1993), 398.

[2]Ibid., 398.

[3]Ibid., 363.

[4]Lutzer, 54.

[5]James Q. Wilson, *The Moral Sense* (New York: Macmillan Free Press, 1993), 249.

[6]Thomas Lickona, *Educating for Character: How Our Schools Can Teach Respect and Responsibility* (New York: Bantam, 1992), 6.

[7]Lickona, see especially pages 13–22 for supporting documentation and the very informative analysis of these data.

10

In Search of a Soul

Harvard Medical School's Dr. Herbert Benson, a cardiologist who practices at Deaconess Hospital in Boston, encourages all his patients to pray and meditate because, whatever their faith or beliefs, he has found that people who pray heal faster. According to a study conducted at San Francisco General Hospital, patients heal faster even when the prayers come from other people, and when the patient has no idea anyone is praying. All across America, alcoholics, drug addicts, and people suffering with various kinds of stress are turning to twelve-step programs such as Alcoholics Anonymous and Al-Anon where they are challenged to seek help from a "higher power." Everywhere you look, God is making a comeback, and sometimes in a big way.

According to surveys by Gallup and the National Opinion Research Council (NORC) in 1992, ninety-one percent of women and eighty-five percent of men in this country say they pray regularly. That includes ninety-four percent of blacks and eighty-seven percent of whites. While thirty-two percent report that prayer simply gives them a deep sense of peace, twenty-six percent said they sense the actual presence of God in their prayers, and fifteen percent regularly receive definite answers to their prayers. Only twelve percent said they feel nothing.

THE RISE OF RELIGION

Everywhere you look these days it is clear that religion is on the rise in America. Just glancing through the best-seller lists in any newspaper or magazine, you cannot help but see that the nation is preoccupied by a fascination with "spirituality." In mid-1994, there were a dozen separate books on spiritual matters, vying for space at the top of the list. Former Secretary of Education William Bennett's new book, *The Book of Virtues*, is a work that includes classic stories and readings on traditional and Christian moral values. It hovered near the top of the charts for several weeks, while Thomas Moore's *Care of the Soul* and Scott Peck's *The Road Less Traveled* remained among the "mainstream" favorites. New Age readers flocked to such hot sellers as *Where Angels Walk*, *The Celestine Prophecy*, *Embraced by the Light*, *Touched by Angels*, and Karen Armstrong's *A History of God*. And the religious book lists featured titles that in many cases outsold the secular competition by hundreds of thousands of copies.

An Associated Press feature in the fall of 1993 reported that there is a new surge of political activism in America that has brought a wide spectrum of Christians and other conservatives into the political arena who, in the past, had simply trusted someone else to deal with the crisis of values in this country. The obvious decline of culture, and especially the election of Bill Clinton, inspired tens of thousands to get active and to put their faith on the line. The Christian Right, the reporter said, is energized as never before, and the non-Christian Left is afraid we're trying to take over. "At issue in this debate," the article reported, "is the public soul-searching over the most divisive of political issues—abortion, homosexuality, sex education, censorship, pornography, school prayer."

The article goes on to quote many leaders on both sides of the debate—from the Christian Coalition to the People for the American Way—and even cites one of my own comments in a ministry newsletter in which I said, "We can't let a misguided army of liberals and homosexuals make a mockery of our country, a mockery of our moral values, a mockery of God's laws." Even though the AP writer could barely disguise his personal feeling that people who hold religious values have no place in the public square, he made it clear that there is an unprecedented surge of religious sentiment in this nation today and that Christians are engaged in a big way.

In just the past year we have seen major cover stories in *Time, Newsweek,* and *U.S. News & World Report* that have focused on "prayer" and issues of "church and state." And along with two recent cover stories in *Life* magazine entitled "The Power of Prayer: How Americans Talk to God" and "Do You Believe in Miracles?" it is apparent that the focus of so much attention on religion is a sure sign that we are a nation in search of a soul.

Perhaps the most surprising finding of the recent surveys conducted by the Barna Research Group of California is the fact that eighty-three percent of Americans now believe that "man is basically good." In light of all the evil we see in our world today, and in light of the Bible's teaching that man is inherently sinful by nature, I find that to be an astonishing discovery. The philosophers and utopians of the French Enlightenment argued that man is a "noble savage." Rousseau's famous remark was that "Man is born free, and everywhere he is in chains." Sure enough, during the last two centuries we have seen a lot of the "savage" side and not much of the "noble."

Additionally, the idea that man is "basically good" is contrary to the historic beliefs of Western civilization. An understanding of the fact that we are born with sinful natures was one of the main factors that prompted our forefathers to become moral people, to take religion and moral instruction seriously, and to achieve great feats of intellect and technology. So where did all these people—the eighty-three percent in the Barna surveys—get the idea that man is basically good?

Dr. Karl Menninger, the famed founder of the Menninger Psychiatric Clinic, wrote a book some years ago entitled *Whatever Became of Sin?* in which he offered some challenging observations about the basic sin nature of mankind. He said that the word "sin" was a good strong word at one time and we all knew what it meant. But today, it seems, we never hear the word "sin" mentioned anymore. Not in school, not in public life, and seldom even in the churches. In one of his early speeches, President Dwight Eisenhower made a passing reference to sin when quoting Abraham Lincoln, who said we should repent of our sins and turn to the Almighty. But after that time, Eisenhower never mentioned it again, nor did the three succeeding presidents. Menninger said, "So, as a nation, we officially ceased 'sinning' some twenty years ago." What other conclusion could he draw from the facts?

Certainly, if you were to take the word of the media today, you would suppose that sin has ceased to exist in America. The word is never mentioned anymore. You can see an awful lot of sin on your television screen; there is plenty of sin described in gory detail in the newspapers and magazines; and the movies and amusements that occupy so many people's lives are filled with the imagery of sin: but it's never called "sin" any more. It is called personal freedom, self-expression, choice, and harmless entertainment.

NOT SIN, JUST DUMB!

In a *Newsweek* article entitled "Why Nothing Is 'Wrong' Anymore," Meg Greenfield says that a long time ago we used to have something called "right and wrong." It was very clear. Everybody knew what was "right" and what was "wrong," "but we don't seem to use the word 'wrong' anymore"—much less the word "sin." In fact, today, she says, "we have developed a broad range of alternatives to 'right and wrong.'" People will accept "right and stupid," for example. They can accept the idea that they occasionally make harmful choices that are just plain "stupid." But "wrong"? We don't talk about the fact that something may be wrong or sinful. We much prefer "dumb."

"Magic" Johnson, applauded all over our country for his athletic prowess, was a veritable ballet dancer in basketball shoes. He dropped balls in hoops the way some of us drop doughnuts in coffee cups—with great ease. But when he made the "brave" announcement that he had tested positive for the HIV virus in mid-1991, what he actually said was, not that he had done anything wrong but that he was "dumb"! He should have practiced "safe sex." There was nothing immoral about what he did! Heaven forbid! It wasn't sinful, just dumb!

How did the press react to Johnson's shocking announcement? *USA Today* reported that the story of Johnson's infection and the way he dealt with it was the "overwhelming choice as the Associated Press sports story of the year." But that wasn't all. A related story in that national newspaper said, "If Magic Johnson is a hero and inspiration to kids, promoting compassion for all through his positive attitude toward adversity, then Linda Ellerbee should be ordained their patron saint of common sense and plain talk." Why should a controversial liberal news pundit be a saint? Because in her televised special with the basketball star, she told millions of American kids, "You don't go to heaven if you die dumb."

"That's what this show is about," she told the nation, "not being dumb." And the *USA Today* reporter went on to say that "*Nickelodeon*, cable's boldest harbor for kids' media-savvy sensibilities, knew what it was doing when it hired Ellerbee to produce no-nonsense news fare for its audience." In other words, they knew that Ellerbee would never say that promiscuity is a sin: She would tell the world that "unprotected sex is just dumb."[1]

I was even more disturbed by one local commentator who, waxing euphoric about the star's courage in the face of death from AIDS infection, said, "Young people, keep your eyes on Magic. Listen to what he says." What does he say? Is he telling young people to "flee from sin"? Is he saying, "Stay away from fornication"? Has he told the young people of the nation, "Look at my example, kids, and keep away from lust and all those other forms of immorality that can kill you"? No. Unfortunately, he didn't say any of those things. He said, "Practice safe sex!"

It seems today that we are no longer concerned with whether or not something is sinful, wrong, or immoral. The only thing we are concerned about is that it is safe. People in America want to have "safe sex" so that they won't have any of those unpleasant aftereffects. They want safe divorces, safe suicides, and safe abortions. Nobody would ever suggest that sex outside of marriage is immoral or that abortions are actually murder! They just want to have them safe and neat and not in some messy back alley where it might be "unsafe" to murder a child. They want approval by the courts and the laws so they can have the nice clinical safe ones.

Safe "euthanasia" and "safe suicides" are becoming more and more popular. Derek Humphry told us in his two books on the subject that "do it yourself" suicide can be awfully messy—sometimes you just foul the whole thing up and you . . . you live! So we need a loved one, a close companion, or possibly a professional like "Doctor Assisted Suicide," Dr. Jack Kevorkian, standing by to make sure we get the job done. Nobody asks if suicide is murder. Nobody asks if euthanasia is a good idea. They just want it to be "safe."

We have lost the concept of right and wrong, of sin and righteousness. So things are "right and stupid," says Meg Greenfield. Or maybe, she suggests, they're just "right and sick." They're not wrong, they're just sick. Sin can never be evil, so it must be sick. Earlier I discussed Dr. Charles Sykes' book, *A Nation of Victims*, in which he describes the rise of psychology in this country and the "therapeutic culture" it has spawned. The psychiatrists will tell us that sickness is a much healthier way to describe our destructive pathologies. It would never do to call them sin.

When somebody shoots a president or murders a half a dozen people in a public restaurant, the public will say, "He must be sick." There is no thought of "punishment" for such crimes. Instead, society demands that we put such people in a hospital where they can be cared for and restored to emotional health. After all, people are basically good. The psychiatrist and the bleeding hearts tell us, "This poor fellow must be sick. But when he gets well, he'll be good as new."

THE CARE OF THE SOUL

Whatever happened to right and wrong, and whatever happened to sin? If we want to know about the basic goodness of man, we should turn first to the Word of God and the lessons of Scripture. From start to finish, the Bible tells us about the blessings of God that are heaped upon the righteous and the damnation that comes upon the sinful and unrepentant. Throughout history, great men and women of the ages have understood that the care of the soul is a matter of confession and humility before God. God can remake an evil heart; He can restore the wounded and bring about wonderful renewal. But renewal always begins with repentance. That is the essence of being "born again."

I think it is especially interesting to note that the greatest saints down through the centuries have all acknowledged themselves to be the greatest of sinners. St. Augustine's book, *Confessions*, is a diary of the progress of the soul from a life of self-indulgence to a life of devotion to God. It is one of the most moving testimonies ever written and is often considered to be second only to the Bible as a work of spiritual inspiration. What the confessions of the great saints tell us is that the closer we draw to the Light of God's perfect truth, the more clearly we see our uncleanness and sin.

The Scripture teaches that man is not good by nature; Christ taught that the heart of man is filled with deceit; and history confirms that man is definitely not "basically good." Anthropologists tell us that one-third of all human beings who have lived on this planet have died at the hands of their brothers—that fully one-third of the human race have died through war, violence, crime, and sudden death at the hands of another human being. If that sounds unbelievable, just consider the atrocities that have been committed in this century alone.

We have seen the Spanish Civil War in which tens of thousands died on both sides; the Nazi Holocaust that killed fifteen million civilians and six million ethnic Jews; two world wars in which as many as twenty million perished, along with tens of thousands of deaths in the prison camps of Germany and Japan. We have now learned of the Gulag Archipelago; the Stalinist purges in which as many as twenty million were murdered or starved to death in prison camps; the ravages of Idi Amin in Uganda who killed as many as three hundred thousand of his own people; and the systematic butchery of more than a million Cambodians by Pol Pot during his four-year reign of terror. Today we see the ongoing massacres in Bosnia and Eastern Europe, as well as in Africa, Asia, and the Middle East.

The brutal massacre of three hundred students and pro-democracy demonstrators at Tiananmen Square in 1989 was only a tiny reflection of the more than thirty-five million Chinese murdered by the Chinese Communists since the beginning of their "Great Proletarian Cultural Revolution." These and many other atrocities make it hard to maintain any pretense that man is inherently good. And it is utterly astonishing to me that anybody with an ounce of sense could hold such a position in light of the history of our race.

Mike Wallace of *60 Minutes* did a story some years ago about Adolf Eichmann, one of the chief architects of the Nazi Holocaust. In that program, Wallace interviewed a survivor of the death camps—a former Jewish prisoner by the name of Yehiel Dinur. Wallace showed Dinur a film clip from the Nuremberg Trials when Dinur came forward to testify against Eichmann. The clip showed Dinur walking into the courtroom, past the box where Eichmann was seated, then turning and looking at him. As he stared at the prisoner, the Jewish man suddenly began to sob uncontrollably, and then a moment later, he fell to the floor in a dead faint.

What had happened? Was Dinur overcome by his hatred? Fear? Terrible memories? No, it was none of these, he said. He told the CBS interviewer that when he looked into the eyes of that terrible murderer, all at once he understood that Eichmann was not the godlike SS officer who had sent so many millions to their deaths. He saw that Adolf Eichmann was an ordinary man. "I was afraid about myself," he explained. "I saw that I am capable to do this. I am . . . exactly like him." Wallace's summation of Dinur's terrible discovery was that "Eichmann is in all of us."

Not only does history attest to it, but the Bible declares it, and Christ affirms it. Jesus said, "All these evils come from inside and make a man 'unclean'" (Mark 7:23). There is a dark and dangerous nature in the heart of man. Even common sense ought to confirm that fact. The evidence of corruption is all too apparent.

EVIDENCE OF CORRUPTION

You don't need to be a historian; all you need is the front page of your local newspaper. By simply going through a few copies of our daily papers in South Florida anyone could find enough to build a pretty solid case against the human race. If man is basically good—as eighty-three percent of Americans apparently believe—why would twenty-three churches have been burned to the ground by arsonists in Florida in less than one year?

Why, if man is basically good, would an intelligent graduate student, jealous of an academic honor bestowed upon a friend, take a gun and shoot his friend along with four others and then kill himself?

Why, if man is basically good, would two angry young men make a video showing themselves with a roomful of stolen goods, bragging, "We're high school dropouts and we steal for a living"? Why, if man is basically good, are a hundred-thousand brochures being distributed in South Florida warning tourists, "If you have a rented car, don't get lost"? Why, if man is basically good, did a woman leave her months-old baby in a garbage can? And why, if man is basically good, were sixteen people murdered in a single year in convenience stores in the state of Florida alone?

The list is endless, and the evidence of the case doesn't stop in my home state. If man is basically good, we need to ask why there is such a growing demand for home-alarm systems? Why did Jeffrey Dahmer, in Milwaukee, kill, dismember and even eat parts of seventeen victims in his apartment? Indeed, even common sense would seem to stand up and shout that man is *not* basically good.

We see a policeman standing on the corner. Why? Is it to help the basically good people across the street? Or is it to go into the bank with you to help you deposit your check? At the bank you will notice the eighteen-inch-thick steel doors that guard the vault where your money is going to be kept at night. Notice the alarm buttons on the floor by the teller's cage. Why all these safety features if man is basically good?

If you stop by the vice president's office to ask for a loan, I assure you that you are going to raise the whole question of original sin in that man's mind. He is going to have some very penetrating questions to ask you about your honesty and your good behavior. None of those questions would even be needed if man were basically good.

Or look at Uncle Sam. He has a little bit more of a level-headed idea about our capacity for evil. Otherwise, why would the government spend billions of dollars on courts, judges, prosecutors, jails, and prisons? Why have we spent trillions of dollars on national defense? Is it to protect us from all those basically good folks out there? Every nuclear missile and every underground silo is a silent and eloquent testimony to the fact that man is basically evil.

How in the world could so many people have become so deceived, even denying the very foundations of this country? One thing is absolutely certain: the founding fathers of this country—to a man—knew that men were evil. Because they knew that men were evil, they believed the truth of Lord Acton's statement: "Power corrupts and absolute power corrupts absolutely." Therefore, they designed a system in which it would be very difficult for too much power to ever be consolidated in too few hands.

As I discussed in the first section of this book, the federal government was divided into three parts—the executive, judicial, and legislative branches—to ensure that no man and no group of men could ever gain a monopoly on power. More than that, the powers of government were to be divided between the federal government and the several states, and those powers not specified by the Constitution were to be reserved unto the people. Even more than that, the powers of the federal government were to be definitely limited and specifically enumerated.

The system of "checks and balances"—including the veto, the power of the Congress to override a veto, and the authority of the courts to challenge laws that they found to be unconstitutional acts of Congress— were all adopted as central features of the United States Constitution, because, as Jeremiah says, "The heart is deceitful above all things and beyond cure. Who can understand it?" (Jer. 17:9).

THE FOLLY OF DECEIT

Today millions of Americans are being misled and deceived by false teachers and false prophets of every description, and from every direction. Movements promising inner healing and "transcendence" are everywhere, and the bottom line is profit and power. Unless we understand that the doctrine of the "nobility of man" is actually a very dangerous deception designed to disguise the wickedness and the deceit in the human heart, then the time is not far off when some benevolent dictator will come forth to take away our liberties and take over every aspect of our lives. If that sounds far-fetched, just remember what happened in the French Revolution. The lesson is much the same, and the dangers today are far greater.

I recognize, of course, that it feels good for our egos to be told that we're such good and honorable people. But an old maxim says, "I would rather believe the most miserable fact than to be deceived by the merriest lie." And that, indeed, is the situation we face today. The condition of the human heart, short of the cleansing and renewal offered only by faith in Christ, is a miserable fact of existence, and to suggest anything else is hypocrisy and deceit.

Chuck Colson said, "In recent decades, popular political and social beliefs have all but erased the reality of personal sin from our national consciousness." How true. We are told that evil is not in us but in society. The American playwright William Saroyan put the secular view succinctly: "Every man is a good man in a bad world, as he himself knows." The evil is out there somewhere. It's out there in the world at large. It's in society. It's in the way we are manipulated by public figures and by big ideas.

The problem, then, is to identify the evil in the world and to repress any suggestion that there may be evil in the heart of man. The secularist's goal is to purge the world of religion—to keep prayer and Bible study out of the schools, to keep religious language and principles out of the government and the universities, and to make sure that any evidence of belief in God or some transcendent vision of faith in Jesus Christ is kept out of public view. The job is to focus all our attention on the innate goodness within us.

But there is one serious flaw in this secular ideology. Speaking a lie does not make it true. And wickedness still resides in the hearts of mankind. Dr. Louis Evans puts it very well when he says, "You can take the man out of the slums, but only God can take the slums out of the man." The problem lies in the human heart, as the eagle eye of Christ surely saw when He said that "out of men's hearts, come evil thoughts, sexual immorality, theft, murder, adultery, greed, malice, deceit, lewdness, envy, slander, arrogance and folly" (Mark 7:21–22). It is out of the heart that the evil of this world comes, and it is only by changing the heart that we have hope.

But even though we have the reality of sin and the ramifications and the consequences all around us, we also have, thank God, the possibility of redemption from sin through faith in Christ. Jesus Christ, whom God has set forth to be a propitiation and to take away the sin of the world, is the answer to the wickedness in the hearts of men. When John the Baptist first saw Him coming across that plain along the Jordan valley, he said, "Look, the Lamb of God, who takes away the sin of the world!" (John 1:29).

We are born in a fallen state, a state of sin and depravity. But we have been assured that God loved the world so much that He gave His only begotten Son as a sacrifice for our sin, and God was willing to take all of that sin and to place it upon His Son. God was willing to punish that sin—not by casting us into hell, which we rightfully deserve, but by condemning His own beloved Son to die upon a cross. God was willing to take that blood and cleanse us and to make us whiter than snow. When *Life* magazine asked its readers if they believe in miracles, any true believer would have to say Yes for this reason if for no other. That God would send His Son to die for our sins has to be the greatest miracle known to man.

John wrote in his first letter to the churches that, "If we claim we have not sinned, we make [God] out to be a liar and his word has no place in our lives" (1 John 1:10). But when we deny that we are basically sinful, we also cut ourselves off from the redemption of Christ. Jesus Christ came, as He said, to save that which was lost. He came to save sinners. He said, "I have not come to call the righteous, but sinners" (Matt. 9:13).

JOURNEY ON THE DARK SIDE

In the very midst of the movement back to God and the attempt to find some sort of transcendence—and while there is some vague notion of "spirituality" in the public mind—there is also a dark side to the spiritual pilgrimage being taken by many people in this land. I am happy to say that we still live in a nation that stands firmly against bigotry and prejudice and racial intolerance, but I am sad to say that there is a new form of bigotry and hatred for Christians, Christianity, and for Christ. Michael Novak, the distinguished columnist who recently won the Templeton Award and its one-million-dollar prize for his writings on religion, once said that it is not possible in this culture today to hold up to public pillory and ridicule any group—whether blacks, American Indians, women, homosexuals, Poles, or any of a number of other groups that have been discriminated against in the past. However, the one group you *can* hold up to public mockery and pillory without fear of reprisal is evangelical Christians.

Can anyone deny the truth of his statement? Our daily newspapers take strong editorial positions against all forms of bigotry and prejudice, yet they think nothing of assaulting Christians and labeling us as bigots, racists, hate-mongers, and misogynists. In Florida, the local daily harbors on its editorial staff one of the most virulent, prejudiced, and hate-filled anti-

Christian bigots in the nation. This is a man who cannot go more than a week without emptying his bile in some fashion against Christians, Christianity, or the various leaders of the church.

Pat Buchanan said that Christian-bashing has become a major sport in America. This hasn't always been true. Until about twenty years ago, the major Hollywood studios regularly produced major films about great Bible stories, the lives of the saints and martyrs, and classic adventures in which Charlton Heston, Kirk Douglas, or Tyrone Power portrayed the great patriarchs or heroes of the faith. Christians were always presented in a positive light, and Jesus Christ was only mentioned reverently. But today, even Christ—the crystal Christ, the spotless and holy Savior, the loving and compassionate Son of God, the only perfect and pure person ever to grace this planet—is held up to savage scorn and mockery.

Just recently on a TV series, a young actress (to whom I will not grant further publicity by naming her) had a role in which she had to take a crucifix and spit on the figure of Christ. Later, she was asked how she felt about doing that, and she said, "I'm an atheist, so it was actually a joy." Spitting in the face of Christ was her idea of fun. And of course, we have been exposed repeatedly to the blasphemies of Andres Serrano and his supporters in the media. This so-called artist, with the support and encouragement of the National Endowment for the Arts, made photographs that were vulgar and sacrilegious, including a crucifix, an image of Christ on the cross, submerged in a glass of the artist's urine. But when the Christian community all across the nation rose up in outrage, bringing pressure against the NEA and government-funding agencies, the press and the liberal elite immediately labeled us as bigots, homophobes, and fear-mongers who were trying to censor creative expression.

Then, of course, we learned of the infamous film, *Last Temptation of Christ*, which took every vile accusation that the most wicked of atheists and unbelievers have ever imputed to Christ and showed them coming out of the mouth of our Lord as self-confessions of a sinful Savior. Through the mouth of an actor, Jesus Christ, the beloved Son of God, was made to say, "I hate God. The Devil lives within me. I constantly lust after women, and the only thing that prevents my consummation of that lust is that I am a coward." Jesus, pure and spotless—Jesus, who had the courage to set His face as flint unto Jerusalem and willingly go to the cross to save mankind from certain destruction—was depicted by evil men as impure and cowardly and filled with lust. Yes, it is unbelievable, but it is being done, and to the great applause of the secular establishment.

We have heard about another film production, apparently made in Canada, which presents Christ as a homosexual. To the pure all things are pure, and to the impure, all things are impure. The attempt to produce such blasphemy simply proves the truth of the Scripture, which says, "since they did not think it worthwhile to retain the knowledge of God, he gave them over to a depraved mind, to do what ought not to be done. They have become filled with every kind of wickedness, evil, greed and depravity. They are full of envy, murder, strife, deceit and malice. They are gossips, slanderers, God-haters, insolent, arrogant and boastful; they invent ways of doing evil; they disobey their parents; they are senseless, faithless, heartless, ruthless" (Rom. 1:28–31).

I also read recently that a law that has been passed in Canada forbidding ministers to preach the Gospel on television. A number of studios where ministry broadcasts were being produced were invaded by the police, records were confiscated and equipment taken, and some ministers were thrown into jail for speaking the Word of God.

THE WAR AGAINST GOD

There is no denying that, in spite of the spiritual hunger of the age, there is an all-out war against Christianity, and it is heating up again in America with much the same ferocity we witnessed in World War II, or that we are seeing today in our neighboring country. And if you are trying to carry on your daily life without alarm, thinking that the prejudice and bigotry will surely go away on their own, then please don't forget where these things can lead. Before a single finger was raised against the Jews in Nazi Germany, before a single family was dragged off to the boxcars, and even before the ovens of Auschwitz were heated up to receive those innocent victims of the Holocaust, there was first an intense propaganda campaign against the Jews not very much different from the media's war against the church in this country today.

Hitler, Goebbels, and Goering first instigated a media blitz against the Jews, calling them the offscouring of the earth. They wrote books and articles against this entire race of people, calling them enemies of Germany who were preventing the progress of the nation. Consequently, when the actual "final solution" was introduced, the people of Germany and Austria had already been prepared by waves of negative, hate-filled propaganda to believe that the eradication of the Jewish nation was for the good of the fatherland.

In recent television programs and motion pictures, Christians have been portrayed as bigots and censors. They are shown to be intolerant, narrow-minded, and ignorant. Those who sincerely believe that Jesus Christ is the way, the truth, and the life are portrayed as a threat to freedom. We are the ones who are a threat to the very well-being of all those decent Americans who just want to live in peace and attain the essential goodness of their human nature. And this is the point at which the view that man is "basically good" has its most damaging impact. Those who want to pursue their own passions do not want Christians to stand in the way. Christians believe in God's standards. They believe that Jesus Christ will soon come in splendor to judge the nations. Our views are absolutely counter to the secular mind-set, and the wicked of this world will not be satisfied until we are silenced once and for all.

We still live in a country with a two-party political system, but as one writer has said, we have a "one-party media." Unlike most countries in the world, we have media that are almost entirely antagonistic to Christianity. According to the Lichter-Rothman Report of media beliefs and values, eighty-six percent of the media elite never or rarely ever attend any church or synagogue. They uniformly support abortion, euthanasia, and no-fault divorce; and they vote for the most liberal candidates. According to a survey by the Center for Media and Public Affairs, only forty-nine percent believe adultery is wrong; forty-four percent of TV leaders think "the government should guarantee employment to anyone who wants a job"; and sixty-nine percent even believe government should "redistribute income" to reduce the "poverty gap." By and large, the men and women who run the major media in this country are anti-religious people who see Christians and conservative "family values" as a threat.

With such a media monopoly, in due time and after sufficient preparation, they could very easily present you to the American secular public as being deranged, demented, and as dangerous as the Branch Davidians. And who is to doubt that the people of America would believe it? Sad to say, reality for most Americans is what they see on the six o'clock news.

The war against Christianity is heating up. This situation did not exist twenty or even ten years ago to this degree. Michael Medved, the co-host of the *Sneak Previews* television show, is one of the finest film critics in America today. He is an observant Jewish believer, and one of the finest friends of the

Christians in this country because he stands up for and upholds the traditional virtues and "family values" upon which this nation was founded. With the single exception of Dr. Ted Baehr, who produces the *Movieguide* reviews, there is no other voice in the film industry with such penetrating insight and understanding of the crisis in America's mainstream media culture.

Hollywood has always said that the bottom line is money, and they make pictures because they make money. But in his outstanding book, *Hollywood vs. America: Popular Culture and the War on Traditional Values*, Medved gives the lie to that argument. He points out in scrupulous detail how the "anti-traditional values" policy of the movies has been part of a relentless and highly unprofitable scheme to overturn America's moral traditions.

In the decade of the 1980s, there were at least ten major motion pictures that absolutely savaged Christianity. Every single one of them lost money. In 1991, Medved reports, PG-rated films averaged $15.7 million each in box office profits, while R-rated films grossed a puny average of just $5.5 million. And while G-rated films blew out all categories, earning an average $18.5 million, sixty-five percent of the films produced by Hollywood were rated R. And many of these lost tens of millions of dollars. Only a twisted sort of logic would persist in producing such fiascoes as *Last Temptation*, *Monsignor*, *Agnes of God*, *We're No Angels*, *The Rapture*, *Guilty as Charged*, and *Nuns on the Run*, which insult and attack the church and its values while also losing enormous amounts of money. No wonder Medved calls it "the poison factory."[2]

A number of studios produced smaller pictures that placed Christians in a favorable light, but interestingly, they were always about people either faraway, like Australia, or long ago, as in *Chariots of Fire*. But those films did portray Christians in a positive light, and every one of them made money. According to Medved's authoritative book, the bottom line is not money but some sort of demonic compulsion that drives these people to lash out against Jesus Christ, against Christians, and against anyone who holds to a sincere belief in God, in spite of the fact that it is going to cost them tens of millions of dollars to do it. They are driven to "make a statement" regardless of the consequences.

DO NOT LOVE THE WORLD

Jesus Himself said that the world would hate us. Why? He said, "If the world hates you, keep in mind that it hated me first. If you belonged to the world, it would love you as its own. As it is, you do not belong to the world, but I have chosen you out of the world. That is why the world hates you" (John 15:18–19). It is clear that the world hates Jesus Christ, but this must be, undoubtedly, the most astonishing fact in all of history. Here is the modern world drowning in its sin, in constant rebellion against God, and deep in every form of amoral, anti-God behavior, already condemned to death by the holy decree of God. He says, "Whoever does not believe stands condemned already because he has not believed in the name of God's one and only Son" (John 3:18). Those who fight against God are condemned already, simply waiting to fall off the precipice into perdition. But the war continues.

Don't forget that where you are sitting is nothing other than "death row." Whether you are at home, in your office, your car, or anywhere else on the planet, every square inch of earth is under the judgment of God. If you go to the moon, it is still "death row." Every person on this planet has been judged, found guilty, and has been condemned to die. Every single day, tens of thousands of people have that death sentence executed upon them. Jesus Christ declared it: "Whoever does not believe stands condemned already," but it was into this world of condemned rebels that the Son of God came on His incredible mission of mercy.

The harmless, sinless, holy Son of God, came with love and compassion to live a perfect life so that we who have failed may have a Redeemer. In His atoning death, which He endured in our stead, Jesus took upon Himself all the evil of our sins and He became sin for us. Then crucified and humiliated, He was held up between heaven and earth on a cross, where the wrath of His own Father was poured out upon Him in our place. He died in our place and purchased for us eternal life. And now, He freely offers a new life to every last one of us, the free gift of eternal life, if we will turn from our doubt and wickedness and trust in Him.

For this anguish, this agony, this trouble of coming into this dark world, He is repaid with the mockery and hatred of the world. To me that is absolutely astonishing. It is incomprehensible. But He answers the question "Why?" Jesus told his disciples, "They hated me without reason" (John 15:25). His only desire was for our good; His only purpose was that we should live "happily ever after." And for that, the unrepentant people of this nation daily give Him their hatred. The Scripture says that the world is at enmity with God. If they hate you, don't forget: "Know that they hated me first." And they hated Him without a cause.

But I am thrilled to be able to say that He also loved us without cause! Did He love us because there was something lovely about us? Did He love us because, as eighty-three percent of Americans claim to believe, there was something "basically good" in us? No! From the top of our heads to the bottoms of our feet, we are corrupt and depraved by nature. We are a stench in the nostrils of God—in mind and heart and soul. The apostle Paul says that even our righteousness is as filthy rags. By nature, from the cradle, we have rebelled against God and broken His commandments. But, praise be to God, *in spite of our unloveliness*, He loved us. He loved us because of nothing in us, but because of something in Him. He is the God of all Grace. He is the essence of love. He loved us without cause, and the world hates Him without reason.

That story has to be the most astonishing and devastating truth we can ever hear. It only shows the deep malignity of our fallen souls. While we like to think of ourselves as "basically good," the fact is that there is dark and malignant evil in our hearts. But, if you are a follower of Jesus Christ, you should understand that the world will hate you, too. The church consists of all those who are united by a living faith in Jesus Christ, and in whose hearts He lives and in whom His Spirit and His love dwell. The world consists of all those who are not connected to God through Jesus Christ; they are the aggregate of the godless.

You will notice that I did not say the church is composed of all of the members of my church in Florida, or your church, whatever your location or your denomination. There are many people within all of our churches who are actually a part of the world. Oh, they wear the costume of Christianity fairly well, and they have a thin veneer of religiosity, but in their hearts, they have never left the world. Their true friends are people of the world. They find their joy in the company of secular and worldly people. Those are the friends they seek out. When those people find friends in the church, it is generally because they have found evidence that the world is in those people as well. So, I must ask: In which group are you to be found? The real church or the world?

Do you remember the story of Herod and Pilate? They were as opposite as any two worldlings could possibly be, but they became friends that fateful day and reconciled because of their common persecution of Jesus Christ. The world will gladly join ranks with anyone who stands against Christians. There are many in the church, and many who are highly visible leaders who claim to speak for Christ who are, in fact, enemies of Christ and of His people.

Jesus says such people have the spirit of Antichrist within them. Interestingly, the worldly people in the church will always join with those outside who want to attack the kingdom of Christ. When the world has bad things to say about the church, there are some in the church who will always join with them. They don't even realize that what they are doing is flying their own flag that says, "I belong to the world!" They join hands with those who have hated the name of Christ. And they hate Him, too, without a cause.

RIGHTEOUS INDIGNATION

What can we do about this war against Christ and Christianity? We cannot do what many would do. We cannot resort to violence. When *The Last Temptation of Christ* was about to be released, more than twenty-five thousand Christians gathered around the office complex known as the Black Tower, in Universal City, California. I was told by one of those present that the people inside were absolutely terrified. They said, "There were just so many of them . . . They were everywhere. The crowd seemed to go on for miles."

They just knew that at any moment the people outside were going to break down the doors and come storming in and trash the building. Some of the studio execs thought the Christians outside were going to try to enter the building and kill people, but the throng did nothing of the kind. Instead, they prayed, sang hymns, and various speakers addressed the crowd, calling on the people to stand firm against the degradation of our culture, urging them to pray and to continue to speak out against evil. And believe it or not, not one single window was broken. The protesters were merely asking the studios to show some restraint—not to release *The Last Temptation of Christ*.

But the film producers said that "artistic integrity" demanded that they produce this vile film and release it to the judgment of the world. Does their artistic integrity demand that they produce a defaming film about Malcolm X? Where is their integrity then? Does their artistic integrity demand that they produce a film defaming Mohammed or Buddha or Confucius? Recall what happened when Salman Rushdie wrote his book, *Satanic Verses*, which Muslims claimed spoke blasphemy against Mohammed. The Ayatollah immediately put a death sentence on Rushdie's head, and the author is still living under that threat. But that is *not* the call of the Christian. That is *not* the way of *Christ*.

No, the war is only *against* Christ, *against* our mild and loving Savior, the Lamb of God who would not strike back when He was smitten and spat upon by the Romans and the Judeans of His own day. But we do have the power of the Gospel, and we can use it to transform the world into the church—because all of us were born as a part of this world. By living lives of moral integrity and love, Christ tells us we can attract the world. And even as the name of Christ is reviled and besmirched by the world, He shines ever brighter in our hearts and in His wondrous glory.

We can share that Gospel. One of the reasons that the war is heating up today is because we have been derelict in our responsibility to do that. So the number of those who are not a part of the church—which Chuck Colson describes so marvelously in his book, *The Body*—that number has been growing and multiplying and becoming stronger, and now they are turning against the church in large numbers. Those whom we have not reached are now looking for a way to unleash their hatred and bigotry against us, our faith, our Savior, and our historic values.

But we should rejoice. Jesus said, "Blessed are you when people insult you, persecute you and falsely say all kinds of evil against you because of me. Rejoice and be glad, because great is your reward in heaven, for in the same way they persecuted the prophets who were before you" (Matt. 5:11–12). The Bible says that all they who live godly in Christ Jesus shall suffer persecution. Have you been persecuted for your faith in Christ? I don't mean for your bad disposition or your critical attitude. But have you been persecuted for your faith in Jesus Christ? If you were arrested for being a Christian, would there be enough evidence to convict you? Have you been persecuted for Christ's sake? If not, then you need to ask yourself: Which camp am I in—am I in the church or in the world?

The real church consists only of those who have a living faith in Christ, and who in spite of trial and tribulation will stand against the evil of the world. I remember a lady who told me about a minister she had known for many years. She said, "In all of those years, I never heard one person speak ill of him. Isn't that wonderful?" My response was, "No. It's tragic." Jesus Christ said, "Woe to you when all men speak well of you, for that is how their fathers treated the false prophets" (Luke 6:26).

The world around us is lost. They are at war with the Spirit of Christ. But there is a ray of hope, for they are also desperately in search of a soul—they are hungry for something to believe in. I challenge you to share the Good News that Jesus Christ is the hope of every heart—the only answer that can offer us a bright and hopeful future. And let your light so shine before men that they will glorify your Father who is in heaven.

In the following chapter, I will examine in more detail, the options before us today, the choices that are available, and then some conclusion about our prospects for the days and years ahead. From there we will turn to the warfare that confronts the church today and our hopes for ultimate victory.✦

NOTES

[1]Matt Roush, "Magic Scores Against HIV; Ellerbee's Candor Earns Assist," *USA Today, TV Preview*, (March 25, 1992), sec. 1D.

[2]Michael Medved, *Hollywood vs. America: Popular Culture and the War on Traditional Values* (New York: HarperCollins / Zondervan, 1992).

11

Alternative Futures

What does the future hold for you? Do you know what tomorrow will be like? Would you like to know? Most people are curious about the future. In fact, whole industries are devoted to trying to satisfy people's curiosity about the future. The producers of the *Back to the Future* motion pictures made a fortune by offering people a glimpse of what life might be like a hundred years or so from now. They found a formula that offered novelty and surprise, but they also offered the optimistic view that past, present, and future are all somehow interrelated. We are not really lost in time and space as we often feel. The film suggested that there's some kind of grand scheme to it all.

What these Hollywood geniuses discovered was actually an ancient truism: When times are uncertain, people will do anything to gain some sense of security. A glimpse into the future—even if it is just a day, an hour, or even a few minutes ahead—offers people a sense of hope. Surely this explains the fascination many people have for psychics, astrology, and other occult practices. They will leap at things that offer some vision of tomorrow even when it is a false vision. We need hope, and for many of us, the best hope is the future.

I think of the enormous success of productions such as *Star Trek* and all the sequels they have generated. What is their great appeal? Is it the intrigue of all those high-tech special effects? Is it the strange creatures and the science-fiction quality of the scripts? No doubt there are many factors involved, but I believe the main reason these space adventures have had such appeal for so many people is that they allow us to experience the future in a way that is safe and objective. These movies are generally positive and upbeat, they demonstrate the victory of human intelligence over difficult circumstances, and they show people with the ability to "transcend" the life-threatening crises that confront them. Such movies and television programs say that the world has a future, that there is hope, and that we can overcome our problems if we just hold on.

FUTURE SHOCKS

The American inventor, Charles F. Kettering, once said it only makes sense to take an interest in the future, since that's where we are all going to spend the rest of our lives. But there are many times when we have to wonder if things haven't already gone too far. Is there still hope for the future? We are surrounded by both good news and bad, and many people have never felt so uncertain about the future.

Most of the time we seem to have very little control over the events of our lives. We are not actually the masters of our fate or the captains of our soul as the humanists once claimed. And in light of all that is happening around us today, the future often seems much too desperate and uncertain. Too many people feel they have nothing to hope for. In the book *Future Shock,* published in 1970, sociologist Alvin Toffler explored the effects of rapid technological and social changes upon society and said that many people in this country are being overcome by the "psychic stress" of modern culture. In times of rapid, unpredictable change, he reported, people lose their ability to cope. There are too many conflicting views of the future, and faced by options that seem equally bad, it is easy to lose control. In the real world, the promise of new technologies and some future "brave new world" may occasionally seem alluring, but they can also be frightening. Toffler said that the future breeds enormous fears, and only an emotional framework for dealing with reality will allow us to regain our sense of security.

The challenge of the future was already on many people's minds at the end of the Second World War. Having recently discovered a wide range of new terrors—including the carnage of war, the great evil that brought about the Nazi Holocaust, and the new threat of nuclear annihilation—the end of the war closed one chapter of fear but opened another. This was one of the things that prompted Air Force General Henry Arnold to set up the first forecasting project to formally analyze the options and prospects for technology in the future. In 1946, Arnold helped establish the concept of the "think tank," and groups such as the Rand Corporation in New York and the Stanford Research Institute in California became the first to apply specialized techniques for thinking creatively about the future.

Since those days, futurists such as Herman Kahn, Daniel Bell, and Buckminster Fuller have tried to predict the look and feel of the future, to comprehend the complex systems that may be ahead of us. They have studied everything from climate and technological advances to future lifestyles and economic conditions. And while the lessons of history are helpful for such studies, the scientists all freely admit that they rely as much on informed hunches as anything else. One type of forecasting, called the Delphi method, has been used to extrapolate models of the future based on the "best guesses" of a panel of experts. But there are also mathematical systems and applications using "computer-aided design" that allow researchers to take these types of analysis a step further.

Today a new generation of supercomputers is being designed by inventors such as Seymour Cray and Alan Huang. Digital processors like the ones used by Lucas Films in producing the special effects for *Star Wars* and other Hollywood productions are capable of conducting millions of digital operations in a split second. With such tools, the think tanks can dabble in "futures imaging" and "reality modeling" that allows scientists to step beyond statistics and theories into three-dimensional models of the world in the twenty-first century. At the same time, some scientists have suggested that researchers are very close to being able to produce microchips not much larger than a postage stamp that can contain as much information as an entire city library. With these marvels of science, computations can be conducted in seconds that would otherwise take years by conventional methods. No doubt these tools will soon become vital components of the futurist's standard paraphernalia.

LOOKING AHEAD

The published results of various studies of the future have certainly done well in the last decade or so. Consider the success of authors such as John Naisbitt and Patricia Aburdene, whose two books, *Megatrends* and *Megatrends*

2000, shot to the top of the best-seller lists and stayed there for years. If you have read either of those books, you know that their main attraction was not the great number of quotes or statistics they compiled, or even the authors' prophecies of the future, but the very positive and upbeat tone of their findings. In light of all the negative news we see each day, these authors were saying that everything is changing for the better and that there is hope for the world. In his endorsement of the second book, John Sculley, formerly of Apple Computers, said, "I come away excited and inspired by the author's insight and optimism." But whether such optimism is warranted in light of our undeniable problems remains to be seen.

All of these success stories are evidence of a basic fact of human nature. When the future seems unclear, and whenever we are confronted by apparent chaos and disorder in society, people need hope. Human nature demands that we look for logical answers and practical options for dealing with our problems. Most of us are concerned with the future these days. We are concerned with what the future may hold for our families, for our financial security, and for society in general. Christians are concerned for the moral decline in our cities and towns, and political leaders are concerned for the fact that government authority and public assistance have failed to bring about the social changes they had once expected. That is why we want to see into the future by any available means.

Perhaps you have visited Disney World in Orlando. If so, you may recall that the men and women who plan and design the amusements, rides, and entertainment facilities at the theme park are known as "Imagineers." They are engineers with terrific imaginations. NASA engineers are something like that, too. They are people with vivid imaginations as well as scientific expertise. As we think about matters of "destiny," it would probably be a good idea to do a little "imagineering" of our own and examine the prospects for our own future. In any event, it seems appropriate that we pause at this point to look at some of the outcomes that we can reasonably expect from the circumstances around us.

One of the popular concepts used by business managers, scientists, and engineers is called the "What if?" scenario. In boardrooms and think tanks, thought leaders get together to brainstorm various options, asking, "What if we do it this way?" or, "What would happen if we took some other approach?" Then, based on the answers they come up with, many believe they can develop more realistic and practical plans. That is what I want to do in this chapter on alternative futures.

In the fall of 1993, we conducted our "State of the Nation Survey" to find out what the people with whom we are in frequent contact through our radio and television broadcasts think about the major issues of our day. We all see polls and surveys being used more and more to determine what is bought and sold in America. Everything from snack foods to federal spending programs seems to be determined by survey results. So we wanted to publish our own findings so that they might be of some use in making policy decisions. If polls of a cross-section of the society are valuable, then we believe our survey should be valuable in taking the pulse of Christians and others who have a stake in the future policies of this nation.

For years people have been writing to me, saying they are concerned with the direction in which this country seems to be headed. Our 1993 survey confirms some of the specific areas that respondents believe need the most attention, and I believe that government needs to take very seriously what these people are saying. The survey was mailed to men and women of all ages all across the nation, to determine the concerns, beliefs, hopes, and leading areas of concern of the American people. In our sampling, taken from the more than 160,000 responses we received, we tabulated the results and then sent them to Washington, D.C., to inform government leaders of the issues we found to be on the people's minds.

WHAT PEOPLE ARE SAYING

According to our survey, a clear majority of men and women believe that the "progressive" social policies being pushed by the government are dangerous to the nation's future. And these people believe that the true source of hope, the Word of God, is being ignored by those in authority. We found that ninety-two percent of the respondents believe that the tremendous growth of the national debt is the result of government's ignoring biblical principles. Thirty percent said that "religious freedom" is their greatest concern, while twenty-five percent listed "abortion," and twelve percent said they were most concerned with the battle over "gay rights." The "economy" and "pornography" ranked fourth as the major concerns of eight percent of the respondents. On other issues, ninety-five percent believe the Surgeon General should declare AIDS a "contagious, communicable, and sexually-transmitted disease"; while eighty-one percent said they fear that legalized abortion will lead to increased euthanasia and "mercy killing" of the mentally handicapped and the elderly.

We also found that ninety-four percent of those surveyed believe that "prayer in the schools" should be restored; ninety-eight percent believe sex-education courses in the schools should promote "abstinence" as the best option for young people; and ninety-eight percent said that "moral character" is a relevant issue in the election of national leaders.

When Gary Bauer spoke at our Reclaiming America Conference in January 1994, he expressed the attitudes and feelings of those who share these concerns. He said that while most people are skeptical about what happens in Washington, D.C., few of us really understand just how different the values of lawmakers are from those of the rest of the nation. The elites in Washington, he said, believe that government can create utopia on this earth. They believe in moral relativism, radical individualism, and a strong central government in control of every area of our lives. While the people of this country believe in personal responsibility, truth, virtue, and faith, the elites in Washington want to build a new world order unimpeded by traditions or religious convictions.

"I know that all of us worry about the economy," said Bauer, "as do our fellow citizens. We worry about having decent jobs and a living wage, and the chance to own a home and educate our children. We all worry about the deficit, which is continuing to go out of control in spite of what the politicians tell you. Between the time that the sun came up this morning and it set this evening, the federal budget deficit increased by one billion dollars. Not because you're under-taxed but because Washington is unable to control itself when it comes to using other people's money."

Economic worries, however, are not the biggest problem in this nation. Bauer went on to say, "I am not worried about America economically, I'm worried because something seems to have gone wrong with the heart and soul of our nation. And millions of our fellow Americans know that something has gone wrong, even if they don't share our faith perspective. You can hear them talk about it at school-board meetings, at the grocery store in their neighborhoods, all of them know something has gone wrong. And our leaders in Washington don't have the answers. They don't even know the right questions to ask."

The speaker recalled that when Martin Luther King made his most famous speech on the mall in Washington, D.C., he said that his dream for this country was that someday we would judge people by the content of their *character* and not the color of their skin. But thanks to government, the media, and the liberal education establishment, children are being told that character doesn't matter. Bauer says this fraud is a terrible violation of King's dream, and the people who give that message to our young people ought to be ashamed of themselves.

Bauer asked, "What happened in America between the time that we understood personal responsibility and a time when there are a thousand reasons to escape the consequences of our acts?" Then he said, "What happened in America is that we forgot God. And having forgotten God, we have unleashed the hounds of hell in our streets, in our homes, and on our children. And until America realizes that, there is no turning back."

Bill Clinton's 1992 campaign slogan was, "It's the economy, stupid!" And all the energies of the Democratic and Republican parties went into talking about the economy. But the real problem in America is not the economy: It's the heart and soul of this nation. Gary Bauer said, "A nation of children without fathers is not going to out-compete Japan. A nation unable to distinguish between right and wrong won't solve the budget deficit. A nation of moral misfits eventually will become a nation of economic misfits. The economy and our moral fiber are linked together, and the politicians just don't get it."

REMEDIES THAT WORK

So what is to be done? Bauer suggests that the first thing that must happen is that government and the media must stop their open warfare on religion in the public square. It doesn't take a genius to see what is wrong in this nation. Half of all marriages end in divorces, a third of all childbirths are out of wedlock. Crime is out of control, the schools have become a violent wasteland, and, as Bauer said, "to listen to our leaders and many in our media, you would think that the biggest threat is that more men and women of faith may go into government. I say we need them, and we need them now." Unless people with moral convictions begin to take a more active role in the leadership of the nation, the situation will only get worse.

Bauer suggests that people in all walks of life are going to have to get over their embarrassment about using words such as *virtue, fidelity, honor,* and *character.* We need people who are willing to push as hard for moral values and self-discipline as the secular culture of our age is pushing society in the opposite direction. And one of the immediate concerns is to restore the quality of education and to teach young people the history of this nation. They need to know who said, "Give me liberty or give me death!" They need to know that when Martin Luther King said, "I have a dream," he was referring to the "character" of the nation. We need to teach them what the Statue of Liberty in New York harbor actually stands for, and why the Berlin Wall came down, and what the forces of liberty were that ended the seventy-year history of Communist oppression.

We need to teach our young people to love the things that have been so vital to the fortunes of this nation, and to honor the things that symbolize our heritage and our freedom. And most important, Bauer told our conferees, "We need to start electing leaders at all levels of government who understand our concerns—leaders willing to talk about the budget deficit and willing to talk about the virtue deficit."

Let us assume that the findings of our survey and the values expressed in our beliefs were once again to provide the moral basis for our laws and the policies that government would enact for this nation. What if we concluded that public policy and economic procedures in the future would be based on biblical principles? And what if we said that the law will guarantee religious liberty, the sanctity of life, and traditional moral values regarding sexuality? This is a short enough list. So what would the outcome of such policies be?

First of all, if biblical economic principles were implemented in this country, the government would be obliged to balance the budget. King Solomon said, "The rich rule over the poor, and the borrower is servant to the lender" (Prov. 22:7). The principle is that debt is a form of slavery, and we are never to allow ourselves or our nation to become the slaves of anyone else. In the New Testament, the apostle Paul wrote to the Romans, "Give everyone what you owe him: If you owe taxes, pay taxes; if revenue, then revenue; if respect, then respect; if honor, then honor. Let no debt remain outstanding, except the continuing debt to love one another, for he who loves his fellowman has fulfilled the law."

In the very next sentence he goes on to tell the people that their duty as Christians is to obey the laws of God. "'Do not commit adultery,' 'Do not murder,' 'Do not steal,' 'Do not covet,' and whatever other commandment there may be, are summed up in this one rule: 'Love your neighbor as yourself'" (Rom. 13:7–9). Obviously, these principles go hand in hand. Respect, dignity, and honesty are intimately related to debt and obligation.

These standards teach honor, duty, and fair dealing, and they teach a level of respect for our fellowman that forbids the kind of wanton exploitation we see in government today.

Second, we would see a new attitude of cooperation between the people of the nation. By reducing its expenditures and its role in managing the lives of people, government would empower people to love, care for, and support each other. The church is a place where people can rally around each other in times of stress, and the community should be the same type of environment. Instead of a nation that works from the top down, we would once again have a nation that works in concentric circles of influence, radiating outward from the individual to the family, the neighborhood, the community, the town, the state, the nation, and then the world. That is the natural balance and the natural inclination of people, but government has turned the equation on its head.

RENEWING OF YOUR MIND

Next, we would see a renewal of the tried-and-proven standards of education. Young people would learn the true facts of their heritage and their history, with special attention to the price our forefathers paid for the liberty we enjoy today. Instead of focusing on racism and exploitation and bitterness, we would be looking for ways to care for and about each other. We would see that we are very fortunate to be here in this great land, and we would want to be sure that every citizen has an equal right to enjoy the great opportunity available here. And with that same spirit of brotherly love and cooperation, we would want to extend faith and values and the lessons we have gained in our own experience to those in other lands who are seeking a democratic model that really works.

As God and His Word have been systematically taken from the schoolrooms of America, young people have become demoralized. Pornographers and the doctrine of "liberation" have exposed younger and younger people to sexually and morally dangerous attitudes, encouraging them to dabble in things that God ordained for marriage. If we were to follow God's standards in this nation, then we would see that the balance is restored. Young people would be taught that they are to respect one another, to respect the emotional and sexual privacy of people, and to abstain from sex until they meet and marry the one person that God has ordained from the beginning of time as their mate. This would, in turn, bring an end to sex outside of marriage, adultery, childbirth out

241

of wedlock, and much of the rampant sex and promiscuity that troubles the world today.

Finally, following God's standards, we would have zero tolerance for crime and abuse of the law. God has always been compassionate to those who try to do the right thing but fail in the attempt. We should also have compassion for people whose motives are good even if they make serious mistakes. But when anyone deliberately flaunts the law and makes a mockery of order, dignity, and social harmony, then swift and certain punishment must be administered. Serious crimes must demand serious sentences, and capital crimes should demand capital sentences. Clearly, this has always been a standard of which God approves. So long as a man, woman, or child wants to live decently and abide by the just rules of the nation, then the law must be tolerant and try to help them to succeed. But if the desire to live decently is somehow lost or disregarded, then offenders must be separated from society, by whatever standards the courts apply—informed by principles of God's Word.

Do you believe these standards are realistic? Do you think this nation would be better off if we tried God's way instead of our own? I certainly do. How stupid of government and of the people who elect our leaders, to presume that we can make up rules by some humanistic standard that will be superior to those ordained by heaven. Yet that is the situation in this nation today. No wonder we are in such terrible trouble.

After the death of Moses, the ancient nation of Israel went through a major transition in leadership, and at first the people were restless and insecure. Knowing that the new leader would need a special blessing, the Lord spoke to Joshua and told him, "Be strong and very courageous. Be careful to obey all the law my servant Moses gave you; do not turn from it to the right or to the left, that you may be successful wherever you go." God knew that there would be many difficult times ahead for the nation of Israel—that there would be trials, temptations, and political difficulties to overcome. But He assured Joshua that the law of God is perfect. If the law was good enough for Moses, it would also be good enough for Joshua. The Lord said, "Do not let this Book of the Law depart from your mouth; meditate on it day and night, so that you may be careful to do everything written in it. Then you will be prosperous and successful" (Josh. 1:7–8).

Later, in his own letter to young Timothy, the apostle Paul said that the Scriptures are our reliable standard and are meant to endure for all time. He said, "All Scripture is God-breathed and is useful for teaching, rebuking, correcting and training in righteousness, so that the man of God may be thoroughly equipped for every good work" (2 Tim. 3:16–17). These instructions are just as valid for us today. What was good for Moses and Joshua is good for us today. When we followed God's law and the teachings of Christ, this nation did prosper. And to regain our place of strength we must return to these standards of truth and wisdom.

LASTING STANDARDS

Unfortunately, the cry we often hear from government is the old cliché that "You can't legislate morality." The secular government believes it can invent rules and a system of order without regard for God's perfect law. But I must be quick to point out, as many others have done, that morality is the heart and soul of the law. When God handed down the Ten Commandments at Mt. Sinai, what He was doing was legislating His morality. He was not giving Moses a set of rules with which to punish the people. He wasn't giving the nations laws to make life more difficult, but to make life happier, healthier, more enjoyable, and generally better. All law, ever since that time, seeks to emulate that standard and to give people a set of values around which a society can be organized.

Morality is the only thing you *can* legislate! *If you don't legislate morality, you legislate immorality.* That is a cardinal lesson of history. You wind up legislating the whims of despots and self-styled rulers. For two centuries, the leaders of this nation understood the moral component of laws, and American laws were just and absolute. They established broad freedoms for self-determination and individual rights; however, they also established firm and absolute penalties for people who willfully break the law. Today we are still legislating morality, but thanks to the new sociological approach that denies the authority of Scripture and the principles of our religious heritage, we are legislating "immorality." And the crime in our streets is a vision of the alternative future that comes from doing things by the world's standard of right and wrong. It is all wrong.

We are coming to the place where, for the first time in the history of this nation, Congress is beginning to legislate immorality. All our laws ultimately come from theology and religious beliefs. If the people honor God, then their laws will reflect their belief in absolute standards of right and wrong. There will be one absolute standard that everyone understands. But if they reject this fundamental source of truth, then there will be no standard, no reliable bottom line, and no source of truth we can all trust.

Dr. Francis Schaeffer once said, "Let me read the laws of any country, and I'll tell you their religion." The actual reality is that laws have always been the legal enactment of ethical and moral values. And morality—yours, mine, and everyone else's—has always arisen out of theology. Laws are based upon morality; morality is based upon theology; and that is simply a fact of life. It is only the atheists, civil libertarians, and others who defy religious truth who challenge this fact in our time.

So for the past forty years, they have been busily enacting laws based upon their value system, which is based on the false theology of humanism, while all the time shouting at the top of their voice to us, "You can't legislate your morality." What they really mean to say is, "You Christians can't legislate *your* morality because we are at work trying to legislate *our* morality." And they are going to tell us that we can't legislate our historic views into law because their objective is to overturn the historic liberties of this nation in order to install a new humanistic, one-world, atheistic, and generally immoral agenda. They are loud, they are forceful, and they are very well funded. And sadly, many Christians have been gullible enough to accept their demands. But can anyone doubt what their future will bring upon us?

In his classic book, *The Road Less Traveled*, Dr. Scott Peck talks about taking the uncommon route to life and discovering the deeper meaning of existence. From the metaphor in Robert Frost's poem for which the book is named, Peck says that the road less traveled is the road that makes all the difference. In our experience, the road less traveled is the road back to the foundational principles and values of this nation. The other road—the one the president, the Congress, and the judiciary are following most of the time today—is a superhighway to hell. If you have any doubts of that statement, just stop to think what is going on in every city in this nation. In many places men, women, and children are already living in a literal hell on earth. Life is increasingly difficult and intolerable. And if we cannot regain our values and priorities, then many people are going to find themselves not only in a hell on earth but in the hell yet to come, which is a future of despair and eternal punishment without God.

REASONABLE ALTERNATIVES

As we look at our circumstances, we soon realize that there are only two hopes for restoring law and order in a nation: One is control imposed from within through moral restraint; the other is control imposed from without by police power and political restraint, which are the only two options when any nation degenerates into gang violence and random lawlessness. Either the people regain control of their emotions and behavior, or the state must come in and beat down the sources of lawlessness. This is the situation we are seeing in South Africa, in parts of Eastern Europe, in Asia and South America, and more often today in the modern American cities of Los Angeles, Chicago, and many others.

In his compelling article called "The Coming Anarchy" in the *Atlantic* magazine, Robert D. Kaplan tells about conditions in the war-ravaged nations of Africa. He describes conditions that have led to unprecedented levels of violence, but the most startling part of his analysis is that the United States appears to be walking right down the same pathway to violence and self-destruction. Why? Because we are falling victim to the doctrines of multiculturalism and ethnic diversity being promoted by the government and other liberals. These views are splintering the nation. We are no longer "one nation under God," and what was once described as a "melting pot" is being divided up into warring camps. Instead of brotherly love, we have ethnic hatred and street gangs. Consequently, religious principles of love, honesty, and compassion are made of no effect.

What does all this bode for the future of our country? Kaplan writes, "Indeed, it is not clear that the United States will survive the next century in exactly its present form. Because America is a multi-ethnic society, the nation-state has always been more fragile here than it is in more homogeneous societies like Germany and Japan." Multiculturalism and historical revisionism are breaking down the social restraints and creating new hostilities in the social structure of the nation that have never existed here before. "A nation-state," he says, "is a place where everyone has been educated along similar lines, where people take their cue from national leaders, and where everyone (every male, at least) has gone through the crucible of military service, making patriotism a simpler issue."[1]

But the writer also notes that our nation is losing its educational foundations and its basis for cooperation between all people. Years ago the novelist Saul Bellow said that when he was growing up in an immigrant family in Chicago, they were not interested in holding on to some kind of foreign identity. They wanted to be Americans. "The country took us over," he said. "It was a country then, not a collection of 'cultures.'" But the multiculturalism being pushed by liberals in government and the universities today is absolutely contrary to the best interests of this nation. And this is only the tip of the iceberg. The dividing-up of the nation can only bring about increased anger, disappointment, and belligerence. Why can't the government and the intellectuals understand this fact?

WHAT'S WRONG WITH AMERICA?

Ultimately, government profits by dividing us up, and that is one source of our problems. In the book, *The Government Racket*, Martin Gross writes, "People are suspicious that something is *fundamentally* wrong in Washington. And they are right. Hundreds of billions of dollars are being taken from them each year under false pretenses. In fact, waste of enormous proportions is built into the federal system, though most of it is expertly hidden. Waste is more prevalent than efficiency; more common than good works. If it continues at its present pace, not only will it bankrupt the nation fiscally, it will destroy us morally as well."[2]

Gross shows how government feeds on special-interest groups, pockets of local support, and the distribution of tax revenues to their constituents. The problems of the federal budget are not due to military spending or to an excess of beneficial programs such as Social Security or Medicare. No, the problem is the excess of "pork-barrel spending" through which congressmen and bureaucrats are funneling your tax dollars to special interests and to their own pet projects instead of into the economy where it is needed. Waste is destroying the economy, and bureaucrats are the problem. They have lost their allegiance to the American people, but they have also lost their allegiance to God.

At a meeting of our state governors some months ago, after listening for several days to other governors bashing traditional Christian values, the governor of Mississippi stood up and made the statement that "this is a Christian nation." No sooner than he had spoken those words than the fur began to fly. First a rabbi jumped to his feet and declared that he was greatly offended because of the governor's remark. Then representatives of People for the American Way said that they were incensed. Then came the representatives of the B'nai Birith, the Anti-Defamation League, the NAACP, and every other minority group with an ax to grind. And I am sad to say, rather than standing his ground, the governor backed away under the pressures. He had no right, the world concluded, to say this is a Christian nation.

Should we apologize for telling the truth? It's interesting that there was no question of whether or not the governor's statement was true. That debate never took place. As we saw in the first section of this book, history and culture and even the law have affirmed the Christian foundations of American society from the year 1607 to the present. In 1947, President Harry Truman said bluntly, "This is a Christian nation." That remark did not cause even the slightest ripple. During World War II, President Roosevelt described the United States as "the lasting Concord between men and nations, founded on the principles of Christianity." Again there was not the least ruffle of feathers. But little by little, the liberal establishment has revised history in their attempt to take Jesus Christ out of the picture. And their victory is America's loss. When we freely confessed that this is a Christian nation, in days gone by, we prospered. We were the "shining city on a hill." Alas, we are no more.

WHOSE VALUES?

Do we even know the constitutional principles of this nation any longer? What about these words: "The church in the U.S. shall be separate from the state and the school from the church"? Do you know that section of the Constitution? Maybe it would help if I filled in the blank, since I omitted a couple of letters. Let me say it again: "The church in the *U.S.S.R.* shall be separate from the state and the school from the church." This phrase does not appear in the United States Constitution at all, but in Article 52 of the Constitution of the Soviet Union—now the Soviet *disunion*. Defunct, because they tried to get rid of God.

We have a nation today that is filled with unbelieving people, and this is what has caused the problems that are ripping the heart out of the nation. Love, honor, duty, respect for others, and love of God. As we have seen over and over, these are the foundations of a great society—they were once the cornerstone of this nation. But, thanks largely to the meddling of government and the liberal ideologies being promoted by educators and the media, many now accept the view that they must retreat back to the churches and hope that someday the unbelievers will go away and let them alone. But, my friends, that is a delusion. It will not happen. Already the barbarians are knocking at the gates, and soon they are going to break them down and come into every area of your life. Unless you and I recommit ourselves to the great task of advancing the Christian faith in this land, and in other lands around the world, there is very little hope of reclaiming the nation or the future.

In his book, *Habits of the Heart*, Robert Bellah says that "Cultures are dramatic conversations about things that matter to their participants, and American culture is no exception." From the earliest days of this nation, there has been an active dialogue about the standards and values that should be perpetuated by society. Our founders held the view that the purpose and goal of the nation is to attain the biblical image of a just and compassionate society. Bellah says that others have offered other standards, and then he adds that, "The themes of success, freedom, and justice . . . are found in all three of the central strands of our culture—biblical, republican, and modern individualist—but they take on different meanings in each context. American culture remains alive so long as the conversation continues and the argument is intense."

In other words, if modern secularism is allowed to crowd out the perspectives of the Christian faith—which it will eagerly do if we allow it to happen—then the culture will be damaged by the loss. No one expects this nation to become a theocracy, where Christianity is the only value, but we do indeed say that the essential values and founding principles of the nation should not be ignored. They cannot be driven from the controversy of ideas. And we cannot hope to prosper as long as we are a nation that rejects the Word and wisdom of God.

America is in dire trouble today. This fact cannot be denied. For the first time in history, we have an administration and a president who have publicly espoused opposition to two of the commandments of God Almighty, the sixth and seventh commandments—dealing with the sanctity of life and with adultery and other forms of sexual perversion. This has never happened before, and I'm not talking about politics; I'm talking about the moral law of God. When a nation sets its face in opposition to the Almighty, it is asking to feel the wrath of God.

The Scriptures give us ample warning, saying, "Blessed is the nation whose God is the LORD." But the Word also says that the nation that forgets God shall be turned into hell, and that judgment begins at the house of God. In light of these things, we all need to ask ourselves some hard questions. What have you done to advance the cause of Christ? What have you done to uphold the standard for which this nation was founded? What have you done to lift up the principles for which the Pilgrims landed on these shores? And what have you done to advance, in their words, "The gloire of God and the advancement of the Christian faith"? In our generation, that marvelous patrimony is slipping through our fingers like sifting sand. Unless something happens very soon, your children and grandchildren are going to live in a godless society where life will be but one tragedy after another. In that day no life will be worth living. Is that an acceptable alternative? Are you willing to let that happen?

PAST AND FUTURE COLLIDE

The apostle Paul was not only an incomparable theologian and a master strategist, but he was also a master at the art of living. By any conceivable measure, his life was one of the most successful, victorious, triumphant lives ever lived by any mere human being. Today, as part of his legacy of successful living, he leaves us a magnificent secret—perhaps the greatest secret that we can ever learn in troubled times like these.

He says, "One thing I do: Forgetting what is behind and straining toward what is ahead, I press on toward the goal to win the prize for which God has called me heavenward in Christ Jesus" (Phil. 3:13–14). Now what Paul is saying, and what the Bible teaches, is very important for our peace of mind. While each one of us must live our lives in three spheres—the past, the present, and the future—we can only live this one moment and this one hour in the present. We cannot step back and relive the past. We cannot jump ahead into the future without destroying our bodies and our minds. Today, this minute, this hour—this is the dimension in which we must do whatever we can for the kingdom of God.

The emphasis of all the think tanks and the engineers and the strategists of the world is focused on the future. But, in reality, they cannot live in the future. They can only plan today for what may come tomorrow. If you are spending all your time in the past or the future, then your anxieties will prevent you from ever being happy in life and also from being successful. I think it is interesting that the words "worry" and "anxiety" both come from the same Latin root. The word means "to choke" or "to strangle." All around us today there are people who are being strangled by their memories, feelings of guilt, and their attachment to a past that is long gone. And all around us are people who cannot simply accept this moment for what it is because they are waiting for tomorrow, for some ideal future, for the day when their real life will begin. No wonder the Latin language described anxiety as choking us to death. Without a realistic sense of our place in time, we are helpless. Unless we learn to deal with the past and the future, not only will we never be as successful and productive as we could be, but we will never enjoy the success we do manage to eke out day to day.

The French philosopher Montaigne said something many of us today will recognize. "My life," he lamented, "has been full of terrible misfortunes . . . most of which have never happened." Indeed, too many of us are like little children living in a dark room full of monsters. Robert Louis Stevenson, who understood very well the world of children, once said, "Anyone can do his work, however hard, for one day. Anyone can live sweetly, patiently, lovingly, purely, till the sun goes down." But when the bony fingers of the past and the unnamed fears of the future reach out to strangle us, we lose our ability to cope and we become useless to ourselves and to others.

Reaching back by faith and forward by hope, we can experience lives of love and purpose. We can experience "the renewing of our minds," as Paul urged us. But the transformation from a life of disappointment to a life of active engagement with the world can only be brought about by faith in Jesus Christ. Have you experienced His love? Have you trusted in His promise? If not, then you have more to worry about than you know. I think worry is a destructive and undesirable thing. But I must also say that there are a lot of people in this country today who really ought to worry more than they do. If they knew that just around the corner, the day after tomorrow, hell is eagerly waiting, they would worry a great deal more than they do. And they ought to! Perhaps that worry would drive them to the Cross, where they could find forgiveness and peace and the free gift of eternal life. For only at the foot of the cross can we as individuals or as a nation find purpose and the fulfillment of our lives. Hope for the future only comes through faith in Christ.

THE HOPE OF IMMORTALITY

A couple of years ago a feature story in *USA Today* told about a man who bet his life that there was good reason to prepare for the future. Tom Donaldson of Sunnyvale, California, was willing to bet that science holds the key to eternal life. He wanted to live forever—at least he wanted to live at some time in the future—and he was prepared to pay a very healthy sum to buy a little more life. "I want to live," Donaldson told reporters. "There's so much to do." But he had one major obstacle: Doctors said he had untreatable brain tumors and very little time left to live.

Facing such a somber prognosis, the forty-seven-year-old computer engineer opted for "cryonics," which is the practice of freezing

250

people—just their heads in some cases—in liquid nitrogen at the time of death in hopes that some time in the future medical science will be able to cure their illnesses and give them a new life.

The reporter said that some four hundred people have already signed up for the cryonics option, paying fees of up to one hundred-twenty thousand dollars for the privilege of being kept in cryonic suspension indefinitely. Each hopes that sometime in the future—perhaps as long as five hundred years from now—they may live once again. To date, thirteen complete bodies and thirteen heads are already being kept in special containers submerged in liquid nitrogen at one of three cryonics centers in California and Michigan. Each volunteer understands that there is no guarantee that they will ever come back. But Donaldson said, "I've got more hope than if they put me in the ground and I turn to dust, don't I?" He hoped that someday he would be awakened in another solar system, cured of his tumors, and that his wife (who also agreed to the procedure) and his pet cat would be resurrected along with him.[3]

Immortality. That's the promise. Eternal life, and the way to get it, people like Tom Donaldson believe, is through the constantly accelerating discoveries of science. But the fact is, we all have the same promise of life in the future—yes, it is an eternal life, and it's not science fiction. There is not even one bit of fiction about it. Jesus said, "I am the living bread that came down from heaven. If anyone eats of this bread, he will live forever" (John 6:51). He invited everyone who would follow Him to share freely in His gift of eternal life. Unfortunately, too many people are looking for some other way, some other god, some other hope. And for the sake of an illusion, they willingly pass up the only future that really matters.

Are you willing to bet your life on the future? Are you willing to bet that science or government or psychology or some new cult will provide you with a reason and a way to live forever? Tom Donaldson's dream was an empty dream. Wherever he is now, he knows that the only future worth having is the hope of heaven in the presence of God. Perhaps you read of the scandal when one of the country's cryonics labs went broke a couple of years ago, and months after the bank had foreclosed on the property they found the rotting corpses of the men and women who had bet their hopes and their futures on science. That was the image of reality, and the truth is that without hope in the One who gives eternal life free of charge, our only hope is self-destruction and an emptiness in the soul. We all have a future in this world, a chance to do something with our lives that will make a difference.

But we also have eternal life waiting for us. Those who come to the cross of Christ will spend eternity in His presence; while those who trust in science, government, or some other illusion will spend the same eternity in hell, without God, without happiness, and without hope. Which do you choose?

Faith is a great and audacious act. Faith steps out on God's promises and takes the challenge to live each day in His Word and by His vision of truth. But faith in God also means a commitment to all God's creatures, to our families, our communities, our nation, and our world. We have a Great Commission from God Almighty to carry that truth to all the world; and we have the mandate of heaven to help influence this world with the Good News of Jesus Christ.

Standing before you today are two options—two alternative futures. You can choose to get involved in the calling of God upon your life and find the joy and purpose that come through being a follower of Christ; or you can be like Tom Donaldson and the others who have found the emptiness and the corruption of the world. In this moment, this hour, I urge you to choose whom you will serve, and put your life in the hands of the Savior of mankind.

The final chapter will look in more depth at the first of these two options and see what the victory of faith entails.

NOTES

[1]Robert D. Kaplan, "The Coming Anarchy: How scarcity, crime, overpopulation, tribalism, and disease are rapidly destroying the social fabric of our planet," *The Atlantic* (February 1994): 44ff.

[2]Martin L. Gross, *The Government Racket: Washington Waste from A to Z* (New York: Bantam, 1992), 2.

[3]Maria Goodavage, "Man Pins His Hopes on a Frozen Future; De-animated, Not Dead," *USA Today*, (September 25, 1990), sec. 6A.

12

The Victory of Faith

In the March 1994 issue of *The Advocate*, a publication for gays, U.S. Surgeon General Dr. Joycelyn Elders said the antigay sentiment in this nation is due to an irrational fear of sex. In the article she endorsed the rights of gays and lesbians to adopt children, she denounced the Boy Scouts of America for being prejudiced against homosexuals and said that conservative Christians are to blame for many of the problems in this nation. "I think the religious right at times thinks that the only reason for sex is procreation," she said. "Well, I feel that God meant sex for more than procreation. Sex is about pleasure as well as about responsibility."

Dr. Joycelyn Elders, Surgeon General of the United States, exercising ethical judgment over the largest health system in the world, thinks that sex education should begin in kindergarten. Condom distribution is the answer to the nation's sexual problems. "We taught [kids] what to do in the front seat," she once told the nation's media. "Now it's time to teach them what to do in the back seat." And she also said it's time for Christians and other pro-life activists to "get over their love affair with the fetus."

Dr. Joycelyn Elders, who was first appointed by Bill Clinton as Commissioner of Health for Arkansas, presided over the restructuring of health services in her own state and chalked up an impressive record. Under Dr. Elders' leadership, Arkansas went from having the fourth lowest teen pregnancy rate in the nation to the second highest. In July 1993, before Elders was confirmed to her office, columnist Cal Thomas reported that under Dr. Elders syphilis infections went up one hundred-thirty percent in Arkansas and the rate of teens who tested positive for HIV went up one hundred-fifty percent. But those facts didn't stop Dr. Elders' Senate confirmation. Dr. Elders says she does not want to outlaw prostitution but to see that prostitutes have access to the Norplant contraceptive. This would free them up, she said, to sell their sex to buy drugs. And in the of fall 1993, just one day before her son was arrested in Arkansas on suspicion of drug trafficking,[1] Dr. Joycelyn Elders suggested that it's about time this country considers the possibility of legalizing drugs.

THE MORALS VACUUM

Dr. Joycelyn Elders does not have the answer to America's health problems. She has instead the failed politics of the radical Left and she and the Administration are intent on imposing their values on the rest of America. According to a study called "Testing Positive," compiled by the Alan Guttmacher Institute, more than twenty-five percent of Americans are currently infected with at least one of more than twenty sexually transmitted diseases at large in the land today. In 1992 there were one hundred-twenty thousand reported cases of syphilis; 1.1 million cases of gonorrhea; four million cases of genital herpes.

The Center for Disease Control reported recently that fifty-four percent of high school students are sexually active. Today we have unmarried mothers under twelve years of age. I recently read of a welfare grandmother, twenty-eight years old. She gave birth to a daughter at age fourteen, who, in turn, gave birth to a daughter at fourteen; and the cycle of illicit sexuality and welfare dependence breeds one generation after another. According to a report by Kristine Napier of the Responsible Social Values Program (an education system for teaching abstinence to kids), the federal government spends more than one hundred-sixty million dollars of our tax money each year to teach kids about "safe sex," while the truth and security of "abstinence" are almost totally ignored.

Why are these things happening? Because there is a moral vacuum in this country that has been created by the radicals and the political elites who have decided that God and the truths of Scripture have no place in public life. In January 1994, *Newsweek* columnist Robert J. Samuelson said that Americans are sick and tired of the smoke screen being put up by the government that maintains that the economy and political issues are at the heart of the nation's anxiety. He says that what troubles America is the raging immorality and permissiveness that are tearing apart the social fabric of the nation.

On one hand is the permissive attitude that is allowing millions of undocumented aliens to flood the nation and draw upon our generous welfare programs. We have school violence that makes the *Blackboard Jungle* image of the 1950s more like a Sunday-school picnic. While the New York-Los Angeles cultural elite are tearing at the framework of morality and telling young people that promiscuity, homosexuality, and deviant behavior are natural forms of expression, they are attacking the traditional and Christian values of the nation and painting conservatives as censors and Nazis.

More and more Americans feel that they are prisoners in their own homes. They cannot go outside without fear; they cannot let their children play outdoors for fear of child molesters and drive-by shootings; their moral and religious beliefs are openly assaulted; and a new politically correct reinterpretation of America is being installed that makes Orwell's *1984* seem like a benign fairy tale. While the liberals accuse conservatives of censorship, they are actively rewriting the history books in our schools to portray whites as slavers and exploiters, while praising "outgroups" and minorities as the true sources of American dignity and worth.

In one newly released history text, the biographies of famous leaders are allocated by race and gender. In the March 28, 1994 issue of *U.S. News & World Report*, columnist John Leo reports that of two hundred Americans selected for special mention in Holt, Rinehart & Winston's textbook, *The American Nation*, fifty-six are white females, seventy-one are white males, and sixty-eight are nonwhites. Of the white males, forty-one were Presidents, leaving thirty lesser lights, among whom one was a notorious spy and the other a defeated general. Among thirteen religious leaders mentioned, just two are non-Hispanic white males—Brigham Young and Ralph Waldo Emerson.

THE WAR AGAINST GOD

What many people do not realize is that when teachers and college professors, or the liberals who control the nation's media, attack the authentic history and the religious values of this nation, they are actually waging war against God. God is *the* absolute. He is *the* Truth. When anyone attacks truth, ultimately they are attacking God's standards and values. We often hear people say, "Well, things are different today. What was true ten years ago isn't necessarily true anymore." And that is certainly accurate if they're talking about science; but it is not true with regard to moral values. God is the same yesterday, today, and forever, and His values never change.

The atheists, however, say that there are no absolutes because there is no God. The Bible is insignificant, they tell us, because God is an outworn concept. Jesus said, "I tell you the truth, until heaven and earth disappear, not the smallest letter, not the least stroke of a pen, will by any means disappear from the Law until everything is accomplished" (Matt. 5:18). But the secular humanists do not want to believe this statement. When people say there are no absolutes, they are saying that Jesus Christ has no authority in their lives; He is not the Son of God; at best, He was merely a "good man," at worst a fraud.

This is the foundation of modern moral relativism. As we saw in chapter three, this philosophy says there are no standards, no source of authority, no principles of right and wrong, and no ultimate truth in this world. Situational ethics, then, demands that we make up our rules as we go and determine by consensus the "values" by which we can more or less agree to abide. In other words, the basis of law becomes what is culturally and socially expedient.

But how odd that while America is going down the road to cultural anarchy, the former Soviet Union is desperately searching for absolute truth and fundamental moral values. On a trip to the United States, former Soviet President Mikhail Gorbachev said the people of Russia are hoping to create a "a state where politics will be linked to morals." He told reporters that within five years he believed his country would "become a democratic society governed by the rule of law and the observance of human rights."

He warned that "It is virtually impossible to carry out such momentous changes . . . without paying the costs, making mistakes and facing aggravated tensions and even crisis." But the former Communist leader understood that moral values and republican virtues are the only things that can save the Eastern nations from total and absolute collapse. "It will be a state open for the world," he said, "and, in many respects, integrated into global civilized processes."[2]

As Gary Bauer of the Family Research Council has said, the only ones who don't understand what basic moral values and virtues are supposed to be are the radicals and the elites who want to deconstruct this nation. Even the Russians, who have lived under atheistic communism for seventy years, now know that moral absolutes have meaning, and that they are the only hope for preventing the disintegration of society. Bauer says, "There's a core set of family values that comes to everyone's mind unless they live in Washington, New York, or Hollywood. The real gap is between most Americans who still believe in those values, still strive for them, and the cultural elite that just doesn't get it, that think all these things are just lifestyle choices."

Those who do not perceive the danger of the course we are on in this country, as we casually accept the degradation of national morality, are like the man who jumped off the Empire State Building. As he passed the twenty-fourth floor, someone heard him say, "Everything's going along pretty well so far." There are many people who want to take this optimistic view and simply go along to get along, but that sort of compromise is self-destructive and very dangerous. To get our feet back on solid ground, we cannot keep going the way we have been for the past three decades. We have to turn things around, and we have to do it now.

RESTORING FREEDOM AND DIGNITY

To restore the essential values and beliefs of America, we cannot stand idly by. We must engage the enemy and take back what we have lost. Young people need to know the words of Patrick Henry who said, "Give me liberty or give me death!" And they need to recall the words of the patriots who wrote the Declaration of Independence, wherein they said that "all men are created equal, that they are endowed by their Creator with certain unalienable rights, that among these are life, liberty, and the pursuit of happiness." Next to life itself, the most highly prized treasure that could be granted to a people is the gift of liberty. But today we are in danger of losing our liberties through casual neglect.

Many people don't realize that liberty is a constant theme through-out the Bible. The Old Testament tells over and over again the story of the fall of man into slavery, and of God's deliverance of His people. It tells of their being taken into the bondage of Egypt, and of God, at length, bringing them out after four hundred-thirty years of slavery. Again, it tells of their falling into idolatry in their own land and being taken away by the Babylonians into seventy years of captivity only to be delivered once again. All of this is but mere foreshad-owings of the great deliverer and the great emancipator, Jesus Christ, who would come to deliver us from the bondage of sin unto the freedom of new life. Christ took upon Himself the penalty of the cross to free us from the slavery of sin so that we might have liberty.

But liberty for many is just a word. It is a high-flown idea from his-tory, or merely a meaningless concept. It is something that we take for granted and to which we give little thought. Liberty is like the air we breathe. Until it is taken away, we are completely unconscious of it. People go for days without ever thinking about the air they breathe, upon which their life depends, and we seldom stop to think what life would be like if we truly lost our liberty.

Americans tend to think that everybody has liberty, but that is not true. One organization that monitors such things tells us that of the more than two hundred nations on this planet, only twenty-six actually enjoy a way of life that includes political and social freedom. Two hundred years ago, free-dom was virtually unknown in the world. And down through the centuries, very few nations have known anything vaguely approaching the freedom and liberty that we have known in this country until recent times. But we would do well to remember the price that has been paid for liberty by the patriots and veterans of this nation. We need to remember those who fought and bled and died that we might enjoy something that many simply take for granted.

THE FOUNDATION OF FREEDOM

It is historically true that wherever the Gospel of Jesus Christ has been preached, and where the Spirit of the Lord has been spread abroad, free-dom naturally follows. Where human hearts have been set free by the Gospel, it has not been long before their nations have become free, and free governments have replaced tyrannies. We have seen this wherever the purity of the Gospel has gone in this world. Those nations that are free today are free because of the power of the Gospel of Jesus Christ.

The American Revolution produced a new and free nation with republican-democratic government, and people more free than any people had ever been before. The French Revolution, coming right after ours, modeled and attempted to emulate the American Revolution. They were encouraged by the fact that we had been successful in defeating a tyrannical monarchy. However, there were several major differences between the two wars. What was the difference? The French Revolution produced the "Reign of Terror" under Robespierre and the philosophers; it produced the guillotine. Nearly twenty thousand heads rolled in the streets of Paris as the newly liberated crowds overthrew the government and the church in search of a new ideal of human enlightenment. Under the influence of the new liberalism, blood flowed like water. The late-eighteenth century in France was a time of fear, terror, and despotism—anarchy that led to tyranny and the reign of Napoleon. But what went wrong? Wasn't liberty enough?

Alexis de Tocqueville said that the essential difference between the two revolutions was that the American war was fought for "freedom of religion," while the French Revolution was a war against "God and the church." The American Revolution was built upon God, upon His Word, and upon faith in the salvation of Jesus Christ. The French Revolution was anti-God, anti-Christ, and anti-Church. One produced freedom and the other produced slavery. Tocqueville said of America: "There is no country in the world where the Christian religion retains a greater influence over the souls of men than in America, and there is no country so free."

The French believed that religion is the enemy of freedom. The founding fathers of this country believed that religion is the essential and indispensable bulwark of freedom. In fact, as I have said earlier, James Madison, the father of the American Constitution, said, "We have staked the whole future of America's civilization, not upon the power of government, far from it. We have staked the future . . . upon the capacity of each and all of us to govern ourselves, to sustain ourselves, according to the Ten Commandments of God."

The American Revolution came out of a nation of people who, because their hearts were yielded to God, gladly attempted to live by His commandments. John Adams said: "We have no Constitution, we have no government empowered to govern an irreligious or immoral people." The Constitution was not written for irreligious or immoral people, he said. It has no power to control such people.

Today, many Americans have sunk to the place where the French people were in the 1790s. They have confused liberty with license; they have forgotten that *true* liberty is being unshackled from the dominion of sin, the tyranny of men, and their inability to follow God, which thereby enabled them to live for Him a godly, righteous, and moral life. They have seen liberty as the freedom to do any blasphemous, ungodly, immoral, unrighteous thing they can get away with. That seems to be the predominant view of liberty in this country today.

But that was also the view of the French encyclopedists and the bloody revolutionaries. That was the godless view of Robespierre, Napoleon, Joseph Stalin, Benedetto Mussolini, and of Adolf Hitler. That was the view of Karl Marx and Vladimir Lenin, and of every atheist leader of the Soviet Union over their bloody seventy-year descent into chaos and destruction.

THE DANGERS AHEAD

As I have repeated many times, our Constitution was written for a godly people. George Washington said that it is vain to think that any nation can be governed well without the aid of religion and moral values. Unless we have absolute standards of truth, then no idea of truth can prevail. There is no way to maintain law and order unless we acknowledge some secure source of truth, some standard that is fundamental to all others. For centuries, that standard has been the Word of God. But today, because many people in this country have acquiesced to the rise of ungodliness and wickedness without protest, the people of this nation are in danger of exhibiting the same attitude toward religion that the French people had two hundred years ago.

Many in our country today look upon religion as the enemy of freedom. Teachers in many of our public schools have acceded to the policies of the liberal teachers' unions to make sure that students from kindergarten through high school will be stripped of any sense of moral or ethical absolutes. Right and wrong are non-issues in our public schools.

Young people today are ignorant of the foundations of this nation, and they have no trust in and no interest in the truths upon which the nation was established. They are so ignorant of history that the majority of our students do not know that George Washington said, "It would be impossible to govern rightly without God and the Bible." Or that President John Adams said, "It would be impossible to govern without God and the Ten Commandments." Too many of our children care more about the latest vulgar song lyrics and hot rock albums than they do about the fact that their liberties are being eroded before their eyes. We are losing one generation after another to the loose liberal lifestyles of the times, and if we cannot stop this slide into relativism, we may yet lose the nation itself.

The courts of this nation have also robbed young people of any connection with God. They have taken prayer out of the schools. They have gotten rid of the Bible and any reference to the religious foundations of the nation in school textbooks. They have gotten rid of the Ten Commandments. And then they wonder why our country is ungovernable. How ironic that the liberals and leftists who establish the policies of education, government, and the media, because of their own vast ignorance of the foundations of this nation, suppose that they can simply invent adequate standards for this great nation. Everything they stand for is diametrically opposite to the principles upon which the nation was built.

In his classic study, *Religion and Culture*, Christopher Dawson writes that "The recovery of moral control and the return to spiritual order have become the indispensable conditions of human survival. But," he says, "they can be achieved only by a profound change in the spirit of modern civilization." The English scholar does not recommend a new religion or a new culture, but a new spiritual *regeneration*. Unless there is a new integration of faith and culture, and unless political values and religious values can be brought into harmony, he says, then there is little hope for restoring law and order in this country.

OVERCOMING TYRANNY

George Washington said, "Let not that man claim the title of Patriot who labors to undermine those pillars" [of religion and morality]. Such a person is no patriot. He is no friend of this nation. He opposes everything upon which this country was built. But daily these standards are under assault by the Left. We have come such a long way in such a short time. When this nation was founded, it was legal to display a crèche at Christmas or to erect a cross on public land. Blasphemy, vulgarity, and public lewdness, however, were looked upon as crimes against public decency. Today, it is *illegal* to put a crèche on public property or to erect a cross. Only artists like Andres Serrano, with funds supplied by the National Endowment for the Arts, can display Christ on the cross—immersed in urine! "If we will not be governed by God," said William Penn, "we will be ruled by tyrants." Truer words were never spoken.

When people do not have Jesus Christ in their hearts, they are in the bondage of sin; they are shackled by every form of immorality, unrighteousness, and ungodliness, and it takes an increasingly powerful external government to keep them from tearing society apart. That is why either we must have self-government under God, or we will have tyranny. A nation without moral restraint cannot exist; it will be turned into an absolute jungle. "Where the Spirit of the Lord is," said the apostle Paul, "there is liberty." But we must also add that where the Spirit of the Lord is *not*, there are tyranny, bondage, and sin.

The great preacher of the last century, Charles Spurgeon, once reflected upon an important text from the first letter of John, which says:

Everyone who believes that Jesus is the Christ is born of God, and everyone who loves the father loves his child as well. This is how we know that we love the children of God: by loving God and carrying out his commands. This is love for God: to obey his commands. And his commands are not burdensome, for everyone born of God overcomes the world. This is the victory that has overcome the world, even our faith. Who is it that overcomes the world? Only he who believes that Jesus is the Son of God.

—1 JOHN 5:1–5

Spurgeon said he very much appreciated the teachings of the New Testament on love, and most of all he appreciated the writings of John, who wrote so eloquently about this subject. But he was somewhat perplexed by the words of the apostle, "This is the victory that has overcome the world, even our faith" (1 John 5:4). Spurgeon said, "The epistles of John are perfumed with love. . . . From the beginning to the conclusion, love is the manner, love the matter, love the motive, and love the aim. We stand, therefore, not a little astonished, to find such martial words in so peaceful a writing. For I hear a sound of war."

The great preacher felt these were the words of strife and contention, of wrestling and agony, of the clashing of swords. John, the apostle of love, used this image of victory over and over again. In fact, it is somewhat camouflaged by his use of the word "overcome," because it is translated from the Greek *nikao,* the same root used for victory.

John tells us that we are to overcome the world; we are to overcome Satan; we are to become overcomers. Jesus said, "To him who overcomes, I will give the right to sit with me on my throne, just as I overcame and sat down with my Father on his throne" (Rev. 3:21). He said, "He who overcomes will, like them, be dressed in white. I will never blot out his name from the book of life, but will acknowledge his name before my Father and his angels" (Rev. 3:5).

So, it is absolutely essential that we be victorious. Unless we are overcomers who claim victory over tyranny in this world, then we shall not be with Christ in heaven. Are you prepared for this message from Scripture? Charles Spurgeon found it surprising, but he found it true and fully in character with the teachings of Christ. Heaven is for victors. It is not the resting place of losers and defeatists who simply gave up and let the secular liberal elite dictate policy and pervert the world. Heaven is a place designed just for those who have overcome the world, who have been renewed by the blood of Christ, who have conquered through the Holy Spirit the terrors of sin and death, and who are given the right to sit at the throne of grace with our Lord Jesus Christ.

Those who overcome shall be pillars in the house of God. Like the columns of the temples engraved with the names of heroes and great patrons in ancient times, we will have a place of honor in the presence of Christ. Those who stand before the Lord are those who have overcome the world. Are *you* one of them?

THE VICTORY OF FAITH

There are three important principles in this view of ultimate victory that we need to recognize. The first is that the world must be overcome. Unless we overcome the world, Scripture tells us, we do not belong to Christ and will not be with Him. What does the world stand for? In the Scripture the world stands for several things. First of all, it stands for the entire worldly system—of which Satan is the god—with all of its lust and greed and hatred and animosity; with all of its self-centeredness and selfishness. This is the world system that is so antithetical to Christ, and this godless world must be overcome.

A second principle refers to the visible world—the world that is visible, tangible, audible, and that crowds in upon us every day. The physical creation is not evil in itself, but the worldly system that has been created by men is indeed capable of great wickedness. And in the hands of wicked men and women, even the physical creation can be made evil in the same sense that you can take something tangible, like a quarter, and use it for evil instead of for good. The coin itself is not evil, but in the hands of an evil person it can be used to accomplish wickedness.

So in the eternal scheme of things, the world is really nothing at all, but it can be given a place of prominence, as an idol to replace the Triune God in our lives. And if we allow such things to separate us from God, then the things of this world can be fatal. We are engaged in a great struggle against the world, against Satan, against the prince of the powers of the air. It is a bitter warfare against the attractions and enticements of this world. Unless we overcome the world by faith, we will be utterly defeated.

The man or woman who does not have faith in Jesus Christ cannot even conceive of such a thing as "overcoming the world." This is why the second principle in this text is so important. "This is the victory that has overcome the world, even our faith" (1 John 5:4). You notice that the apostle changes the subject here from the Christian who is to engage the world to the source of victory. In the first verse he speaks of "everyone who believes that Jesus is the Christ is born of God." But the source of victory is in the neuter form, because John is referring to a thing, and that thing is our "faith." Our faith comes from the regenerating power of God. For that which is born of God overcomes the world. And the source of victory—that great power that overcomes sin and adversity and tribulation—is the work of Christ in our hearts, even our faith. So it is faith born of God that overcomes the darkness and disaster of the world.

We must be born of God. Otherwise we cannot understand what it means to overcome the world. We cannot even conceive of thinking about overcoming the world, because Jesus made it clear when He said, "I tell you the truth, no one can enter the kingdom of God unless he is born of water and the Spirit. Flesh gives birth to flesh, but the Spirit gives birth to spirit" (John 3:5–6). So we must be born again.

This is not the view of some little group somewhere. It is not some "evangelical" fad. No, it is the commandment of our Commander-in-Chief. It is the imperial declaration of the Lord God Almighty, the Son of the Ever-lasting God, that One who created heaven and earth, and who will decide who enters heaven. Jesus said, "Most assuredly, I say to you, unless one is born again, he cannot see the kingdom of God." And He also says that unless we are born again, we cannot even see the kingdom of heaven. Therefore, for anyone who is lost and apart from God, it is unrealistic to even think about overcoming this world.

For such a person, this world is all there is. Those who long for the treasures of this world are ripe for the wiles of the so-called "prosperity preachers." This is the "name-it, claim-it, and frame-it" gang. The trouble with these shortsighted people is that they have completely lost sight of the goal. They teach people how to seek after this world's goods—how to become better citizens of "Vanity Fair." Jesus said that we should not lay up for ourselves treasure on earth where moth and rust can corrupt, but we are to lay up treasures in heaven. What the "prosperity preachers" are doing is teaching people how to lay up treasures on earth. They use "faith" to accomplish worldly ends, and thus they have distorted and corrupted Christ's teachings. No wonder they have suffered such public humiliation.

SLAVE AND MASTER

How do we overcome the world? We overcome it when we see the world for what it really is with all of its tawdriness, and in the case of the worldly system, in all of its evil. In the case of the physical world, we see it in its brevity; we see it only as that which should lift us up unto God. Unfortunately, there are many people who think they have overcome the world when they have simply gained a large chunk of it. But this is not what Jesus means.

I think of a man who started out well. He did well in business. He would have illustrated John Wesley's saying, "Make all you can, save all you can, give all you can." He was tithing his income regularly, and God blessed him in doing that, and he became more and more prosperous. Then one day the man went up to Peter Marshall, the famous chaplain of the United States Senate, and said, "Dr. Marshall, I have a problem. I have been tithing now for some time. It wasn't too bad when I was making twenty thousand dollars a year. I could afford to give the two thousand. But, you see, doctor, now I am making five hundred thousand dollars a year and there is just no way I can afford to give away fifty thousand dollars a year."

Dr. Marshall said, "Yes, sir. I see that you do have a problem. I think we ought to pray about it. Is that all right?"

The man agreed, so Dr. Marshall bowed his head and said, "Dear Lord, this man has a problem, and I pray that you will help him. Lord, reduce his salary back to the place where he can afford to tithe."

The man was so startled he let out a yelp. "No, Dr. Marshall, that's not what I meant!" But the point was made very well. Who is the master, and who is he that overcomes the world? We are to have mastery over things, not to let things have mastery over us. It has often been said that money makes a wonderful servant but a terrible master. And yet there are many people in this country—and many Christians, I'm afraid—who are completely enslaved by money. They give all of their thought to it. If they are not thinking about how to get more of it, they're thinking about how to hold on to what they have. That is indeed a form of slavery.

Consider the story that Jesus told about Lazarus and Dives, the rich man who lived sumptuously and had the finest of everything. Lazarus was the beggar who sat at his door, eating crumbs from the master's table. Eventually, they both died. Lazarus went into heaven, to Abraham's bosom, and Dives went to hell. Who really was the victor in all of that? One man had made and spent a fortune, the other had accomplished almost nothing in this world. As the parable continues, the rich man cries out:

"Father Abraham, have pity on me and send Lazarus to dip the tip of his finger in water and cool my tongue, because I am in agony in this fire." But Abraham replied, "Son, remember that in your lifetime you received your good things, while Lazarus received bad things, but now he is comforted here and you are in agony. And besides all this, between us and you a great chasm has been fixed, so that those who want to go from here to you cannot, nor can anyone cross over from there to us."

He answered, "Then I beg you, father, send Lazarus to my father's house, for I have five brothers. Let him warn them, so that they will not also come to this place of torment." Abraham replied, "They have Moses and the Prophets; let them listen to them." "No, father Abraham," he said, "but if someone from the dead goes to them, they will repent." He said to him, "If they do not listen to Moses and the Prophets, they will not be convinced even if someone rises from the dead."

—LUKE 16:24–31

There have been many good people who lived in a tiny garret or cottage and managed to gain very few of this world's goods. Yet their hearts were right with God. There are some today who have a concern for the kingdom of Jesus Christ, a passion for bringing others into that kingdom. They are people who witness faithfully to others wherever they go. These are people who have overcome the world. I am thankful there are some who, because of the grace of God and their faith, have been blessed by God with success and have managed to accumulate a certain amount of wealth. And yet they have continued to serve Christ and to witness for Him. Whether in poverty or plenty, what Christ wants is our hearts.

LAYING UP TREASURES

I once had the pleasure of knowing a man who was phenomenally rich in the things of this world. He had hundreds of millions of dollars, and yet his great zeal was to be a witness for Jesus Christ. He never saw anyone, I don't believe, with whom he didn't find a way to share the Gospel. He was a victor over this world. But no one will ever do that unless he has been born of God. Those who belong to this world cannot enter the kingdom of heaven—they can't even see it. Therefore, it would be ridiculous in their eyes to try to overcome the world; all they want to do is gain more and more of it, not realizing that they are becoming more and more enslaved to the things of this world. We overcome the world only through faith. Faith is the victory, the apostle John says, and as a well-known hymn declares: "Faith is the victory! . . . that over-comes the world."

If anyone has any doubt about this being the true meaning of "over-coming the world," then he or she needs to look upon Jesus Christ, because that is where John was looking when he wrote these words. No doubt he recalled that great solemn night, the night that Jesus went into Gethsemane to pray, the night before He was stripped and beaten and nailed to the cross. After they had finished their supper, Jesus said to them, "In this world you will have tribula-tion. But take heart! I have overcome the world" (John 16:33).

That was truly a most astonishing statement. Here is a person who has none of this world's goods. The Son of Man does not even have a place to lay His head. All that He owns He has on His body, and even that will be taken away from Him before twenty-four hours is past. Here is one who is being hounded and searched for, one who has been hated and soon will be taken and killed—a person who is apparently an utter, total failure by the standards of this world. Yet this Christ says, "In this world you will have trouble [whether persecution or heartache or trials]. But take heart! I have overcome the world."

Jesus was an overcomer! He was not deceived by this world. He wasn't grasping for the things of this life. He saw the world for what it was and His eyes were fixed on the eternal kingdom of God. He knew the world for what it really is. It is only by faith that we can reach out and be connected to Him, the Great Conqueror. It is only by faith that we have the victory in Jesus. For we now partake of the victory that Christ won on the cross, so that we no longer merely struggle toward victory, but rather we go from victory unto victory. The battle is won. The war is won. We are the victors in Jesus Christ if we trust in Him. Our faith is trusting in Jesus Christ and believing that He will give us the victory.

I think of the story of a young man I greatly admire. He was a com-mitted Christian—one of those who is sold out for Christ—a man whose eyes were fixed upon the Lord. His great desire in life was to serve Christ and to glo-rify Him and to make Him known to others. He was enrolled in a freshman chemistry class at a Canadian university. The professor, an atheist, was an arch-enemy of Christians and used every opportunity to mock the faith of his stu-dents. Being concerned about the warfare that was being waged against people of faith, the young man went to the campus religion counselor and talked to him about the problem. The counselor said, "You haven't seen anything yet. Wait until you get to the *pièce de résistance* later in the course. He goes through this same little drama every time, which consists of holding a test tube out over a concrete floor and asking if anyone in the class believes that *prayer* can keep that test tube from breaking when he drops it.

"Of course, all of the students see what is happening, and most of them are afraid to accept that challenge. So they just keep silent, and the professor mocks them and says, 'Just as I thought. Nobody really believes in the power of prayer. Obviously, prayer is just a hoax.'"

After hearing this, the freshman said to the counselor, "Will you enter into a covenant with me to pray every day until that big event that God will overcome and Christ will gain the victory? I intend to challenge the professor when the time comes." And so they agreed.

The weeks went by, one by one. Every day they prayed that Christ would gain the victory. Then, finally, the big day arrived. The professor took a test tube, held it out over the concrete floor and said, "Is there anyone here that really believes in prayer?" The young man stood up and said, "Yes sir, I do."

Startled, the professor said, "Well, what do you know? We've got a live one this year! Young man, are you willing to pray that if I drop this test tube on the concrete floor that it will not break?"

"Yes, sir, I am," said the student. So he bowed his head and started praying: "Dear Lord Jesus, You know that there are believers in You who have been praying that You will gain the victory today; that You will keep that test tube from breaking. We pray that You will glorify Your name and that You will overcome in this instance. In Thy name, Amen."

Whether because the professor had bent his elbow a little bit more than usual, or perhaps turned toward the class and didn't realize how he was standing, but in the electric silence that filled the room when he dropped that test tube, it glanced off the toe of his shoe and skidded across the concrete floor, and it didn't break! Suddenly the whole class burst into laughter and loud cheers. Finally someone had taken on this Goliath of an atheist and defeated him. And Christ gained the victory!

LESSONS FROM THE EAST

Corrie ten Boom used to say, "Jesus is Victor!" Jesus is always victorious, even in defeat. But how often we accept defeat without gaining the victory for Christ. When we look at the condition of the sin-sick world around us, I often wonder what it will take for the Christians in this nation to wake up to the challenges being thrown in our faces by the world? Will we wake up to the crises around us and stand up for our faith? Do we even understand that we are enduring a crisis of faith?

Recently I read in *Foreign Affairs* magazine a very informative interview with the former Prime Minister of the nation-state of Singapore. Perhaps you know that Singapore, under its powerful leader Lee Kuan Yew, has become one of the richest and most dynamic nations in the East. It has a booming economy, a gross national product that exceeds that of Great Britain, and is the third largest refiner of oil and gas in the world. Manufacturing, shipping, and distribution services in that tiny country have been ranked among the finest in the world.

Much of the credit for this incredible success goes to the former Prime Minister who kept a firm hand on the government and made sure that law and order were never sacrificed for the sake of progress or "new ideas." Most recently, Singapore has made headlines for its stand on carrying out the "caning" of the American student, Michael Fay, who was convicted of vandalizing automobiles and other property in that nation. The same sense of values the world witnessed in the caning incident demonstrates the leader's attitude concerning justice, fair play, and personal responsibility.

At one point in the interview, the magazine reporter asked this brilliant man what he thought might be the problem with the American system. Lee said, "It is not my business to tell people what's wrong with their system. It is my business to tell people not to foist their system indiscriminately on societies in which it will not work." He meant that he does not like for the United States or other nations to try to push their systems—many of which are less successful than Singapore's—on his own country. But after some further prompting, the distinguished leader made some startling but insightful remarks about the conditions in the United States today.

The reporter asked, "Would it be fair to say that you admired America more twenty-five years ago? What, in your view, went wrong?"

Lee responded, "Yes, things have changed. I would hazard a guess that it has a lot to do with the erosion of the moral underpinnings of a society and the diminution of personal responsibility. The liberal intellectual tradition that developed after World War II claimed that human beings had arrived at this perfect state where everybody would be better off if they were allowed to do their own thing and flourish."

Then he continued, "It has not worked out and I doubt if it will. Certain basics about human nature do not change. Man needs a certain moral sense of right and wrong. There is such a thing as evil, and it is not the result of being a victim of society. You are just an evil man, prone to do evil things, and you have to be stopped from doing them. Westerners," he said, "have abandoned an ethical basis for society, believing all problems are solvable by a good government, which we in the East never believed possible."

Then after a few more questions, Mr. Lee came to a very important point that seems to have been missed by some of the brightest minds in this country. "In the West," he said, "especially after World War II, the government came to be seen as so successful that it could fulfill all the obligations which in less modern societies are fulfilled by the family. This approach encouraged alternative families, single mothers for instance, believing that government could provide support to make up for the absent father." And he added, "there is grave disquiet when we break away from tested norms, and the tested norm is the family unit. It is the building block of society."[3]

WHAT ANYONE CAN SEE

Family values, punishment for crime, immediate incarceration and treatment for drug offenders, respect for tradition, and reverence for spiritual values. All these things that have contributed so greatly to Lee's success in Singapore are routinely ignored by the political and cultural elites in the United States today. How is it that an Asian, who does not even live in this country, who is not a Christian, and who has absolutely no input into the affairs of the United States government, can come to such an incisive and astute evaluation of the problems in this country when the leaders of our own government are seemingly blind?

How is it that Dr. Joycelyn Elders, Surgeon General of the United States of America, a medical doctor who is charged with the health and well-being of more than two hundred-fifty million Americans, has so obviously missed these obvious truths? While the sirens wail around her, Dr. Elders chooses to parade her own immoral agenda before the world, loudly and adamantly, calling evil good and good evil. And virtually every policy she prescribes, with the full support of the president and the United States Congress, contributes to the inevitable destruction of the nation.

How ironic. While the United States wallows in defeat and immorality, following the failed ideas of the radical Left, men and women thousands of miles away have no problem seeing the folly of our self-destruction. Commenting further on the problems in this country, Lee Kuan Yew says he finds parts of the American system totally unacceptable—guns, drugs, violent crime, vagrancy, unbecoming behavior in public—"in sum, the breakdown of society." And then he says, "The expansion of the individual's rights to behave or misbehave has come at the expense of orderly society." And what can we expect the result of such stupid policies to be? You complete the answer. Unless you happen to be a member of Congress or the federal bureaucracy, the answer should be perfectly clear.

Jesus said, "This is the victory that has overcome the world, even our faith." But I must ask, have *you* overcome the world, or has the world overcome you? Have you been born of God, or, as Christ said of the Pharisees, are you the child of your father, the Devil? There are two families of this world, the children of God and the children of the Devil. To which family do you belong?

What you must know is that we were all born into Satan's family, and if we hope to spend eternity with Christ, we must be *born again* into God's family. Only through new life in Jesus Christ can anyone in this world ever hope to enter God's family. And we only obtain the victory by faith, by the marvelous work of the regenerating power of the Holy Spirit. Without that faith, without the new birth, and without that overcoming and that victory, we will not, indeed, we cannot, enter the victory that Christ has made available to His own.

My fervent prayer is that God will grant to each one of us the will to stand against the darkness and tyranny of this world. And I pray that He will grant us the wisdom, the tenacity, and the will to claim the victory that overcomes the world. Through commitment to Christ, and through a renewed commitment to a strong moral character, we still have the opportunity to restore the fortunes of this nation.

Ultimately the destiny of mankind is in God's hands; but He has empowered us to serve Him here and now. He has given us the power and the resources to overcome the world. Will you join with me, and with the millions of others who are dedicated to this goal, in reclaiming America for Christ?

NOTES

[1]*The Economist*, Jan. 22, 1994, 26.

[2]John M. Simpson, "Gorbachev's Vision: a Nation of Morals," *USA Today,* (June 5, 1990), sec. 1A.

[3]Fareed Zakaria, "Questions and Answers with Lee Kuan Yew," *Foreign Affairs* (March/April 1994).

Conclusion

The Destiny of Man

We have traveled many miles in these pages. We have examined a lot of difficult social and political issues, and we have reviewed comments and perspectives from many well-informed people on these subjects. What I have tried to show is that the demoralization of the American people and the deconstruction of our historic values over the past four decades have introduced dangerous forces within society, which, unless checked, will destroy this nation.

Christians have avoided the dirty business of politics for too long. While Christians have withdrawn into their holy huddles, the nation has been taken from us and transformed by secular liberals and humanists into a nation we no longer recognize. Because we were not there to be counted—and because we consoled ourselves with the silly notion that we could be a "silent majority"—people who have a very different agenda for America have stripped the nation of its pride, dignity, and honor.

Christians have avoided the political arena because they have been silenced by the false doctrine of "the separation of church and state." But, as I have said over and over again, that silence is a luxury we can no longer afford. As government attempts to intrude in our lives, in our homes, and even in our most sacred institutions, it is up to men and women of faith to take matters back into their own hands. It was Christians who founded this nation, and only people empowered by dynamic faith can save it. Whatever anyone may believe about such a statement in this day of "diversity" and "tolerance," I maintain that this view is simply true as stated. Unless we regain the moral authority upon which the nation was founded, and unless we return to the godly principles that allow society to function in harmony, there is very little hope that this nation can avert imminent disaster.

But even while I insist that Christians bear a great responsibility for the political future of this nation, through their devotion to truth and moral values, at the same time we must all reach out to people of every background and every perspective and work to build coalitions of men and women who share our concerns. We must appeal to all those who care about the issues that we care about. We do not have to agree on every aspect of every issue, but we must unite with like-minded citizens and work together as a mighty force for good in the world.

The object is to gain new allies for a good cause. We must not allow the doctrines of diversity and multiculturalism so much in vogue today to divide us and make us a splintered society. We are still the "United" States of America, and if we expect to continue without commitment to "life, liberty, and the pursuit of happiness," we must work for political and moral unity. It is time for us to take back this nation so that we might once again be a nation with a brilliant future and a glorious destiny, but we must also be committed to the general welfare and prosperity of all Americans.

BREAKING SILENCE

The place to start is at the local level, in the schools, on the zoning boards, town and county councils, in the local courtrooms, and serving on state advisory committees. " Every skirmish in the "culture war" counts. Every battle is important. Every act and every deed that helps to bring about positive change and renewal matters for the future of this society.

During a dinner meeting with our Leadership Council in Fort Lauderdale, Mr. Quayle made one of his most perceptive remarks. He said that in his encounters with liberal leaders, the media, and other secular organizations, he found that there is just one thing those people want from Christians: our silence. I am sad to say that they have been all too successful in getting it from us to date. But we cannot allow that situation to continue. We must break silence and get back into the arena.

Throughout this book I have dealt with many of the issues that should be of concern to Americans today. I have examined the fact that we are enduring a "crisis of culture" and a "crisis of moral authority." We saw the dominant issues of the day and how the assault of secular liberalism has made us "a nation at risk" and a nation whose destiny has suddenly become very uncertain. In the first section of the book I explored in depth the objectives of the Great Commission and the cultural mandate given to us by God Himself. Then I urged each of you to get into the fray by speaking out for freedom and reclaiming the heritage our founding fathers fought and died for.

In his remarks, Mr. Quayle observed that some Christians have avoided the political arena because they have been silenced by the false doctrine of "the separation of church and state." But, he said, that silence is a luxury we can no longer afford. As government becomes more and more intrusive in our schools, neighborhoods, homes, and now even our health care, we must scrap any notion of retreat and come home with a vengeance. Christians need to come back to the public square as Charles de Gaulle came back to France at the end of World War II. "Their goal," said Mr. Quayle, "was to restore Paris as the 'City of Light.' Our goal is to restore America as the 'Shining City on a Hill.'"

Mr. Quayle suggested that, if we expect to be effective and successful, we must reach out to people of every background and every perspective. We must appeal to all those who care about the issues that concern us. We do not have to agree on every aspect of every issue, but we need to build coalitions with those whom we agree with on key principles so that, together, we can become a mighty force for good in the world. The object is to gain new allies for a good cause. "Religious America," he said, "should not allow itself to be broken into immigrant believers, native-born believers, white, black, and Hispanic believers. Scripture tells us that all of our divisions disappear in Christ. It's time for us to take that to heart." It is time for us to take back this nation so that we might once again be a nation with a brillian future and a glorious destiny.

In the final section, I focused specifically on issues of character and destiny, on the various claims on the soul of this nation, and on the alternative futures before us. It is my hope, in each of these chapters, to show that the power for renewal has already been granted to us by Jesus Christ, who has told us that we can be "more than conquerors" through the wisdom of His Word and the power of the Holy Spirit who lives within every Christian's heart. The only thing that prevents us from claiming the victory is the level of our personal commitment and dedication to the task, whatever the cost.

Already the secular world is collapsing around us. People are dying for the truth of God's Word that can break their bondage to sin. As one social program after another fails, as taxes skyrocket out of control, as government spending puts us behind the eight ball of history, and as the social fabric of our cities degenerates into gang warfare, crime, and every form of abuse, the people of this nation know that some sort of change must come, and soon. The Administration in power has pulled the wool over the eyes of the voters, but suddenly people are beginning to wake up. There has never been a better time for Christians to get active and go on the offensive than now.

THE CALL TO COMMITMENT

I hope that in the process of looking at the pros and cons of all these issues, and in seeing just how far this nation has strayed from the truth that sets us free, you may now have a better idea of the risks and the responsibilities before you today. I hope that every reader of this book will have gained a new sense of self-determination and a commitment to no longer be part of the "silent majority" but to speak out.

First of all, I urge you to tell others about the Gospel of Jesus Christ, and then about the values of the cultural mandate. There is no way this country is going to be changed without a renewal of faith and a new commitment to our Savior. But we must also speak out about the principles upon which this nation was built. All too often, in our own timidity, we have cowered outside the public arena and left the platform to the atheists and secular liberals who want to "redefine" America and take us down the pathway to socialism. Because we have not spoken out and taken a stand for the things that truly matter, we have put our lives—and the lives of our children—in great jeopardy.

But I believe with all my heart that if we bring the good news of the Gospel to men, women, and children who are lost, then we will see yet a magnificent rebirth all across this land—a regeneration of faith and values and a restoration of what America has always meant to the world—not only a beacon of freedom and democracy but a land where justice, honor, and virtue prevail. Our hope is that America might once more be a land of *character* and a bastion of moral integrity.

The fact that we want to see a restitution of Christian values in this nation does not mean that we demand that everyone in this nation believe as we believe or do as we do. The Constitution, and the original intent of the founders, was that every person in this nation would be free to believe as his conscience dictates. Christians support with all their hearts the ideal of "religious liberty." And furthermore, we do not hate anyone, as our critics so often claim. We do indeed desire that those who are lost and who do not know the Savior would come to the cross of Christ; we do indeed hope that those who are spiritually blind would have their eyes opened to the way of truth; and we do indeed pray that those who are bound in the chains of sin and brokenness might be delivered and emancipated from the world of darkness. But we have no desire to force our beliefs down anyone's throat.

We want to see those who are pulling this country down lifted up. Our faith—and the Word of God—tell us that the only joy is to be found at the right hand of God, not in the pigsty of the world. But we do not intend to *force* anyone to believe as we do. We want people to be joyful because they have opened their eyes to God's Word and their hearts to Jesus Christ, who alone is the source of joy in this world.

The angel said that first Christmas night, "We bring you good tidings of great joy!" Every Christian should be determined to share those good tidings with everyone he meets. It is wonderful to see lives turned around and transformed by the wonder-working power of the Gospel. Believe me, I know what it means to have your life transformed. I have been there. I became a Christian at the age of twenty-four. My best friend, drinking buddy, and fellow carouser, had been converted the year before. He told me later that he had once considered coming to share the Gospel with me, but he said, "No, that Jim Kennedy is beyond hope. He is beyond being reached even by the grace of God, and if I talked to him about Jesus Christ he would probably punch me in the mouth." So he never came.

No one in twenty-four years ever came to tell me about the Gospel. I had to hear it for myself on a radio program from fifteen hundred miles away. After all those years, a radio preacher touched my heart, and his message awakened me to the "Good News" of forgiveness and eternal life. Until that time, even though I had rubbed shoulders with many Christians, no one told me that I could have new life in Christ. Everyone concluded that I was beyond hope. That's why I say we must be *silent no longer*.

GOD'S PURPOSE FOR YOU

God is in the business of building character. What interests the Creator of the universe is not how much wealth or power you attain in this world. He is not interested in the size of your home, your car, or your bank account. God does not keep His eye on you to see if you are a "winner" in this life; He is much more concerned with how you live each hour, how you love those around you, and how you prepare your heart for life in the kingdom of God. He cares most about your integrity, your conscience, your heart, and your soul. God wants you to be filled with the love of Jesus Christ and the indwelling power of His Holy Spirit. He wants you to be an "overcomer," a follower of the Savior who confronts this sin-sick world with faith and conviction. He want you to be one who helps to bring renewal and repentance. In short, God's interest in you begins and ends with your character.

If you look around in any direction, you will see the evidence of God's judgment upon this world. The crime raging through the land is a sign of judgment; broken homes and ruined lives are evidence of judgment. Storms, floods, tornadoes: All these things are a wake-up call to this nation to get right with God. As just one graphic example, I read recently that the earthquakes that blasted Southern California in January 1994 devastated at least seventy pornographic film companies housed in the San Fernando Valley. Those companies were responsible for ninety-five percent of the X-rated videos made in the Unites States each year. A report in the *Seattle Post Intelligencer* said that the epicenter of the quake was precisely where the X-rated video industry was headquartered, in a tightly clustered area in the town of Northridge. The front-page story even said that the level of destruction was "apocalyptic," and the reporter quoted a businessman who once supplied actors to the porn industry, who said, "It's enough to give you an attack of religion." My reaction was, "Congratulations! At least one person got the message. But what is he going to do about it now?"

The important thing from God's perspective is not merely hiding the truth in our hearts but sharing it with the world around us. It is not enough to hide our light under a bushel, as the verse says, but to reveal the light of truth to a world dying in sin. When it comes to sharing our faith and impacting our culture, silence is far from golden. If the one thing the world desperately wants from Christians is our silence, then I hope that you will make up your mind that you will no longer accept that sentence of silence. I hope that you will resign your membership in the "silent majority" and burn your draft card in that defeated army.

I urge you to speak out, first of all, about the Gospel of Jesus Christ—to be obedient to the Great Commission. This country will never be changed unless individuals are put in touch with the life-changing message of salvation through Jesus Christ. Second, I urge you to become involved in the cultural and political life of our nation. Write letters, register to vote, speak out in public forums, run for office, and stand up in whatever way you can for those principles on which America was built. Politics may be a dirty business, but so long as you and I leave it to the secularists and atheists, we can't expect it to get any better. But if we remain silent, we shave no right to complain when things get worse.

Now is the time for men and women of conviction to break silence, to fulfill the Great Commission, to take up the cultural mandate, and to reclaim this nation for Christ. Let's not just break the silence, let's break the "sound barrier" both in sharing the good news with others and in applying biblical truth to the problems of our day.

THIS PRODIGAL NATION

Everyone knows the story of the Prodigal Son. But in bringing this work to a close, I would like to paraphrase that familiar parable and tell you another one—the story of the prodigal nation. The story might be entitled "One People's Pilgrimage to the Pigsty," and that certainly has been the course that America has been on for some time. But one thing is certain: like the Prodigal Son, this prodigal nation began its life in a godly Christian home. For those who have followed along with me through the record of our history, there can be no reasonable doubt of that fact. Massive efforts are being made to eradicate the legacy of faith from the collective consciousness of the nation. But all the effort in the world can never remove the truth of history. The historical record speaks for itself.

Like the Prodigal Son, this prodigal nation was also enticed by dreams of a far country—a far country that bears the name of "secular humanism" and "sensual self-indulgence." The ads on television, the radio, and the magazines were stunning. It truly looked like a dream come true, and the travel brochures were beautiful. There was license and liberty without law. All your wildest fantasies could come true. There was nothing to restrain your passions. You were free to enjoy it all. Keep in mind that secular humanism is nothing more than atheism with a Madison Avenue makeover, and it has been painted in brilliant colors by the secular humanist media of our day. Atheism is negative: It says there is no God. But modern humanism wanted to put on a positive face—surely the power of positive thinking could transform a negative into a positive. Atheism said, "Down with God." But humanism says, "Up with man"—and, while we're at it, "Down with God." The ideal of humanism is that man is to be seated on the throne. There is no room for God there. So, swallowing all these deceptions, we ran off to the far country of the humanist dream.

What is it like in this far country? Steve Turner, a noted British journalist, wrote a tongue-in-cheek view of what might be the "Apostle's Creed" of the humanist's dream of that far country. Every week the faithful stand and recite their creed. This, of course, is decidedly tongue-in-cheek, so maybe we should call it the "Apostate's Creed." I hope that you are able to grasp the irony of what he says:

> We today believe in Marx, Freud, and Darwin [the holy trinity]. We believe everything is okay, as long as you don't hurt anyone, to the best of your definition of "hurt," and to the best of your definition of "knowledge." We believe in sex before, during, and after marriage. We believe in the therapy of sin. We believe that taboos are taboo. We believe that everything is getting better despite evidence to the contrary. The evidence must be investigated, and you can prove anything with evidence. We believe there is something in horoscopes, UFOs, and bent spoons. Jesus was a good man, just like Buddha, Mohammed, and ourselves. He was a good moral teacher, although we think his good morals were really bad.
>
> We believe that all religions are basically the same—at least the ones that we read were. They all believe in love and goodness. They only differ on matters of creation, sin, heaven, hell, God, and salvation. We believe that after death comes nothing, because when you ask the dead what happened, they say nothing. If death is not the end, then the dead have lied, and it is compulsory heaven for all—except perhaps for Hitler, Stalin, and Genghis Kahn.
>
> We believe in Masters and Johnson. What's selected is average, and what's average is normal, and what's normal is good. We believe in total disarmament. We believe there are direct links between warfare and bloodshed . . . We

believe that man is essentially good; it's only his behavior that lets him down. This (of course) is the fault of society. Society is the fault of conditions, and conditions are the fault of society. We believe that each man must find the truth that is right for him and reality will adapt accordingly. The universe will readjust, history will alter. We believe that there is no absolute truth except the truth that there is no absolute truth.

HEADED FOR HARD TIMES

For all its good humor, this really is the credo of the humanists who inhabit the far country today. The intellectuals and liberal elites of our culture are naturally opposed to the traditions and standards of our culture. For them, moral truths are merely relative. They would have us believe that all lifestyles are of equal value. They do not acknowledge the sacred value of the traditional family, made up of one mother, one father, and their dependent children. For them, any group of consenting adults equals a family. And despite the fact that such a view can destroy the very foundations of American culture, these "opinion leaders" have succeeded in convincing the majority of Americans that their views are correct. The traditional Judeo-Christian view of "family" is being eroded before our eyes.

How does Christianity fare in the far country? The *SCP Journal* says, "Christianity, which is becoming ever more politically *in*correct, is increasingly at odds with the emerging monolithic creed of this present time, which sees as one of today's root problems the fact that God is not tolerant of 'sin,' that He stands in judgment over sin (which He defines as evil.) God is not 'open-minded.'" Indeed, that is a problem for those who want to fly by their own rules. The "sacred cows" of the far country—such as abortion and homosexuality—are by contrast among the most defiling sins according to the biblical worldview. What one system calls good the other calls evil.

It seems that it is even impossible to teach good and evil, right and wrong, ethics or morals in the universities of the far country. A few years ago, things had become so chaotic in the business world, with so many scandals and evils, that the distinguished professors of the Harvard Business School felt obliged to establish a "Chair on Ethics." A good idea, perhaps, but in case you think the liberal deans and tenured radicals had suddenly come to their senses, think again. Those who took the Harvard course on ethics discovered that the purpose of the curriculum was not to teach people how to be more ethical but to analyze decisions that businesses should make to stay out of trouble with the law. The bottom line, we discovered, was, "Don't do anything that will get your name in the newspapers!" The standard was not morality or even ethics but newsprint. If it won't look good in print, then don't do it. Those are the morals of the far country.

Not long ago Chuck Colson wrote an article contending that it just might be impossible for Harvard to teach ethics today. Real ethics, he noted are based on a genuine understanding of right and wrong, and Harvard long ago abandoned any belief system based on absolute truth. "Harvard's philosophical relativism," Colson says, "precluded the teaching of real ethics." And he adds, "No wonder the best they could offer was a course in pragmatics."

In the far country nothing is ever right and wrong, except, of course, those who say there are things that are right or wrong. But the more he indulged in sin and vice and sexual immorality, the more the Prodigal began to think that perhaps things were not as wonderful in the far country as the travel brochures had led him to believe. After he had wasted all of his inheritance in riotous living, there came a famine in the land. We have not quite reached that point yet in our prodigal nation. Some of our citizens have perhaps gone further, and some not quite as far as others. Indeed, some have gone all the way to the bottom of the barrel.

When the Prodigal Son woke up to find that he had spent all his fortune, he also saw that the land was besieged by a great famine. And when we do finally spend all our fortune in our riotous living, charging the tab to our children and grandchildren in terms of an outrageous federal deficit, there is going to come—some economists say it will come in the next seven to ten years—a time when the total interest on the federal debt will equal the total budget of the United States government. The balloon will burst, and then comes the famine.

A DANGEROUS DIAGNOSIS

The Prodigal Son ended up in a pigsty feeding the swine, and that is exactly where our prodigal nation is headed as well. Some of our citizens have already arrived, via the quicker shortcuts of drugs, immorality, sex, and alcohol. But the rest of the nation is rapidly following their footsteps. Thanks to the hedonism of the "Me Generation" and the "new morality" of the sixties, this country has undergone what some have called a "sexual revolution." The startling fact is that there are fifty-six million people in America who now carry the scars of sexually transmitted disease. That's not just a toboggan ride down the slippery slope, it's a supersonic transport. And the number is growing at twelve million new cases diagnosed every year. That means that in just five years, there will be an additional sixty million people suffering from humiliating and potentially life-threatening illnesses brought on by sexual immorality. Add up those numbers and you have a total of one hundred-sixteen million Americans with STDs; and that is over half of all of the people in this country over the age of twelve. The name of that place is called the pigsty, and we're rapidly approaching it.

However, the story of the Prodigal Son doesn't end in a pigpen. As the Phillips translation of the Bible puts it, when he finally came to his senses, the young man got up and said, "I will return to my father's house. I perish from hunger." I am absolutely convinced that this is what is going to happen in America. I am an optimist, and the reason I am an optimist is that I have read the last chapter of the Bible. I know we win in the end, and that is very good news. How long it is going to take for our prodigal nation to come to its senses, though, no one can say for sure. The signs all seem right at this moment, but the conditions of the cultural mandate make it clear that the outcome of this situation depends very much on us, the Christians of this world. Will we get involved and get the Gospel to the lost, or will we just slip back quietly into the shadows, embarrassed to take a stand for Christ? I believe God has put this test of character before us to see what we are made of.

But, dear friends, whatever chastisement must come upon this prodigal nation, and whatever miseries must come upon the land of the humanist pigsty, we will all be partakers of those miseries. Because we are guilty, too. We who have been enlightened by heaven, we who have been brought to our senses by the Spirit of God, we who have come to understand the Gospel of Christ, have not been reaching out to this benighted and insane world that is plunging into the mire and the muck of the pigpen. We have run from their slurs and their screams of rage, and thus we have not been there to help bring the men and women of the nation back to their senses and home to their Father.

So it all depends on how faithful we Christians are. If every Christian in this country were to lead someone to Christ next week, the whole nation would be transformed . . . in one week. But what do we do? Most won't even bother to invite someone to church. That, indeed, is tragic. The prodigal son will come home. The only question is: What is it going to take to bring him to his senses?

THE HOPE OF RENEWAL

But there is good news. There is evidence that at least part of the collective prodigal nation is awakening from its long slumber, and this somnolent state may be coming to an end. You can see signs of an awakening in numerous articles appearing in magazines and newspapers. Numbers of books have also appeared in the last few year expressing the fears and concerns of those who see the evidence of our moral degeneration. Not long ago I ran across a headline that said, "Statistical Vital Signs Show America Today is Definitely a Sick Patient." This is just a sample of hundreds of articles spelling out the bad news. Slowly but surely, people in secular America are beginning to see that everything is not wonderful in the far country. They are beginning to see that there are problems in the pigsty.

Joan Beck wrote a column in the *Chicago Tribune* entitled, "We Cannot Ignore the Value of Religion." In that article, she talked about Yale law professor Stephen L. Carter's new book, *The Culture of Disbelief*, which talks about the damage that has been done to this country by the suppression of religion. Many will recall that President Bill Clinton responded strongly to the book, cited it in some of his addresses in early 1994, and even invited a group of twelve evangelical Christians to a private discussion in the White House to find out how the Administration might address some of the concerns described by Carter in that work. Clearly, the loss of religious values impacts people in all quarters.

Then in *Newsweek* magazine, which is one of the most liberal news publications in the country, I happened across an article entitled, "Losing Our Moral Umbrella: Politicians Appeal to a Judeo-Christian Tradition." Surely it must be good news when politicians start appealing to the historic Christian moral position. The *Los Angeles Times* published an article that declared, "Programs won't solve social problems: only high morals will." The headline says it all, but we have already lost our way in this humanist utopia. We have been seduced into a prodigal pigsty and, thanks to the offensive rulings of the justice system, we still can't teach morals in our schools and universities. Only "high morals" will solve America's problems; but when will we once again make "moral values" legal in public?

The *Sun Sentinel*, which is our local newspaper in Fort Lauderdale, recently published a column by William Raspberry saying that former education secretary William Bennett is right in his view that "Society must reassert moral, ethical values." The harbingers of the secular paradise seem to be singing a different song these days. All over the nation we hear voices crying out, saying that something is wrong in our humanist utopia. And some have gone so far as to suggest that maybe we need to return to our Father's house. Can they still print such things in the far country? Aren't they worried about separation of church and state? Well, I am happy to say that, little by little, such things are being said today—and that is a very encouraging sign.

And there are some other hopeful signs. Statistics published recently by the Institute of World Missions (IWM) showed that there is an incredible multiplication in the number of people around the world who are coming to a saving knowledge of Jesus Christ. Earlier, in chapter four, we saw how the Gospel spread from Jerusalem to Judea and Samaria and then to Rome and the farthest reaches of the globe. The IWM report offers a similar perspective, from the time of Christ to the present, but with a somewhat different focus. They report that in the year 100 A.D., an average of one hundred persons per day worldwide were being converted to Christianity. The rate continued to climb steadily until 1900 when the average was nine hundred-forty-three per day. By 1950, the number grew to four thousand-five-hundred per day, growing at a pace that surpassed the "population explosion."

By 1980, the average number of conversions had increased to twenty thousand per day; and by 1993, fully eighty-six thousand new converts were coming to the cross of Christ every single day. This makes Christianity the fastest growing religion in the entire world, by far. At the current rate of growth, by 1995, the number of those converted to Christianity will surpass one hundred thousand every single day of the year. And by the turn of the century, it will top two hundred thousand per day!

Just think what that means. The number of souls being won to Jesus Christ and the number of persons who will experience the new life of faith will have increased two hundred times in a single century! God is doing a marvelous work in our time, and He has called us to be a part of His glory and His victory in the world. He allows us to share in His joy by sharing His love with a world that desperately needs hope and regeneration. Most of the growth in the church today is taking place outside the United States, but there is a great deal going on in this country, and the prospects for revival in this nation have never been greater. The problem is that eighty-six percent of Americans claim to be Christians already. A part of our task is to lead those who are merely "nominal" Christians—Christians in name only—to a true encounter with the Messiah.

THE WALK OF FAITH

A minister told me not long ago that he had just led a man who was a member of another denomination to Christ. The new believer was joining his church that Sunday. A man who had already professed himself to be a Christian recognized his sin and came to a genuine "born again" experience. Today that man is still a professing Christian, and, at least statistically speaking, nothing has happened to the number of believers in the world.

It struck me that this was an example of a "stealth conversion"—it was invisible like the stealth planes used by our armed forces. But, don't let the statistics fool you. In reality, something tremendous happened in the life of that man. It was something that will make a world of difference in his life now and forever. "This my son was dead," said the father of the Prodigal, "and behold he is alive." And thanks to his rebirth in Christ, he is going to begin showing signs of the new life that is within him. The evidence of the new Christian is the walk of faith he undertakes.

In the *West Palm Beach Post* a few weeks ago, there was a front-page headline that said: "Christians take over Jacksonville, Florida." The message, from the humanist point of view, was that the city was in danger! Alas and alack, who do these Christians think they are? Do they think they can govern a city? But look, they have also taken over the school board! They have instituted abstinence-based sex education! They are calling crime a sin and saying that moral renewal is needed in the state of Florida! Good heavens, what were the people of Jacksonville going to do about it? What would happen to the young people!

The bad news for the secular humanists is good news indeed for the world. For wherever faith in Jesus Christ is found, new life begins. Sin, hatred, violence, and other self-destructive behaviors will disappear. God has good news for the world, and we are His emissaries. But, sadly, too many Christians are still sitting on the sidelines.

If I could say only one thing in these pages to touch your heart and make a difference in your life, it would be to urge you to join the army of the Lord, to accept His challenge to become a part of the greatest movement of the Spirit of God in the history of the world.

The challenge is not just to preachers and teachers. It is to you: first to come to the throne of grace, to humble yourself before the Almighty God of heaven, and then through His Spirit to reach out to the prodigal nation around you with the Gospel of Jesus Christ. Bring the men, women, and children where you live into the church where the King of kings can bring genuine renewal—new life, new hope, and a new character. Share the good news that the walk of faith is the only way to true joy and happiness. When you shake off the deadly sleep of the humanist dream, you will awaken to the brightest vision of hope you have ever known. Our nation has been seduced into the far country. Now, with God's help, we shall reclaim this land and awaken this world to an eternity of wonderful blessings. And when this nation desperately searching for its soul finally returns to its Father's house, there will be rejoicing in heaven and on earth!

At the conclusion of the parable of the Prodigal Son, we read that there was music and feasting, and all those called into the father's house shared in the excitement and the happiness of the young man's return. The parable is a lesson for all of us. This is what God has in store for us right now. It is not slavery, not self-righteous prudery, not sadness and intolerance. There is no tyranny in God's house, but freedom and joy and excitement. The Devil's lie is exposed for what it is, and the rejoicing does not end at midnight. It lasts forever—in this life and in the next.

Are you a part of this great story? Are you engaged in the struggle for the soul of America? Are you a part of the solution to the "crisis of character" that has racked this nation for the past forty years? Or are you just one of those poor, listless Christians sitting on the sidelines, watching the destruction of your hopes and dreams?

My prayer is that God will grant each one of us today a new beginning. With all my heart, I pray that every single one of us will determine, right now, in this hour, that we will stand firm, that we will join the mighty army of the Lord, outfitted with spiritual armor, fully prepared to engage in the battle for the soul of America. And to overcome the world for Christ.

Bibliography

Augsburger, Myron. *The Christ-Shaped Conscience*. Wheaton: Victor Books, 1990.

Ball, William Bentley. *In Search of a National Morality: A Manifesto for Evangelicals and Catholics*. Grand Rapids: Ignatius/Baker Books, 1992.

Barrett, David B. *World Christian Encyclopedia: a Comparative Study of Churches and Religions in the Modern World, AD 1900–2000*. New York: Oxford University Press, 1982.

Barton, David. *America: To Pray or Not to Pray?* Aledo, Tex.: Wallbuilder Press, 1991.

Bell, Jeffrey. *Populism and Elitism: Politics in the Age of Equality*. Washington, D.C.: Regnery Gateway, 1992.

Bellah, Robert N., et al. *Habits of the Heart: Individualism and Commitment in American Life*. New York: Harper & Row, 1985.

Bloom, Allan. *The Closing of the American Mind: How Higher Education Has Failed Democracy and Impoverished the Souls of Today's Students*. New York: Simon & Schuster, 1988.

Burkett, Larry. *The Coming Economic Earthquake*. Nashville: Thomas Nelson, 1993.

Collier, Peter, and David Horowitz. *Destructive Generation: Second Thoughts about the Sixties*. New York: Summit Books, 1989.

Colson, Charles, with Ellen Santilli Vaughn. *The Body: Being Light in Darkness*. Dallas: Word, 1992.

Dawson, Christopher. *Religion and Culture*. New York: Sheed & Ward, 1948.

D'Sousa, Dinesh. *Illiberal Education: The Politics of Sex and Race on Campus*. New York: Vintage, 1992.

Davidson, James Dale, and William Rees-Mogg. *The Great Reckoning: Protect Yourself in the Coming Depression*. New York: Simon & Schuster, 1993.

Eyre, Linda, and Richard Eyre. *Teaching Your Children Values*. New York: Simon & Schuster, 1993.

FitzGerald, Frances. *America Revised: History Schoolbooks in the Twentieth Century*. New York: Random House, 1979.

Flood, Robert. *Men Who Shaped America*. Chicago: Moody Press, 1976.

Graham, Billy. *Storm Warning*. Dallas: Word, 1992.

Martin L. Gross. *The Government Racket: Washington Waste from A to Z*. New York: Bantam, 1992.

Guinness, Os. *The American Hour: A Time of Reckoning and the Once and Future Role of Faith*. New York: Macmillan Free Press, 1993.

Henry, Carl F. *Christian Countermoves in a Decadent Culture*. Portland, Ore.: Multnomah, 1986.

Josephus. *The Antiquities of the Jews*, in William Whiston, ed., *The Works of Josephus: Complete and Unabridged*. Peabody, Mass.: Hendrickson, 1987.

Kennedy, D. James. *Why I Believe*. Waco, Tex.: Word, 1980.

Kilpatrick, William Kirk. *Why Johnny Can't Tell Right from Wrong: Moral Illiteracy and the Case for Character Education*. New York: Simon & Schuster, 1992.

Kimball, Roger. *Tenured Radicals: How Politics Has Corrupted Our Higher Education*. New York: Harper & Row, 1990.

Kirk, Russell. *The Roots of American Order*. Washington, D.C.: Regnery Gateway, 1992.

Lewis, C. S. *Mere Christianity*. New York: Macmillan, 1960.

Lickona, Thomas. *Educating for Character: How Our Schools Can Teach Respect and Responsibility*. New York: Bantam, 1992.

Lutzer, Erwin. *Exploding the Myths That Could Destroy America*. Chicago: Moody, 1986.

McWhiney, Grady, and Robert Wiebe, ed. *Historical Vistas: Readings in United States History 1607–1877*. Boston: Allyn & Bacon, 1963.

Medved, Michael. *Hollywood vs. America: Popular Culture and the War on Traditional Values*. New York: Harper-Collins / Zondervan, 1992.

Meldan, Fred John. *Why We Believe in Creation, Not in Evolution*. Denver: Christian Victory Publishing, 1959.

Millard, Catherine. *The Rewriting of America's History*. Foreword by D. James Kennedy. Camp Hill, Pa.: Horizon House, 1977.

Naisbitt, John, and Patricia Aburdene. *Megatrends 2000: Ten New Directions for the 1990s*. New York: Avon Books, 1990.

Phillips, J. B. *Your God Is Too Small*. New York: Collier Macmillan, 1961.

Robertson, Pat. *The New Millennium: Ten Trends That Will Impact You and Your Family by the Year 2000*. Dallas: Word, 1990.

Schaeffer, Francis A. *A Christian Manifesto*. Westchester, Ill.: Crossway, 1982.

_____. *How Should We Then Live? The Rise and Decline of Western Thought and Culture*. Westchester, Ill.: Crossway, 1976.

Solzhenitsyn, Aleksandr. *A World Split Apart:Commencement Address Delivered at Harvard University, June 6, 1978*. New York: Harper & Row Publishers, 1978.

Sproul, R. C. *Lifeviews: Make a Christian Impact on Culture and Society*. Old Tappan, N.J.: Fleming H. Revell, 1986.

Sykes, Charles J. *A Nation of Victims: The Decay of the American Character*. New York: St. Martin's, 1991.

Tarnas, Richard. *The Passion of the Western Mind*. New York: Ballantine, 1993.

Thomas, Cal. *The Death of Ethics in America*. Waco, Tex.: Word, 1988.

Tocqueville, Alexis de. *Democracy in America*. Translated by George Lawrence. New York: Harper & Row, 1969.

Wilson, James Q. *The Moral Sense*. New York: Macmillan Free Press, 1993.

Topical Index

About the Author

D. James Kennedy is Senior Minister of the 8000-member Coral Ridge Presbyterian Church (PCA) in Fort Lauderdale, Florida, and host of the nationwide television broadcast, "The Coral Ridge Hour," and a daily syndicated radio program, "Truths That Transform." He holds A.B., M.Div., M.Th., D.D., D. Sac. Litt., Litt. D., D. Humane Let., and D. Sac. Theol. degrees, as well as his Ph.D. from New York University. He is founder and president of Evangelism Explosion International, founder and Chancellor of Knox Theological Seminary, and founder of Westminster Academy and Christian radio station, WAFG.

His books include *Evangelism Explosion*, with more than one million copies in print, as well as *The God of Great Surprises*, *Truths That Transform*, *Turn It to Gold*, *Why I Believe*, and sixteen others. Dr. Kennedy was Moderator of the General Assembly of the Presbyterian Church in America in 1988–89 and offered the opening prayer for the Republican National Convention in August 1992.

Jim Nelson Black is a writer and researcher, and author of the book, *When Nations Die: Ten Warning Signs of a Culture in Crisis*. He holds M.A. and Ph.D. degrees in the humanities from the University of Texas at Arlington and pursued doctoral studies and dissertation research at the Sorbonne, in Paris, France. He has collaborated on more than a dozen best-selling books.